THE PUFFIN

THE PUFFIN

by M. P. Harris

Illustrations by

KEITH BROCKIE

T & A D POYSER

Calton

ISBN 0 85661 038 0

First published in 1984 by T & A D Poyser Ltd
Town Head House, Calton, Waterhouses, Staffordshire, England

Text set in 10/11½ pt Linotron 202 Ehrhardt, printed and bound
in Great Britain at The Pitman Press, Bath

Contents

6   *Contents*

List of Plates

List of Figures

List of Tables

Introduction

There can be few people who cannot recognize a painting or photograph of an adult Puffin. However, most have a preconceived idea that it is a penguin-sized bird and are shocked to hear that stands only 18 cm high and weighs 400–500 g. But I doubt if more than a tiny fraction could draw even the most approximate likeness without reference to a book such as this. In it I try to describe the Puffin and summarize what is known of its life and its relations with man in terms understandable to the normal person but in detail enough to satisfy the scientist. It obviously draws heavily on my own studies but I have attempted to give a balanced view and include the opinions of other people.

The only previous book on the Puffin is that of Ronald Lockley, based on his pioneer seabird studies on the Welsh islands carried out before and just after the Second World War. The book was published in 1953 and has long been out of print. If the reader can get hold of a copy he will find that Lockley's personalized approach gives a vivid description of seabird life. My book complements rather than supersedes his.

THE STUDY OF PUFFINS

Up to now the study of Puffins has been based on watching birds at nesting colonies, catching and marking them, and examining the burrows. Puffins live in some of the less accessible parts of Europe and North America and, more importantly, much of their life goes on under ground and they do not take kindly to too much detailed attention. We have already learnt much but further progress will need skilled and patient workers. Perhaps, in the future, someone will be able to extend our knowledge to the bird at sea, for, as with most seabirds, we are largely ignorant of what our bird does there.

1   Location of colonies where the main studies on Puffins have been carried out.

There many references in the literature to Puffins, but as will become apparent, there have been few detailed studies and I should first describe briefly the islands where these have been made and give due credit to the workers whose results I use so much in the succeeding chapters.

SKOKHOLM AND SKOMER

These two islands, a few kilometres apart off the coast of Dyfed (formerly Pembrokeshire) in south-west Wales between St Brides Bay and the oil port of Milford Haven, have large numbers of seabirds including auks and tens of thousands of shearwaters. Skokholm, the southern and smaller of the two is 106 ha in extent and bounded by cliffs of Old Red Sandstone 15–30 m high. The middle of the island is covered with bracken but at the edge the vegetation is stunted due to extremes of wind, salt spray and grazing by the multitudinous rabbits. The 2,500 pairs of Puffins are restricted to a narrow band along the cliff-edge except for a couple of slopes where they compete for burrows with shearwaters. Skomer is almost three times as big (290 ha) and composed of two large, mainly flat-topped igneous masses joined by an isthmus only 10 m wide. Again Puffins breed mainly at the top of the 50 m high cliffs or in a few of the steep slopes above. Many of the 6,000 pairs nest along the fringes of two large bays which help form the isthmus. The vegetation here is much taller than on Skokholm and a few of the colonies are in tall bracken. Earlier this century Puffins were far more numerous than at present (e.g., 20,000 pairs on Skokholm in the 1930s) and on both islands some nested far inland in places now occupied by shearwaters, rabbits and gulls.

The first scientific studies on Puffins were done by Ronald Lockley (1934–38) on Skokholm between 1927 and 1939, rather as a sideline to his pioneer work on the biology of the Manx Shearwater. During this period Skokholm became the best known seabird island. After the war he turned his attention to Skomer and later (1953) published his monograph *Puffins*. This described the main outlines of Puffin biology and behaviour, in very evocative prose. In 1969, Peter Corkhill (1972–73) started a new era in Puffin research on Skomer and this was carried on by Ruth Ashcroft (1976–79) and Peter Hudson (1979–83) with special emphasis on the factors influencing the breeding, the growth of young and the dynamics of the Puffin population.

ST KILDA

This is the most isolated island group in Britain being 66 km west of the Outer Hebrides. There are four islands – Hirta, Dun (almost joining it), Soay and Boreray (6 km away). All are cliff-bound, difficult of access and have extremely large seabird populations including about half the British Puffins and a quarter of all the Gannets in the North Atlantic. My studies have been carried out at the colony on Dun (32 ha, highest point 175 m) where 40,000 pairs of Puffins burrow in steep slopes covered with sorrel and mayweed (Plate 2). Once a landing has been made (and we linked Dun and Hirta with a breeches buoy) this is an excellent place to study Puffins because of the large numbers, the markedly different density of burrows in different sub-colonies and a thriving population of Great Black-backed Gulls which eat mainly Puffins during the summer months. One might detest these predators but they are an important aspect of the Puffin's life (and death).

My own studies started in 1972 when I was employed by the scientific branch of the Nature Conservancy, which later became the Institute of Terrestrial Ecology, part of the Natural Environment Research Council. My research was to describe the changes in the numbers of Puffins around Scotland and to determine the cause of a large decline in numbers at some of the western colonies. I compared Puffin biology and population dynamics at two very different colonies, St Kilda, where the population has declined this century, and

the Isle of May where the population has increased spectacularly. The rationale was that if I could detect any difference between these two populations I could then look for the reason why the former population had declined so dramatically this century and why the latter had increased. This research was documented in papers, listed in the bibliography. In later years Kenneth Taylor (1982) has studied the behaviour of Puffins both here and on the Isle of May.

ISLE OF MAY

This is a small island of 57 ha of greenstone in the entrance to the Firth of Forth east of Edinburgh. Along the west and south-west sides of the island there are 50 m high cliffs, stained white by the droppings of Guillemots, Shags and Kittiwakes; elsewhere the grass and campion covered slopes fall gently to the sea. Up until 1956, the 5–10 pairs of Puffins nested in holes or cracks in the top of these cliffs but following the recent dramatic increase (to maybe 10,000 pairs in 1982) they now compete with the extremely numerous rabbits for burrowing space in the shallow soil over most of the island (Plate 4). The population of Herring and Lesser Black-backed Gulls increased rapidly to 17,000 pairs in 1972. Then the number was reduced to about a third by killing adult gulls. Surprisingly, there is no evidence that these gulls had any adverse effects on the Puffins although they did have a profound effect on the vegetation which would doubtless have resulted in severe soil erosion in the future.

LOVUNDEN AND RØST

Just south of the Arctic Circle in Norway, Svein Myrberget (1959–80) studied the biology and feeding of some of the 60,000 pairs of Puffins breeding on the island of Lovunden in Lurøy Township, Nordland Province, from 1952 to 1957. The nest density was fairly low, at one per every 2–5 m² of colony, and the main colony covered only 10 ha. Very few burrows were accessible because, unlike the other study areas, Puffins here make their nests either among large piles of rocks or dig burrows in the small patches of turf between boulders. His data are the few we have for Puffins nesting among boulders.

Puffins on the Lofoten Islands to the north of Lovunden have come upon hard times. Breeding has failed virtually completely in 13 of the last 15 years, apparently due to lack of food. Sad as the situation is, studies on the small but steep burrow-riddled island of Hernyken (Plate 17) by Gunnar Lid (who, tragically, was drowned during his field studies in 1983) and his helpers (1979–80) have produced valuable information on how Puffins try to cope with these adverse conditions.

RUSSIAN COLONIES

The Murmansk coast of Russia stretching between the Norwegian border and the entrance to the White Sea has some fine seabird colonies. A lot of work has been done on several species of seabirds but unfortunately the language problem has resulted in much of this being unknown to western ornithologists, with the notable exception of *Ecology of sea colony birds of the Barents Sea*, written by Belopol'skii which was published in English in 1961. The Puffin is one of the less common seabirds, and has little commercial potential for eggs or flesh so has attracted less attention than the Guillemot and Eider. Despite this, more was known about the biology of Russian Puffins than about any others until the recent British studies. Even in translation the papers convey some of the atmosphere of a Puffin island and obviously the authors had a definite 'feel' for the bird.

The first Soviet work was undertaken in 1937 and 1938 in eastern Murmansk. Kaftanovskii (1941–51) compared the breeding biology of the various auks nesting on the Kharlov Island and later published details of the biology of the Puffin here and on nearby islands. The Bolshoi and Malyi Zelenets are small islands bounded by low cliffs, above which a 30° slope leads to a central plateau 30–40 m above sea level. Both the slope and the plateau are covered with a peaty soil, in which the Puffins dig burrows. Most Puffins nest in the slope but some go 150 m inland among crowberry and cloudberry. On the Kharlov Islands most pairs breed in small groups of burrows dug in the shallow soil right at the cliff-edge. Most other Russian studies have been made on the 260 ha of the two Ainov Islands where 12,000 pairs (or 75% of Russian) Puffins nest. The colonies are well defined, with an average density of 0.4 burrows/m² of peat in the main colony. Sometimes the burrows are so dense that it is impossible to walk over the area without causing severe damage. Some colonies are up to 400 m inland, in a thick carpet of daisy-like chamomile, dock, red campion and other herbs and grasses. Between 1958 and 1962, Skokova (1962–67) and Korneyeva (1967) studied both the breeding biology and social behaviour. Skokova was well ahead of the time in wondering whether some of the communal displays might have allowed birds to exchange information on the whereabouts of food. Excellent summaries of the breeding biology are given by Kozlova (1957) in *The Fauna of USSR*.

The tantalizingly little information we have on the biology of the large-billed race of the Puffin which inhabits the high-arctic comes from Uspenskii (1956).

GREAT ISLAND

Much of our knowledge of the Puffin in the west Atlantic is due to David Nettleship's (1972) studies in 1967–69 of the impact of the 1,500 pairs of Herring Gulls on the Puffins of Great Island, one of three uninhabited islands composing the Witless Bay Seabird Sanctuary off the south-east coast of the Avalon Peninsula, Newfoundland. It is about 1.4 by 0.7 km and bounded by steep cliffs and has peaty soil. On the cliff tops the slopes are grassy and hummocked, but inland there is raspberry-grass meadow and a coniferous forest – a marked contrast to European colonies. There were at least 100,000 pairs of Puffins, most of which bred within 50 m of the cliff-edge (Plate 3).

Although this study site, at 47°11′N, is further south than any colony on the eastern Atlantic, the climate is cool and humid due to the frequent fogs and cooling effect of the Labrador current. In recent years young from here have been taken to Eastern Egg Rock, Maine, as part of a re-introduction programme undertaken by Stephen Kress (1977–82) for the National Audubon Society and Canadian Wildlife Service. These young are now coming back to breed at their foster colony and producing important data on the timing of return of immatures.

I draw widely on published work of these and other studies and have also been ably served by many researchers who have kindly answered questions and allowed me access to unpublished data. I have tried to give credit where it is due without overburdening the text with citations and I apologise for any oversights. It should be possible to trace the original data from the reference lists. My special thanks are due to Mike Hornung, Kenneth Taylor, Stephen Kress and Kees Swennen for supplying details on their own research. The chapter on the distribution abroad would have been impossible without the help of Robert Barrett (Norway and adjacent areas), Ake Andersson (Sweden), Mike Hill and Roger Long (Channel Islands), Jean-Yves Monnat and Eric Pasquet (France), Erik Mortensen (Faeroes), Aevar Petersen (Iceland), Finn Salomonsen (Greenland) and David Nettleship (North America). Arne Nørrevag and Chris Mead improved the sections on fowling and ringing recoveries. Various Bird Ringing and Banding Offices allowed me access to ringing recoveries, Stuart Murray and Kenneth Taylor helped with much of the fieldwork, David Jenkins and Sarah Wanless made valiant attempts to improve my English and Vivienne Anderson and Pat Andrews struggled to type my disgraceful writing.

I have been extremely lucky to have Keith Brockie do most of the illustrations. He obviously knows Puffins well. The distribution maps, graphs and other diagrams were prepared by John Turner, and Bernard Zonfrillo drew the diagram of the moult of the bill plates. Many people allowed me to see their photographs and I thank these as well as those whose results are displayed in the book.

CHAPTER 1

Auks

The Puffin is perhaps the best known member of the auk family (Alcidae) which is distantly related to the gulls, terns, skuas and waders. There are no auks in the southern hemisphere, and no penguins or diving petrels in the northern hemisphere. The resemblance of the larger auks to penguins and the smaller auks to diving petrels is due to convergent evolution, a process by which completely different birds have, over untold generations, been moulded to a similar appearance by similar environmental pressures. Now these groups seem to occupy similar ecological niches in the different hemispheres. Despite this, no penguin has developed such an elaborate bill as a Puffin, although the crested penguins have gone in for flamboyant head plumes such as are found in some auklets.

There are 22 species of living auk and one other, the Great Auk, which was persecuted to extinction in the 1840s, divided into seven tribes as shown (page 23). For interest I have added the approximate ranges (including the Bering Sea with the North Pacific, and the Arctic Ocean with the Atlantic). The average weights (from Bédard 1969) give an indication of body size. The Least Auklet is by far the smallest and Brünnich's Guillemot, now the largest, is about ten times as heavy. The flightless Great Auk was about five times as heavy again.

The Puffin tribe is usually placed at the end of the classification, linked to the auklets by the Rhinoceros Auklet which, despite its name, is a puffin and not an auklet. The fact that the Common Puffin is at the extreme end need not mean that it is the most specialized species. Subjective judgement is needed to decide whether the gaudy Puffin which carries the fish for the young, so attractively

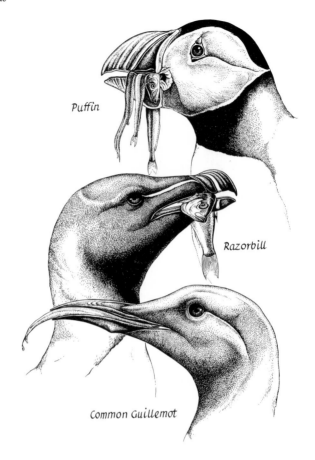

Puffin

Razorbill

Common Guillemot

2   North Atlantic auks carrying food for their young. Three species carry fish crosswise: the Puffin can manage up to 60 fish, although the usual range is 4–10, the Razorbill 1–5 fish and the Black Guillemot only a single. The Common and Brünnich's Guillemots carry a single fish but hold it longitudinally with the head down the throat. The Little Auk carries a mass of crustacea in a throat pouch (see facing page).

hanging from the bill, has evolved further than the Little Auk or some of the murrelets which have developed gular pouches for carrying large quantities of plankton. The latter group might well be the more efficient; e.g. Cassin's Auklet can carry more plankton than a Puffin can carry fish, yet it is only about one third the size.

EVOLUTION OF THE AUKS

Because the fossil record is very sparse we must rely heavily on zoogeography

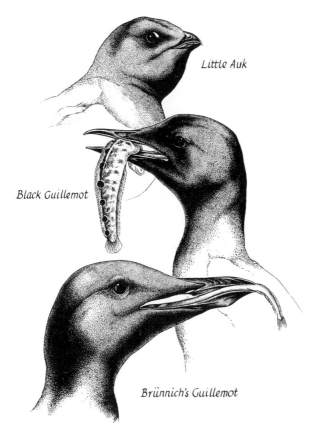

Little Auk

Black Guillemot

Brünnich's Guillemot

when speculating how the various puffins evolved. Eighteen species of auks occur in the North Pacific and 16 are endemic. This compares to just four endemics in the Atlantic – the Common Puffin, Little Auk, Black Guillemot, Razorbill, five if we include the extinct Great Auk. Common and Brünnich's Guillemots are found in both oceans. The few population estimates suggest that approximately similar numbers of auks occur in the two oceans.

Udvardy (1963) suggested that the family evolved in the Pacific where there are fossils from the early Tertiary (50 million years ago). Speciation occurred early and some auks had already become extinct by the Pleistocene (1 million years ago). Some early auks, including a proto-little auk and proto-puffin, apparently reached the Atlantic via the North American Arctic when the Bering Strait was open. Later, when this seaway closed, these birds were cut off and developed in isolation.

We guessed that the ancestral puffin entered the Atlantic about 5 million years ago and there evolved into the Atlantic or Common Puffin – whereas at the same time the ancestral stock isolated in the Pacific evolved into the diurnal Tufted Puffin and nocturnal Rhinoceros Auklet. The Bering Strait re-opened during the first inter-glacial in the Pleistocene so allowing the Common Puffin to re-enter the Pacific. Apparently, evolution had by then gone so far that the puffins did not inter-breed. In this new environment the Common Puffin evolved into yet another species, the Horned Puffin, and even today the similarity between the species is obvious. Auks still move between the oceans, albeit rarely, as four Pacific species have been reported from the Atlantic or adjacent waters in historic times. These were a Tufted Puffin obtained and painted by Audubon from the mouth of the Kennebec River in Maine, a Parakeet Auklet captured on Lake Vattern in Sweden, a Crested Auklet in summer plumage shot north of Iceland, and Ancient Murrelets captured in Wisconsin, Toronto and on Lake Erie.

The auks have evolved many and peculiar habits. Some species breed within burrows or in piles of stones from which they come and go by day or night, depending on the species; other species lay their eggs on exposed cliff ledges and take their young to sea when only partly grown. The Marbled Murrelet sometimes lays its eggs on a horizontal branch 45 m up a large tree. The comparative biology and ecology of auks is a fascinating topic but is outside the scope of this book.

THE PUFFINS

The present book is concerned solely with the Atlantic or Common Puffin (which is called the Puffin from here on). However, for the sake of completeness the appearance, range and numbers of the other species (taken from Wehle 1980) are given below.

Tufted Puffin

This is the largest puffin, standing some 30 cm high and by far the most strikingly marked. The bird is all-dark, except in summer when the forehead and cheeks are white and there are spectacular long white or yellow tufts of feathers dropping down behind the eye and curling on to the shoulders. The legs and feet, eye-ring and bill are startlingly orange or reddish-orange, the base of the upper mandible is greenish and the outer part has several very distinct grooves which curve the opposite way to those on the bill of the Common Puffin.

The Tufted Puffin is the commonest Pacific puffin with 6–8 million birds (compared to maybe 15 million Common Puffins) spread from Alaska south to Hokkaido Island in Japan and California in North America. In winter they disperse widely through the north Pacific. These puffins usually breed in earth burrows near the cliff edge, partly because it is easy to dig there, partly because these are the heaviest of puffins and have difficulty in taking off from flat ground. The colonies are sometimes very large, with many tens of thousands of pairs. The biology is 'typically puffin'. A single egg is incubated for six weeks

	Weight (g)
1. (Great Auk *Pinguinus impennis* North Atlantic – now extinct)	5000
Razorbill *Alca torda* North Atlantic – widespread	740
Common Guillemot (Common Murre) *Uria aalge* Widespread in North Atlantic and North Pacific	930
Brünnich's Guillemot (Thick-billed Murre) *U. lomvia* Widespread in colder parts of North Atlantic and North Pacific	980
2. Little Auk (Dovekie) *Plautus alle* Only found in very north Atlantic and the adjacent Arctic	170
3. Black Guillemot *Cepphus grylle* Widespread in North Atlantic	430
Pigeon Guillemot *C. columba* Widespread in North Pacific	480
Spectacled Guillemot *C. carbo* Restricted to Asian side of North Pacific	(?480)
4. Marbled Murrelet *Brachyramphus marmoratus* Widespread in North Pacific	230
Kittlitz's Murrelet *B. brevirostris* Restricted range in northern parts of North Pacific	240
5. Xantus' Murrelet *Endomychura hypoleuca* Restricted to California and Baja California	160
Craveri's Murrelet *E. craveri* Breeds in Baja California	150
Ancient Murrelet *Synthliboramphus antiquum* Widespread in North Pacific	230
Japanese Crested Murrelet *S. wumizusume* Restricted to Japan	(?230)
6. Cassin's Auklet *Ptychoramphus aleuticus* East North Pacific	170
Parakeet Auklet *Cyclorrhynchus psittacula* Northern North Pacific	320
Crested Auklet *Aethia cristatella* Northern and west North Pacific	280
Least Auklet *A. pusilla* North and west North Pacific	90
Whiskered Auklet *A. pygmaea* North and west North Pacific	120
7. Rhinoceros Auklet *Cerorhinca monocerata* East and west North Pacific	570
Common Puffin *Fratercula arctica* Widespread in North Atlantic	510
Horned Puffin *Fratercula corniculata* Northern North Pacific	650
Tufted Puffin *Lunda cirrhata* Widespread in North Pacific	840

and the young are fed on fish and squid (sometimes caught well away from the colonies) for six to seven weeks before fledging.

Horned Puffin

About two-thirds the size of the tufted species, the Horned Puffin has blackish upperparts, white underparts and sides to the head, and a large, brightly coloured beak. The main differences between this and a Common Puffin are the pointed fleshy protuberances which point devilishly to the sky from above each eye, and the inner part of the bill which is creamy yellow, the outer part red. The legs and feet are orange.

The species has a more northerly distribution than the Tufted Puffin, although the two species occur together over about half the breeding range. Some birds move south in winter and many winter in the open sea. The total population is some 2–4 million birds. The Horned Puffin generally nests among rocks or in cracks in the cliffs, perhaps because in its northern range the ground is often too frozen for burrowing, or perhaps because of competition with Tufted Puffins. The single egg is incubated for six weeks and the chick fed for another six weeks on fish and squid caught fairly close to the colonies.

Rhinoceros Auklet

This species is about the same size as the Tufted Puffin, its upperparts being sooty-black and underparts whitish. The upper breast, throat and sides of body are browny grey resulting in a slightly dirty appearance. The bill is not so flattened or as deep as in other puffins, but in the breeding season it has a large 'horn' pointing upwards and slightly forward from the base of the upper mandible. The breeding garb is completed by two pairs of whitish plumes, one plume set behind each eye, the other pair at either side of the gape.

It breeds in large colonies in two fairly separated areas – first, the Gulf of Alaska east and south to California (where there are only a few hundred birds) and, second, from the western end of the Aleutian chain down the coast of Asia to Japan. The total population of probably less than a million birds winters inshore, just to the south of the breeding range. Unlike other puffins, this species is usually nocturnal on land, visiting its burrow, dug in the soft soil among dense vegetation or in a cave, only during the hours of darkness. Apparently it is then safe from predatory gulls while crashing into or floundering among the bushes and tall herbs. The single egg is incubated for six weeks and the young fed for seven to eight weeks.

CHAPTER 2

Morphology of the Puffin

Before we can consider the ecology, biology and behaviour of the Puffin we should describe the bird and trace its development from the un-puffin-like fledgling which leaves the burrow at night, through to the bird which returns two years later as a recognizable but unfinished immature, and onward to the fully-developed five-year-old. Between fledging and breeding the Puffin undergoes four or five major moults during which it is unable to fly. These are hazardous times when many die if they are caught by severe weather or an oil slick.

EXTERNAL FEATURES

A full-grown Puffin is strikingly marked – the upperparts (perhaps better termed the back, considering the upright stance) are black in fresh plumage, brown by the end of the breeding season, and the underparts are white except for a rather variable black necklace across the front of the neck. White underparts probably make the bird slightly less obvious to fish which view the Puffin from below when it is silhouetted against the sky. There are two well defined whitish-grey face patches, each taking up most of one side of the head. The patches run backwards to points which almost, but not quite, meet at the nape. Sometimes a few greyish feathers complete the join. The top of the head is usually black or dark grey, but sometimes brown, and obviously paler on the forehead. The sexes look almost identical and a Puffin probably tells the sex of another by behaviour and the overall size of the bill which is much larger in the male.

The bill is large, compressed sideways and brightly-coloured in summer with a pale ridge separating the outer bright orange or red part from an inner bluish area. The upper bill is separated from the feathers by a pale rather fleshy plate, or cere, dotted with pores and small feathers. Although the bill is partly composed of horny plates, the anterior bone of the skull is much enlarged and flattened. There is a bright yellow, wrinkled rictal rosette at each corner of the mouth. The eye is dark or hazel-brown surrounded by a bright red ring and further set off by patches of cornified skin above and below and a distinct crease in the feathers behind. One could hardly design a more contrasting eye.

Legs and feet are usually bright orange, occasionally lemon yellow. The toenails are strongly developed (for digging) and can give scratches just as painful as a tweak from the beak. When the bird is standing, or even flying, the inner toe and its very large markedly curved nail are turned inwards. Coues (1868) described this claw in a good example of the morphological description of birds which occurred last century.

> The peculiar position, no less than unusual shape of the inner claw of this genus is a strongly-marked character, not found in any other but *Lunda* (Tufted Puffin). The great curvature and extreme sharpness of the claw could not be maintained were it vertically placed like the other claws, as it would be worn down by constant impaction against the rocks which the birds habitually alight upon. But in the usual attitudes and movements of the birds it lies perfectly flat on its side, and is so preserved intact. The birds make great use of this claw in digging their burrows or in fighting; and the preservation of the instrument for these purposes is evidently the ulterior design of the peculiar direction of its axis. The birds have the power of bringing it, on occasion for use, into a vertical position.

Puffins walk and dig more than the other auks. For instance, you never see a Guillemot, even on a colony as flat as a table top, set off for anything but the shortest walk to see what its neighbour is up to; Puffins appear to delight in such activity and will rush yards to view a fight. The mobility probably explains why the tarsi are not laterally flattened as is usual in many aquatic birds. Although the webs are strong, they are often torn or punctured in fights with other Puffins.

In flight the Puffin flaps its rather inadequate-looking small wings extremely rapidly. Only when held aloft by strong up-currents near the cliff-edge, or when gliding down from the cliffs in the beautiful moth-flight display, do Puffins fly with anything but the usual frantic 300–400 beats per minute (Meinertzhagen 1955). During the moth-flight display the feet are usually crossed, which probably explains the rather hunch-backed appearance (Plate 1). The smaller wings result in Puffins having a high stalling speed so that in calm conditions, or when forced to ditch downwind, they do not so much land as stop flying and crash onto the sea or the grass. Nonetheless, into a sufficient wind they can land with the gentleness of a helicopter. Wings are used for propulsion underwater and the feet act as rudders. Large wings are then a disadvantage as they offer much resistance; underwater even those of the Puffin are too large so have to be kept slightly bent. Thus, the wings are a compromise between the needs of

flight (large area) and swimming underwater (smaller paddles).

Puffins fly deceptively fast, and have been timed with a stopwatch over a known distance at 77–82 km/hr. Lockley (1953) noted that they could make headway against gales of 100 km/hr wind over land and progress at 15 km/hr against similar winds at sea. However, they gave up the struggle and sat on the water during a 150 km/hr storm. Observations made during speed trials of naval vessels give more direct results. On the Clyde, Vaughan (quoted by Lockley) clocked Puffins flying at 80 km/hr and Maurice (1958) recorded that a Puffin held position alongside a boat travelling at 70 km/hr and then drew ahead. I have no records of the speed underwater but dives usually last only 20–30 seconds; rarely, if scared, a minute.

Partial albinos occur in many colonies and are normally not noticed as the white is usually restricted to patches on the head, neck and back. Even when the Puffin is almost entirely white the primaries remain black. This is because black feathers are structurally stronger than white feathers, and primaries are subject to much wear as the bird goes in and out of burrows. In the late winter, just before the bird moults, the outer primaries are sometimes little more than shafts. This difference in the strengths of white and black feathers can be assessed by looking at the outer primary of a gull – the black always lasts longer than the white 'mirror' at the tip. I have not heard of a Puffin with pink eyes or legs, although a few chicks have white patches on their legs or feet. Leucism, in which the normal pigmentation is diluted, giving a very pale brown, almost cream-coloured Puffin occurs but is even rarer. Melanism has not been recorded in a Puffin and is extremely rare in auks. Sometimes grey or white edgings to the feather of the back and rump give the bird a silver-grey back. This is not albinism nor is it a sign of age as it occurs in immatures. The significance, if any, is unknown.

White Puffins figure in the folklore of many communities which depended on birds. One was said to have come back to the same place in the Faeroe Islands for some fifty years. The last ten years or so it was never seen to land on the cliffs but it still returned to near the island on sunny days (Williamson 1970). The St Kildan bird-fowlers explained these partial albinos as Puffins which had escaped half-way through being plucked. Both these and Faeroese knew the monetary value of the albino Puffins and Guillemots – there are drawer's full of both in some museums!

THE WINTER PUFFIN

Many people are surprised by the Puffin in its winter garb. Such a bird is so changed that it was once thought to be a different species. The face patch is dusky, sometimes almost black, especially in front of and just around the eye; the bill is not so brightly coloured nor so hard and looks rather odd because it is constricted at the base. The eye ring is dark which, with the shedding of the eye ornaments, gives the bird a 'wide-eyed' expression. The legs and feet are pale yellow.

The changes in the beak were described by Bureau (1877) and I can do no better than to translate his century-old writings. This observant Frenchman noticed that the two distinct types of Puffins had very different beaks and were found at different times of year. He thought that they were probably different plumages of one species. But when and how did the changeover occur? His first clue came when he collected some specimens at the Breton colonies in early August.

> Their beak, which in spring time formed a horny case, solid and homogeneous, now came apart like a suit of armour, the beautiful rose at the corners of the beak and the red circles around the eyes were atrophied and discoloured, the scaly areas above and below the eye had either fallen off or were separating, the feet which during the breeding season were beautiful vermilion-red were now orangey and, finally, the moulting of the plumage was beginning (except for the tail and wings) in some specimens.

He worked out that the Puffin owed its nuptial regalia mainly to three changes in the bill – a slight increase in size, a general increase in the colourings, and the production of the horny or scaly plates on the posterior part of the bill. The basal half of the bill is covered by plates which separate and fall off at the end of the breeding season. The upper mandible has a horny rim (Fig. 3), a nasal shield, two sub-nasal plates and two orange or transparent lamellae which overlap the hind edge of the first bill ridge. The horny rim on the border between the upper mandible and the plumage is shaped like an inverted U. It is pierced by numerous evenly spaced holes through which poke rudimentary feathers. Early in the breeding season this horny rim is translucent and skin-coloured but in July it becomes yellow and dead-looking. When the horn is shed the underlying skin is exposed. This is black and membranous with the same rudimentary feathers. The nasal shield and two sub-nasal plates are a beautiful lead-blue colour in the spring but they also lose their sheen and fall off to expose much darker skin underneath.

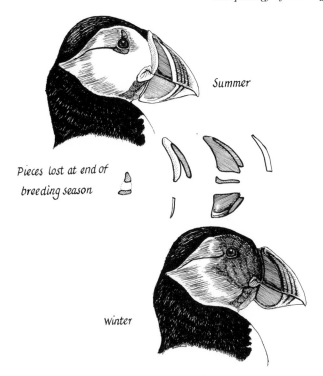

Summer

Pieces lost at end of
breeding season

winter

3   *The transformation from summer to winter plumage by the loss of the bill plates and eye-ornaments, the shrivelling of the atrophic triangle and the darkening of the face. (From a drawing by Bernard Zonfrillo).*

The lower mandible has two border pieces and a chin plate. In the spring the border pieces are bright orange, but when they drop off in the late summer, they expose a yellow membranous hind margin to the bill although this soon darkens. The chin plate is either lost in one piece or in small fragments, exposing the main fabric of the bill including a triangle of membranous yellow skin. This is called the atrophic triangle because it gradually shrinks. According to Bureau, the remnants of this triangle lodge in the cavity formed by the slight drawing apart of the two sides of the lower mandible. It is the shrinking of this membranous area plus the loss of the horny rim of the upper bill that gives the winter Puffin its peculiar head shape. The wide-eyed look is accentuated by the loss of the plates above and below the eye and the ill-defined patch of dark feathers in front of the eye.

IMMATURES

The adult Puffin is such a very striking bird that it is not surprising that it takes the bird several years to attain adult plumage.

At fledging the juvenile is rather like the winter adult but only three-quarters of the size. The beak is stubby and dark all over, and the dark area in front of the eye is more extensive and blacker. The legs and feet are greyish. Young Puffins are frequently mistaken for Little Auks, but Little Auks lack pale face patches, and have white eyebrows, white trailing edges to wings and even stubbier bills. About half of the juvenile Puffins lose the black face patches during their spring moult, and then resemble adults except for their small dark beaks; other juveniles retain scattered black feathers during their first summer. The differences may be due to the different timing of hormone secretions in individuals, but why or how they arise is obscure. It takes four or five years for a Puffin to reach maturity and full weight. During this time the wings continue to grow. The bill reaches its full length by the end of the first winter and later attains a greater area – often a 25% increase – by becoming deeper and, to a lesser extent, by an increase in the curvature of the top edge. Whereas the beaks of one- or two-year-old Puffins are pointed and triangular, those of breeding adults are more rounded. In many immatures the smooth outline of the upper edge of the bill is broken by a kink or steep rise where the bill meets the cere (the waxlike membrane at the base of the beak). Although this is sometimes seen in adults too, it is then far less obvious. With age, the bill becomes more brightly coloured, with more distinct markings, and with each breeding season the eye ornaments get larger and the eye ring brighter. Examples of these various types of beaks are shown in Plates 6 and 7.

The bill also develops grooves on the outer, red part. Although there is great individual variation, the older the Puffin the more grooves it is likely to have (Table 1). Typically one-year-olds have only a trace of a groove, two-year-olds one or an incomplete groove, three-year-olds normally one and a half, rarely two, and most four-year-olds have two grooves. About half of older birds have more than two grooves but many never gain more than two. This development has been documented by following birds ringed as chicks (Petersen 1976b, Harris 1981) but the general principle was common knowledge to bird-fowlers years ago.

Bill grooves are critical to adult Puffins as they, apparently, cannot hope to find a mate until they have two grooves. The few breeding Puffins without these grooves, have deformed or damaged bills. The grooves presumably have some secondary sexual function so how then do the birds with deformed bills manage? Possibly the shape or area of the bill may be important (and the grooves incidental). Birds with deformed bills may be at a disadvantage unless they bred before the beaks became damaged or deformed. Birds usually retain their mate from one season to the next, and after breeding once presumably recognize each other by other features. Any bird with two fully developed bill grooves is almost certainly sexually mature even though many birds fail to breed at this age, apparently because they cannot obtain a burrow.

In the winter beak the grooves, although still present, are less distinct. The diagonal ridge dividing the bill into two parts is then often dark and not obvious, so care must be taken not to include the groove posterior to this ridge when estimating age. Winter birds are best classified just as adults (bill with two or more grooves), juveniles (bird small, bill relatively smaller, primaries pointed), and immatures (bill intermediate).

SEXING

Male Puffins are, on average, slightly larger and heavier than females but large samples are needed before the differences are statistically significant (Table 2). However, males have significantly longer and deeper beaks than females, giving them 10% more bill area. An immature can be mistaken for a female unless the shape of the bill and the number of grooves are noted. Puffins obviously do not make this mistake. Although there are large overlaps in the bill measurements, if the bill depths of birds of known sex from a single colony are plotted against their bill lengths as a scattergram, two clusters of points are formed, with males in the top right and females in the lower left (Fig. 4). A line can be calculated which best separates the sexes and this information used to sex living Puffins. This sexing must be restricted to birds from the same colony as there are marked differences between birds from different colonies.

WEIGHT

Puffins are present at the colonies for most of the summer. Much of the time is spent down burrows, standing around or flopped, breast-down, on a rock

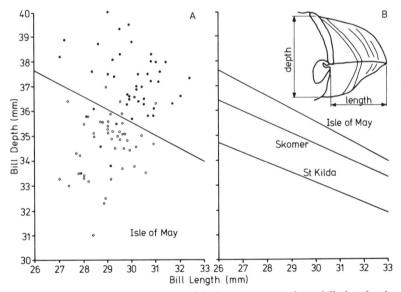

4 *Sexing Puffins by bill measurements. Males have, on average, larger bills than females and most adults can be confidently sexed by the use of a discriminant line calculated from birds sexed by dissection (A). This line varies greatly from colony to colony (B).*

with eyes closed, all of which expends little energy. But at other times they are digging, fighting or just rushing around to see what their neighbours are doing. As the breeding season progresses they gradually lose weight so that at the end they are, on average, 5% lighter than when they returned at the start of the season. This is presumably associated with the strain of getting and retaining a burrow, laying an egg and raising a chick. The low point is reached when the birds are feeding young and there is a slight recovery in weight immediately after the young have fledged. Immatures also have this pattern of weight changes; they probably expend much energy trying to get themselves established. Birds do not, however, stress themselves too far and give up breeding if conditions become too bad. About 95% of adult Puffins survive over winter to the next breeding season, so it is a better strategy to lose a chick than to risk dying for it.

TAXONOMY

Although the Puffin breeds over a wide range there are no geographic differences in plumage. Birds are, however, larger the further north they live (Table 3). Puffins in southern Britain have a wing length of 158 mm and weigh some 400 g, those in Spitzbergen have wings of 186 mm and weigh up to 650 g. A partial exception is that birds from western Atlantic colonies are larger than those from British and Faeroese colonies in the same latitude. This is, presumably, because the seas there are much colder than those at similar latitudes in the east. One would expect cold-water Puffins to be larger than those in warmer climes since larger size reduces the ratio of body area to mass and so heat loss (Bergman's Rule). However, expectations are not always realized and Puffins nesting in east Scotland are significantly larger (mean weight 397 g, mean wing length 162 mm) than those in the west (374 g, 158 mm) – an intriguing and unexplained difference.

Historical background

Birdwatchers and even the most serious ornithologists can become upset if the scientific name of a well-known bird is changed and will tend to mutter against 'splitters' (that is, taxonomists who divide one species or subspecies into several) or 'lumpers' (those who combine two or more species or subspecies). They do not realize how lucky they are! Ornithological taxonomy at the species level is now reasonably stable and they should be glad that they are not involved with intestinal worms or even plants. This stability is, however, a fairly recent phenomenon, and *Fratercula arctica* had many growing pains.

Up to the 1960s it was generally agreed that there were three subspecies of the Atlantic Puffin differentiated solely by size: the very large *naumanni* in the high-Arctic, Spitzbergen, and north-west Greenland; the small *grabae* in Britain, Ireland, France, Channel Islands, southern Norway and (formerly) Heligoland and Sweden; and the intermediate *arctica* of eastern North America, Iceland and most of Norway. The dividing line between *grabae* and *arctica* in

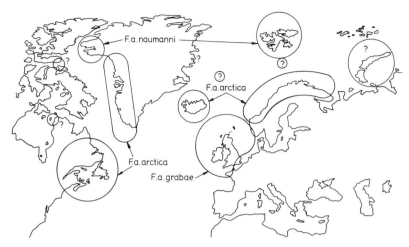

5   *The breeding ranges of the three subspecies of Puffins. There is doubt as to which
subspecies occur on Novaya Zemlya, Bear Island, Jan Mayen and in northern Canada.*

Norway was the 200 km-gap in the species distribution between Stavanger and
Husoy, north of Bergen (Fig. 5). The populations on the Murmansk coast of
Russia, Novaya Zemlya and Jan Mayen, were difficult to place, being apparently
intermediate although some difficulties were due to the limited material
available for examination. This situation took many years to sort out and some
of the correspondence in the scientific literature, especially *British Birds*, in the
early part of this century was spiced with more than a little rancour.

One of the problems was that when Linnaeus described the Puffin as *Alca
arctica*, he failed to give a type locality. He just referred to 'Habitat in rupibus et
praecipitiis montium maris atlantici, praesertim in insulis' (lives in the Atlantic
on rocky and steep sea cliffs and especially on islands) in his Fauna Svecica.
This seems more likely to refer to north Norway than Sweden, but it is most
unfortunate that Puffins from these two areas have wings 6–12 mm different in
length. Obviously Linnaeus did not know about this! Hartert (1917) designated
the type locality as the Vesterålen Islands but this was a little late.

Brëhm (1831) described *Mormon (Fratercula) grabae* from the Faeroes. He
thought that this race was the smallest Puffin, though he had not seen
specimens from further south. Galliard (1875) and Vian (1876) considered that
French Puffins should be designated *Mormon grabae*, but they did not say
whether they had compared their specimens with anything but birds from
Spitzbergen (the very largest individuals). These Spitzbergen birds had already
been designated as a separate species called *Fratercula glacialis* in 1865 by the
conservative Newton (1865) but 30 years later Ogilvie-Grant (1898) demoted
these birds to *F. arctica*, refusing them even subspecific status. Bureau (1879),
also, detached French birds into a separate species *armoricana*. In 1911 Zedlitz

and Roi identified the population on Bear Island as being the Scandinavian race, that is distinct from the Spitzbergen birds.

The Handlist of British Birds published in 1917 recognized the British and Faeroese birds as belonging to the subspecies *F.a. grabae.* This sparked off a row in *British Birds* where Sclater and Mackworth Praed (1917) took exception to this, noting 'that there is no distinction between the Norwegian and British birds worth recording', but Hartert (1917) excused his earlier judgement (in the Handlist) by saying that their opinions were 'hasty and valueless, because they are based on quite insufficient material'. This was true, because they were based on only one Norwegian adult, but Hartert himself only had five! Sclater and Mackworth Praed were 'not altogether satisfied' pointing out that the birds from Kristiansund (at 63°N), 550 km further south in southern Norway, were much smaller than those from the Vesterålen Islands and that nobody really knew where Linnaeus got his specimens from. They had great admiration for the extreme accuracy and thoughtfulness of Hartert's work but felt that 'he has gone too far in what the Americans conveniently term speciation'. The parting shot from Hartert was – 'I believe that they will in time agree with me in principle and interpretation of the facts'. The editors of *British Birds* then drew the discussion to a close until more skins from Norway were available.

Salomonsen (1944) in a thorough review of the more numerous specimens then available reinforced the suggestion of three subspecies. He pointed out that the birds from southern Norway were akin to those in Britain rather than to those further north in Norway.

The present

Some more recent authors have again expressed doubts about the validity of the subspecies despite the marked difference in sizes of Puffins from different areas. The problem is to distinguish a species showing clinal (continuous) variation from that which has distinct geographically differentiated subspecies. Most recognize the large high-arctic subspecies *naumanni* (Plate 11) but lump the more southern *arctica* and *grabae.* I consider that there is something to be said for retaining the two southern subspecies, if only for convenience, while admitting that there are undoubted grey areas. There is a break in the Puffin's distribution in southern Norway which coincides with a distinct change in size of wing and egg. Puffins from Kjør (near Stavanger) have a mean wing length of 163 mm, while those from Runde (400 km north) have a mean of 167 mm. The best course is to put off judgement until the present large-scale ringing of Puffins in several countries shows how much interchange there is between various colonies. We already have a British reared Puffin breeding at Kjør; if it had been much further north I would seriously consider forgetting *grabae.*

MOULT

Moult may be a basically simple process but it is a critical time for birds because it takes much energy, needs specific proteins, reduces the thermo-insulation properties of the plumage and, when primaries and tail feathers are shed, reduces the efficiency of flight. Breeding and moult are the most important events in a bird's calendar. The process, timing and ecological adaptations of moult have been studied in many landbirds but in relatively few marine birds, because moult occurs outside the breeding season when sea birds are difficult to study or even shoot.

As soon as breeding ceases, the Puffin's bill loses its bright colour, the sheath flakes off, and head and neck feathers are moulted. Only much later are the main wing and tail feathers replaced. This occurs more or less synchronously, probably as part of the pre-nuptial moult, and the bird is flightless. Despite the synchronous moult, the inner primaries complete their growth first. This is probably because the longest outer feathers take longest to grow, but the outer feathers may start growing slightly later as happens in the Guillemot (Birkhead and Taylor 1977). Extremely rarely one or two primaries are not replaced, resulting in a mixture of old and new primaries. It is difficult to know what might have caused this breakdown of the normal synchronous shedding of primaries. The moult of head and neck feathers, and the development of the beak plates, complete the transformation to summer plumage. The development of the beak and primaries is not directly correlated, but the summer face pattern and beak sheath in adults develop at the same time. Adults with black faces and incompletely developed bill sheaths are sometimes seen at the colonies (Plate 8). A few breed but most do not.

The wing moult occurs well away from land, so it is difficult to get direct observations on its timing. Most records are birds washed up dead on beaches and it is possible that moulting birds are more susceptible to adverse conditions; if so the sample will be heavily biased. The bulk of adults complete the replacement of their primaries before they return to the colonies in early spring, but a very few may still be growing the outer one or two primaries. The proportion of such birds varies from colony to colony. For instance, on St Kilda, 45 out of 227 birds examined in late April and early May had some incompletely grown outer primaries, mostly just one or two in each bird but all ten in one case and four in another, whereas only a single bird, which had been ringed as an adult three years before, of 914 adults handled in March on the Isle of May was growing its primaries. Dead flightless adults have been found all months from October to April inclusive.

Many birds in their first year of life replace primaries some time between March and July whereas others retain their primaries until the November of the year following hatching, by which time they are extremely worn. The pattern of moult of older immatures is confusing, probably because there are several age classes involved but most are flightless January to March, i.e. at the same time as adults.

The replacement of the main wing and tail feathers just before breeding is unusual. It does not occur in other Atlantic auks and hence needs explaining. The primaries of Puffins probably have to be in especially good condition for the summer when they suffer much abrasion and bleaching. Even though the wing feathers are new at the start of the season, they are very brown and battered by August. If they had been used for a whole year they might have been virtually useless. Puffins spend a greater proportion of their time swimming than do some other auks, e.g. Guillemots, so abraded primaries may not be unduly disadvantageous to them when not breeding. The few birds moulting primaries in the autumn may be those with exceptionally worn feathers which must be replaced before the birds can migrate to winter quarters.

FLIGHTLESSNESS

Members of several unrelated groups of birds become flightless when they are replacing their primaries. These include auks, diving petrels, divers, grebes, ducks, swans, geese and rails. The species have 'gambled' on getting the feather replacement over as quickly as possible. This necessitates finding a place safe from predators and the worst of the weather and, unless the species lay down large fat reserves, a good and predictable food supply. Many of these birds go to considerable lengths to find suitable areas; for instance most of the 100,000 Shelduck of western Europe go to the German Waddenzee to moult. Any threat to these areas, be it change of habitat or oil spillage, puts these flightless birds at grave risk. Puffins do sometimes get caught out. For instance, after the wreck of the oil-tanker *Amoco Cadiz* in March 1978 in Brittany, many more Puffins than other species were found dead. Being flightless, they just could not escape.

Within a natural taxonomic group there is often a gradation from species with a normal moult pattern to those which have a flightless moult. All the Atlantic auks and some of the Pacific species are like the Puffin in having a synchronous primary moult and a flightless period. In contrast the small Whiskered, Cassin's, Least and Parakeet Auklets moult their primaries one or two at a time like most other birds (Stresemann and Stresemann 1966). The slightly larger Marbled and Kittlitz's Murrelets are intermediate and have an accelerated moult in which the feathers are shed rapidly and the birds can only just fly. This pattern of moult probably evolved in response to two separate and conflicting ecological pressures (Storer 1960). First, the wing is used for flight. In the largest living auks the wing area/body weight ratios are among the lowest of any birds. The wing loading approaches a point at which the wings can sustain flight only with a great increase in size of the pectoral muscles. The loss of even one or two primaries would reduce the wing area sufficiently to make the bird flightless or at least to create extreme difficulty in taking off. As it is, these auks fly with more rapid wing beats than most other seabirds and have difficulty in becoming airborne in calm conditions. They are the species which have 'capitulated' and moult as quickly as possible. The smallest auklets have a much larger wing area/weight ratio and so can afford to lose a primary or two without seriously impairing flight. Second, auks use the partly folded wings as paddles to 'fly' underwater: wings suitable for flying are inefficient underwater. The wings of the largest auks are probably still large enough to be used underwater even when primaries are missing and the bird is flightless. The wing of a Puffin which has shed all its primaries is only 60% normal size when held in the flying position, but 80% when part-folded, with the 'wrist' half-bent as it is in the underwater position. The smallest auks have a wing area near to the critical underwater size so that the loss of one or two primaries would hardly be noticed in a partly folded wing. The wing of the flightless Great Auk was very small in relation to the size of the bird; presumably it was the most efficient size for swimming. It replaced its primaries irregularly one at a time so as to keep the wing area relatively constant.

The development of the diving petrels parallels that of the smallest auks (Watson 1968). The Little Auk and the Peruvian Diving Petrel are about the same size, and both have synchronous moult and hence become flightless. However, even though the small auklets and the Common Diving Petrel, are very similar in size, the former does not become flightless, the latter does. The reason for this difference is not clear.

SUMMARY

As well as being aesthetically attractive, the Puffin is a very specialized bird, even down to its sideways-twisted inner toe. Its wings are a compromise between paddles for swimming underwater and aerofoils for flight. Despite its small wing the Puffin commonly flies at 80 km/hr.

The distinctive bill is transformed in winter when the nine horny plates which give it much of its colour are shed. The eye ornaments are also lost.

It takes four or five years for a Puffin to reach maturity. During this time the wing continues to grow, the bill increases in area and grooves develop on the outer part. The bird also gets heavier. It is possible to age immature Puffins by the development of the bill grooves.

Male and female Puffins are indistinguishable in plumage but the male has, on average, a noticeably larger bill.

Puffins from north-west Greenland and Spitzbergen are markedly larger than Puffins elsewhere and belong to a distinct subspecies *F.a. naumanni*. Puffins from the Faeroe Islands and southern Norway, Britain and France are considered to belong to *F.a. grabae*, leaving the bulk of the world's Puffins in *F.a. arctica*.

The main moult occurs in late winter just before the birds return to the colonies. Immatures moult slightly later than adults. During this moult, Puffins are flightless.

CHAPTER 3

Distribution in Britain and Ireland

Most people know what a Puffin looks like but apart from active birdwatchers only a few ever manage to see one. If they do, it is usually after making a special boat trip to one of the few accessible colonies like Skomer off south-west Wales or the Farne Islands off Northumberland. Most Puffins live on isolated islands or in other out of the way places where they escape notice, and it comes as something of a shock to learn that there are between a half and three-quarters of a million pairs in Britain alone. The Puffin is among the commonest of British seabirds. This chapter maps the colonies in Britain and Ireland and summarizes what is known of the change in numbers since historic records began. We start in western Scotland, move to north Scotland and the northern Isles and then progress clockwise around east Scotland, England, Wales, north Irish Sea and Ireland. The Channel Islands are dealt with in the next chapter. As will become evident, there are now many fewer Puffins than there were at the turn of the century.

The great difficulties in even estimating the approximate numbers of Puffins, let alone accurately counting them, are discussed in Chapter 4. All figures given here must be considered approximate and I have omitted the *approximate, order of,* and *about* which prefix most totals. In 1969–70 all the known seabird colonies in Britain were visited during 'Operation Seafarer' and most estimates of Puffin numbers date from this time, hence the frequency of these years in the following colony accounts. Sources of other specific counts are given in Appendix B.

SCOTLAND

Outer Hebrides
These islands have always had the largest colonies of Puffins in Britain and in

1969 about 60% of British and Irish Puffins nested here. By far the largest colonies, totalling 300,000 pairs in 1975–78, are on St Kilda, and these are treated separately in Chapter 4. There were once many more, here and at the other large Scottish colonies. To judge from contemporary accounts the colony on the isolated island of North Rona must have been very large in the last century. However, there has been a great decrease since then, to 6,000 pairs in 1972–76. There are also great numbers of Great Black-backed Gulls here but these kill few Puffins. A decline in numbers on nearby Sula Sgeir occurred between 1932 and 1949, possibly due to soil erosion, and there were 350 pairs in 1972. The main concentration of Puffins on the Flannan Islands is on the main 90 m-high island of Eilean Mor (4,000 burrows in 1975), and there could be several thousand pairs on the other islands. A few hundred birds occupy most of the available habitat on Haskeir Rocks off North Uist.

Most visitors to the Shiant Islands have been impressed by the numbers of Puffins; for example:

> In countless thousands. The sea, the sky, and the land seemed populated by equal proportions, each vast in itself – a constantly moving, whirling, eddying, seething throng of life, drifting and swooping, and swinging in the wind, or pitching and

6   *Puffin colonies in mainland Scotland and the Hebrides.*

heaving on the water, or crowding and jostling on the ledges and rocks, arising from, and alighting on, the boulder-strewn slope, or perched like small white specks far up in the cliff-face amongst the giant basalt columns.

Harvie-Brown and Buckley (1888) thus considered this the densest British colony. Later visitors found fewer Puffins, or perhaps the earlier authors had got carried away, but in 1947 James Fisher ranked this population as the largest in Britain after Foula and St Kilda. A detailed census in 1970 found 77,000 occupied burrows mainly in boulder scree, and a much-reduced area of earthy slope. Although there was a 20% decrease between 1970 and 1971, annual counts since then suggest that the decline has stopped. It is impossible to determine when the decline started. Rats reached the islands in 1900, and certainly eat many Puffin eggs, but there is no direct evidence to show that they were responsible for this decline. Indeed, the previous owner, N. Nicolson, did not notice any decline until about 1959.

The other large colonies in this island group are on Mingulay and Berneray at the southern end of the island chain. In 1888 Harvie-Brown and Buckley wrote of the 50 m-high stack of Lianamul, Mingulay:

> The Puffin has complete hold over the whole upper crust . . . Later in the year the whole surface is one sticky compound of mud and dung, feathers, bad eggs, and defunct young Puffins, ankle-deep or deeper – waiting perhaps to be scraped away some day from the rocky floor on which it rests, and be spread far and near over the worn-out pastures by future generations of farmers – truly a filthy if a fruitful compost.

By 1949 the numbers on Mingulay were 'not impressive' and 1,100 pairs were estimated in 1969. A fuller survey in 1975 suggested 5,700 pairs with 200 pairs on Lianamul. In 1871, the towering 180 m-high cliff of Barra Head on Berneray was described as a 'crowded beehive' for Puffins but there were only a few hundred birds in 1964 and 1969. Some hundreds of eggs were collected on Barra in 1919 but the colony there is too small for this to be done now. Elsewhere a total of a few hundred pairs nest on Coppay, Gasker, Causamul and Pabbay.

Inner Hebrides

The colonies here are very small and scattered. There are now 20–30 pairs on the low-lying Ascrib Islands off Skye, where Harvie-Brown (1895) found them breeding in immense numbers in the turf and under rocks, and 'hoped that they will remain in a minority as these "comics" are quite abundant enough already . . . I fear that they are too much on the increase'. Likewise there must have once been many more Puffins on the small islands off the north of Skye. In 1842 they were 'literally covering the rocks and ledgy cliffs (of Fladda-chuain) with feathered thousands' (Wilson 1842); there were 200 burrows in 1969.

The colonies on Rhum declined from 1,000 pairs in the 1950s to 25–30 pairs in 1977 but there has since been a definite increase to maybe 50–70 pairs in 1982. Possibly some birds moved the 3 km to Canna where the maximum counts gradually increased from 1,200 individuals in 1962 to 1,800 in 1974 before declining to 800–1,100 in 1978–79. This may have been a recovery following a decline as there were 'fine colonies' here in 1933 and 1936. In recent years there has been a redistribution of birds and now there are more on the north cliffs, possibily due to erosion of colony area on the isolated stacks. A few hundred pairs breed on Muck Island but the several hundred pairs which bred on Eigg between 1926 and 1934 had gone by 1953.

Further south there are colonies on islands off Mull. Those on the scattered Treshnish Islands have increased in recent years and there are now several thousand birds on Lunga and 250 pairs on Staffa. Again, this may be an increase following a decline. Certainly these populations were expanding in the 1890s when Harvie-Brown (1892), who obviously feared the Puffin, wrote: 'Puffindom is spreading rapidly, and an increase is observable at many places every successive year; they will ere long banish other species'. There are a few pairs on Eilean Mor off northern Coll and a few hundred Puffins on the grass-covered Reidh Eilean off Iona. The species is rare on Jura and Islay, though the odd pair sometimes breeds on some of the scattered islets in this area.

Firth of Clyde

'They come twelve raik a day and 156 million thousand at a raik', – a tale told by a fisherman about Ailsa Craig in 1888 (Gibson 1951). Although this must be the greatest of the many exaggerated tales of Puffin numbers, the colony referred to must once have been spectacularly large. In 1696 Puffins were 'darkening the sky', in 1866 they were breeding 'everywhere a patch of soil is found in which it can burrow' (Walker 1868), and in 1871 Gray remarked 'their numbers seemed so great as to cause a bewildering darkness, and as they approached near enough to be touched by an outstretched arm, I was not sorry when they came to their senses, and began to settle on the ground'. Immense numbers were still present in 1890–1900, a slight decline was noted in 1910, the island was practically deserted by 1934 and only 30 birds were seen in 1947. There was a short-lived recovery to 250 pairs in 1950–51. Since 1961 there have been 20 or less pairs, all nesting in crevices in the steep cliffs among the fragmented granite which used to produce the finest curling stones. The decline has been attributed to the combined effects of man, rats (which arrived in 1889), oil and gulls.

Three new nearby colonies may have absorbed a few of these missing birds (Gibson 1970). Peaty Glunimore was colonized about 1920, the population increased to 200 pairs by 1955, but much of the habitat was destroyed by a rock fall in the early 1960s. The colonization of adjacent grass-topped Sheep Island occurred at about the same time and there were 250 pairs in 1971. Two pairs bred on Sanda in 1951 and in 1978 there were 250 pairs. One or two pairs nest on the Mull of Galloway, Burrow Head, and the low Scar Rocks in Wigtownshire. Up to 12 pairs have bred on the Mull of Kintyre.

North-west Scotland

The colonies at the north-east approaches to The Minch are small and the species is now extinct on the Summer Isles. Further north, rats were blamed for driving thousands of Puffins off the main island of Handa and the 300–400 pairs recorded there since 1959 have been mainly confined to the isolated Great Stack. To the south there are a few pairs on Meall Mor, to the north a few hundred pairs on the rocky Am Balg.

Between Cape Wrath, and the Kyle of Durness, the 300 m-high cliffs of Clo Mor have by far the largest mainland colony in Britain with, it is guessed, 25,000–50,000 pairs. The eastern edge of this colony is part of the only mainland naval gunnery target area in Britain, which probably explains why only a few birds nest at that end of the cliffs despite much apparently suitable habitat. Slightly further east 2,000 pairs of Puffins nest at low density in the solidified sand cliffs of Faraid Head. Despite much human disturbance the colony flourishes.

Shetland Islands

Nothing in the old accounts even hints that there were ever any more Puffins than there are now. The three largest colonies are at Hermaness and Burra Firth in the extreme north, Foula in the extreme west and Fair Isle between Orkney and Shetland. The very large colony of at least 50,000 pairs at Hermaness is scattered along several miles of boulder screes and heavily-grazed steep slopes. It was once much smaller for Saxby and Saxby (1874) described how it was a difficult climb to get to the Puffin slopes; now this is one of the easiest colonies to walk to. Increasing numbers also nest on the isolated Muckle Flugga, Rumblings and Vesta Skerry, at the extreme northern tip of Britain.

Foula is one of the most spectacular of islands with kilometre after kilometre of towering bird-covered cliffs. Its seabird populations match its grandeur. Pennie (1948) described how the species breeds in almost astronomical numbers with Puffins issuing like smoke from the honeycomb of burrows half-way down the 330 m-high Kame. This is still the main colony although part of the ground in which the birds burrow has slipped into the sea. In 1976 Foula had 70,000 Puffin burrows (Furness 1981). The population nesting on the isolated stacks and almost vertical grass slopes of Fair Isle has increased this century to maybe 20,000–30,000 pairs. The only other Shetland colonies with even a few thousand birds are Fetlar (1,500 pairs), Noss (2,000 pairs), Uyea (2,000 birds) and Sumburgh Head (5,000 birds occupying all available ground near the lighthouse). The last is a very ancient colony as Puffin bones are common in the ninth and tenth century dwellings at nearby Jarlshof. There are many other small colonies sprinkled around the outer edge of Shetland and several, such as those near Loch of Spiggie and at Colsay, have increased in size in the past 100 years, while other islands have been colonized, e.g., Inkster in 1951. There may also have been some redistribution of numbers; Haaf Gruney,

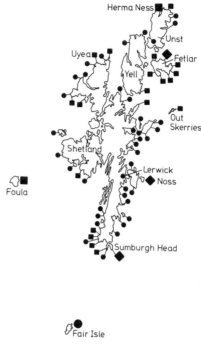

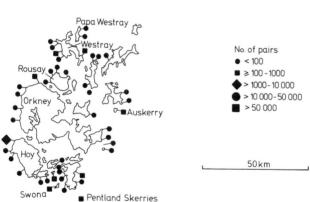

7   *Puffin colonies in Orkney and Shetland.*

for example, apparently gained birds when the soil blew off the top of one of the outlying stacks, after men had dug up the ground to get at burrows (Raeburn 1888).

Orkney Islands
Puffins burrow throughout the 5 ha of suitable ground on Sule Skerry and

almost threaten the lighthouse by their presence. Recent population estimates have been 60,000 pairs, 44,000, 36,000, 35,000 and 44,000 burrows in 1967, 1975, 1979, 1980 and 1982 respectively. All but the first estimate were obtained in basically the same way and so indicate no recent change. Most other Orkney colonies are very small. The only ones known to have more than 100 pairs are near the 335 m-high St John's Head, Hoy (? 2,000 pairs), Swona (250 pairs), Switha (250 pairs), Muckle Skerry (300 pairs), Costa Head (150 pairs), and unknown numbers at South Ronaldsay, Rapness, and Swine Dale-Inga Ness, Westray and Auskerry.

North and east Scotland

There are colonies on many of the steep and isolated cliffs from the northern Caithness/Sutherland border around past John O'Groats to Ord Point. Little has been written on the past history of these colonies and even now because they are difficult to get to the population estimates are probably unreliable. The largest colonies, maybe totalling 15,000–20,000 pairs, are at Duncansby Head, Ceann Leathad, and at Dunnet Head. Puffins have never been common on the east coast of Caithness and under 2,000 Puffins were found between John O'Groats and Helmsdale in 1977 (Mudge 1979), a tenth of the 1969 estimate.

Further south at Troup and Pennan Heads there were thousands of birds in 1895 (Harvie-Brown and Buckley 1895), 'many' in 1945 (Baxter and Rintoul 1953) but just a couple of hundred pairs now. There are small but mostly rapidly-increasing colonies on most suitable headlands from here south to St Abb's Head. In many areas nest sites are probably limiting the numbers, and the Puffins burrow in the few grassy ledges half-way up precipitous cliffs or nest in cracks in the cliffs themselves, rather in the way northern birds manage.

The most spectacular recent increases in Britain have occurred on the grassy islands in the Firth of Forth. Between 1959 and 1982 the Isle of May population has increased from five pairs to 10,000 pairs. Craigleith had 25 pairs in 1889, 1,500 burrows in 1978. Inchkeith and Fidra had no Puffins until 1965 and 1967, respectively, but in 1978 they totalled 1,100 birds. Ringing has shown that many of these birds are immigrants from the Farne Islands. Rather surprisingly, the population on the Bass Rock has remained less than 50 pairs for more than a hundred years.

ENGLAND

East Coast of England

The largest colony in the North Sea is on the low-lying bird-covered Farne Islands. The population has expanded steadily this century to 15,000–20,000 pairs. These islands have only a thin layer of soil, and severe soil erosion caused by the activities of the Puffins, gulls and seals (page 81) has resulted in a redistribution of the Puffins among the islands. Now there are only a few hundred pairs on the Wamses, which were honeycombed with burrows in 1885, but many thousands of pairs on Wideopens, Staple and Brownsman Islands.

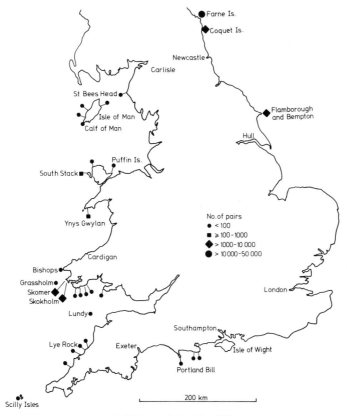

8 Puffin colonies in England, Wales and the Isle of Man.

Puffins were first seen ashore on Coquet Island, which only rises a few metres above the sea 40 km to the south, in 1962, successful breeding was recorded in 1966, and there were 1,500–2,000 pairs in 1982. The most southern colony in the North Sea is on the high, steep cliffs of Bempton and Flamborough Head, Humberside. At the start of this century there were many Puffins but the population temporarily declined between 1906 and 1952. Subsequently there has been a gradual increase, with 1,000 birds in 1969, 6,000 in 1978.

South Coast of England

No Puffins now breed on the Channel coast. The small colonies in Kent, and possibly Sussex, became extinct in the early part of the last century. The Puffin was never numerous on the Isle of Wight but there has been a steady decrease since 1923; for example, there were 300–350 birds at Freshwater Cliffs in 1937 but only 12 in 1961. A very few pairs may still breed near The Needles, where last century boats used to take out Puffin-shoots. The situation is little better in Dorset, for between 1964 and 1974 Puffins disappeared from several long-established colonies, and the numbers present at the few remaining sites decreased. The population of the east part of the county dropped from 35 pairs in 1964 to 17 in 1975 and 11 pairs in 1980. The species was more numerous early this century and eggs were taken for food near Lulworth Cove in the early nineteenth century. Further west, 2–3 pairs bred at Portland 1976–79 and 4–5 pairs in 1980–81. There are now no Puffins on the south Cornish coast where there were once colonies at Godrevy Island (perhaps until the lighthouse was built in 1860), on the Lizard Peninsula (where 60 dozen were killed on Gull Rock in 1860) and at Land's End (Penhallurick 1969, 1978).

Puffins were once used to pay the rent for the Scilly Isles and their value increased seven-fold between 1300 and 1440, though whether this was due to a decline in numbers or to inflation is unclear (Penhallurick 1969). Puffins were still very numerous at the end of the nineteenth century and the population on grassy Annet was put at 100,000 Puffins in 1908. There were smaller colonies on several other islands, but there has been a major decline since. There were still considerable numbers on Annet in 1924 but only 70 pairs in 1978. There are only scattered pairs on other islands.

Bristol Channel

The story is similar here (Penhallurick 1978). The once large Cornish colonies have all but disappeared and, in recent years, breeding has been proved or suspected only at Long and Short Islands (17 pairs in 1982), Lye Rock (2,000 birds in 1948, nil in 1982), The Sisters (one pair in 1967), The Mouls (20 birds in 1981) and Carter's Rock (8 burrows in 1967). The county total is probably less than 50 pairs. Nearby Lundy has a long association with Puffins. In 1892 it was 'impossible to form any conception of the incredible number . . . there would not be room for another Puffin'; in 1939 there were 3,500 pairs, in 1953, 400. The decline continued, with 40–45 pairs in 1969–71, but the colony appears to have now stabilized at about 100 birds. Rats and pollution have been suggested as possible reasons for the decline.

WALES

In 1894 Mathew wrote that 'we do not believe that we should exaggerate were we to say that the Puffins, in number, are then equal to all other birds in the county (Pembrokeshire) added together'. The population soon collapsed; for instance there were hundreds of thousands of Puffins on Grassholm in the 1890s but only 200 in 1928 and a handful of pairs now. Part of this decline was caused by the birds destroying the habitat (page 79). The largest Welsh colony is now on Skomer, but again this is a fragment of its 1894 size when there was said to be scarcely a yard of ground free of burrows. In 1946 the population was estimated at 50,000 pairs but the decline continued until the population stabilized at some 5,000–7,000 pairs in 1963 and perhaps 6,500 pairs in 1982.

Some of these birds may have been responsible for the increase on neighbouring Skokholm to 20,000 pairs in 1930–40. This latter colony then gradually declined to the 1969–79 level of 2,500 pairs.

Until 'quite recently' (Wintle 1925) the soil of Caldey Island was honeycombed with burrows (a favourite turn of phrase for Puffin colonies); there are now none of the main island although a few pairs remain on St Margaret's Island. There were 25–30 pairs on Cardigan Island in 1924 but none in 1930, perhaps due to rats which got ashore in 1924. Ramsey Island never had many Puffins and now has none. Other small colonies occur on Middleholm, on the Bishops west of Ramsey, and on a few mainland sites in Dyfed. Great tenacity has been shown by Puffins at Worm's Head, Gower where breeding still occurs in cracks in the steep cliffs despite the maximum count this century being only eight birds.

There are now only a few small colonies in North Wales, again remnants of much larger ones. Although Forrest's (1907) account of hundreds of thousands nesting in turf burrows on the very small St Tudwals Islands was probably an exaggeration, there were certainly very large numbers. In 1935 there were still many thousands of burrows, but rats reached the east (but not the west) island in the 1940s and by 1951 the bulk if not all of the Puffins had gone from both islands (Thearle *et al* 1953). Although rats may have wiped out the last few pairs on one island, the main decrease in numbers took place before rats were recorded. In 1774, Puffins on Puffin Island (or Priestholm) off Anglesey, were likened to swarms of bees, yet they had (apparently) been exterminated by rats in 1835. Soon after 1880 Puffins returned in numbers, reaching a peak of 2,000 pairs in 1907 due, it is said, to the extermination of the rats during this period. Rats were not seen again until the 1970s, yet by then the Puffins had declined to 300–400 pairs. There are now less than 50 pairs.

Other colonies in this area have always been relatively small, e.g. Ynys Gwylan-fawr (500–1,000 pairs), Ynys Gwylan-fach (50 pairs), South Stack off Holyhead (478 birds in 1977) and Ynys Arw (Skerries). Previously, there were mainland colonies near Aberdaron, on the Lleyn Peninusula. Puffins ceased breeding in the early 1950s on the Great and Little Ormes near Llandudno where they were 'swarming' in the eighteenth century but were 'seldom numerous' at the start of this century.

NORTH IRISH SEA

The Puffin is a rare bird here. The only breeding site in north-west England is St Bees Head, Cumbria, where up to 20 pairs nest among the other auks. It was once very numerous on the Calf of Man but numbers declined to 10–20 pairs in the early 1960s though they have since recovered slightly to 35 pairs in 1981. Elsewhere on the Isle of Man the species has never been common in historical times and there have been about 35 pairs for the last 20 years.

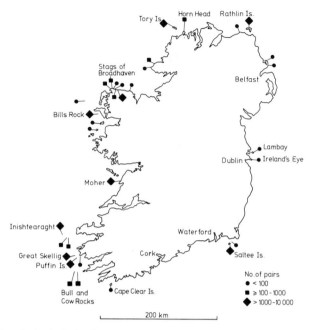

9   *Puffin colonies in Ireland.*

IRELAND

Irish colonies are poorly documented but the population was increasing at the end of the last century and a general decline was noted between 1925 and 1960s (Ruttledge 1966). There are now some 30–40 colonies but only seven have more than a thousand pairs.

About half of the Irish population is on the Kerry Islands. Inishtearaght, a rocky pyramid of an island with the most westerly seabird colonies off continental Europe, once had the largest Irish colony. The population appeared to decline from 20,000–30,000 to 7,500–8,000 occupied burrows between 1955–68 and 1969–73; this has been disputed but the doubters produced no more figures. Disagreement over even such large possible changes indicates yet again the difficulties in monitoring Puffin numbers. Other large colonies are on Great Skellig or Skellig Michael (6,000–6,500 pairs in 1969–73), and Puffin Island (somewhere between 4,000 and 10,000 pairs 1967–81). There were once 'incredible numbers' on Little Skellig (Turle 1891) but there are now few, possibly due to Gannets taking over part of the nesting areas. Puffins were numerous on Great Blasket earlier this century but now there are extremely few. Two colonies to increase in recent times are on Inishnabro (116 pairs in 1966, 600 in 1973) and Inishvickillaun (300 pairs in 1969) – both of these appear to be returns to previous levels.

Further north there are several thousand pairs on the 8 km of Cliffs of

Moher, Co. Clare, whereas the two large colonies in Co. Mayo on Illanmaster (2,000 and 5,500 pairs in 1969 and 1976) and Bills Rocks (at least 5,000 pairs in 1939, 1,000 in 1967) are on islands. Other nesting areas are Clare Island, Stags of Broadhaven, and Blackrock (totalling 1,700 pairs in 1954, far fewer in 1969), Pig Island, Inishturk, Kid Island (500–1,000 pairs) and cliffs near Porturlin. In Co. Donegal there are colonies on Tory Island (1,200–2,000 pairs in 1954, less in 1969), Tormore Island and the nearby mainland (maybe 500 pairs) and at Horn Head (maybe 250 pairs).

The main colony on the north coast is on Rathlin Island (2,000 pairs) at the North Channel entrance to the Irish Sea. The other colonies in Co. Antrim are small, at Muck Island, The Gobbins, Carrick-a-rede, Sheep Island and Larrybane Head. There was previously a colony at Hulin Rocks off Larne but this was deserted following the building of a lighthouse (Thompson 1851). The only east coast colonies are on Lambay Island (300–400 pairs in 1907, 1,000 pairs in 1939, 100 pairs in 1970) and Ireland's Eye (1,000 pairs in 1939, eight birds seen offshore in 1969). Rats and human interference have been suggested as reasons for these declines.

The main southern colony in Co. Wexford is that on Great Saltee. In about 1895 there were many thousands of pairs burrowing in the earthy top of the island and the colony appeared to be expanding in 1913. Numbers later fell but there were 3,000 pairs in 1949. The population declined to about 750 pairs in 1969 and remained there until 1979 before increasing slightly (Lloyd 1982). The island has some rats though they do not appear seriously to affect the Puffins, perhaps because the rats avoid the cliffs. There are also a few pairs of Puffins on neighbouring Little Saltee. The only other colonies on the south coast of Eire are on Cape Clear Island, and Bull and Cow Rocks in Co. Cork.

BRITISH AND IRISH POPULATIONS

The above account should have warned the reader to be wary of accepting glib statements of counts. However, it seems part of human nature to want to know how many of anything there are. Therefore I give my best qualified guesses of the various populations (rounded off and expressed as pairs) in 1982:

Outer Hebrides	400,000	England	20,000
Inner Hebrides	2,500	Wales	10,000
Firth of Clyde area	500	Ireland	45,000
Northwest Scotland	35,000	Isle of Man	50
Shetland	125,000	Channel Islands	300
Orkney	45,000		
Northeast Scotland	20,000		
TOTAL Scotland	625,000		

These suggest a total of about 700,000 pairs which will probably surprise many people. In 1975, I speculated that there were about 550,000. This large increase is partly real and partly due to better coverage of the major colonies.

CHAPTER 4

Monitoring numbers in Scotland

There are plenty of old, extravagant and picturesque descriptions of Puffin colonies which contrast markedly with the relatively modest numbers present at the same colonies today and thereby suggest massive decreases in numbers. Some descriptions were obviously written by the inexperienced who were overawed by the spectacle of a few thousand Puffins, but others were probably true. The evaluation of the past status of the Puffin needs subjective judgements and is, therefore, unsatisfactory. Modern ecology requires a more numerate approach. Here I give details of some attempts to satisfy this need, set a base-line against which future changes can be measured and give case histories of changes in Puffin numbers at two very different Scottish colonies. Details are also given of the results of monitoring Puffin numbers at four other colonies.

THE PROBLEMS

Counting large numbers of Puffins is difficult and the interpretation of such counts is almost impossible due to great diurnal and seasonal variation in the numbers visiting the colonies. Counts of birds are used only as a last resort where the nest sites are on inaccessible cliffs or deep among boulder screes. Counts at small colonies give some idea of the colony size but it is impossible to convert such counts to the actual number of pairs at a colony.

Counting occupied burrows in colonies where Puffins dig burrows is a much more worthwhile exercise. Such burrows are usually easily distinguished from unoccupied ones because of fresh excavation, droppings, hatched eggshells or fish in the entrance. The burrows of rabbits, which occur in many Puffin colonies in Britain, are larger, have well-worn runs leading to them and usually have distinctive droppings nearby. There is no easy way to distinguish between a Puffin and Manx Shearwater burrow but luckily these two species coexist on only a few islands. Counts are best made in late April or May, that is just before or during laying when the birds are digging new or cleaning out old burrows. An added advantage is that the sometimes luxuriant vegetation has not grown up and covered the burrow entrances.

It is possible to convert such counts to breeding pairs by following the fate of a sample of burrows. For instance, on St Kilda 132 out of 208 burrows (63%) which had been classified as occupied were definitely used for breeding that year and in two areas on the Isle of May, 78% and 93% of occupied burrows later had eggs. The remaining burrows were mostly still being dug or were too short for Puffins to use. Single checks are insufficient to determine whether or not a burrow is used for breeding; some pairs may not have laid and others may have already lost their eggs. A much simpler, and probably more valid, way to follow the changes of the population is to compare counts of occupied burrows which are made at approximately the same time each year.

It often pays to be suspicious of counts of burrows, or indeed of anything, since their accuracy is frequently more implied than real. As regards Puffin burrows, the best results are obtained when one observer counts burrows in fairly small areas (e.g. $30\,m^2$). Repeat counts then are usually consistent (in most cases to within 5–10% of the mean) if the area counted is small. However, variation reaches 20% if the area is large, probably because the counter 'gets lost' in large featureless areas and either misses burrows or double-counts some. A series of counts of the same area can reduce this error but this is often undesirable because regular crossing of densely burrowed areas causes the collapse of burrows. A more important, and as yet largely unquantified source of error, is that due to the counts being made by different observers in different years. Different observers probably have slightly different criteria as to what constitutes an occupied Puffin burrow.

Estimating the numbers of Puffins nesting in boulder scree is difficult. One method is to count the number of loads of fish being taken to young in a known proportion of the colony, and to compare this with the number of feeds taken to a known number of young during the same period. However, this assumes that the feeding rate is the same in the two areas, but since the feeding rate changes with the age of the young, and the laying dates vary greatly within a colony, this method is probably invalid.

In very small colonies it may be possible to count all the burrows directly. However, this is generally impracticable, so sample areas must be selected. Monitoring is usually carried out by counting burrows each year in a few fixed transects 3 m wide running through the colony (Plate 10). This method is useful for detecting changes in the boundary of the colony and in burrow density in both the central and peripheral parts of the colony, but the accuracy of such counts is difficult to determine as the sample size for statistical purposes is the number of transects.

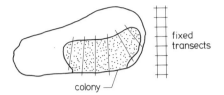

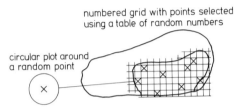

10   Two methods of monitoring the numbers of burrows in a Puffin colony. The upper has fixed transects running across the colony, the lower has circular plots positioned at random in the colony.

A statistically more reliable method is to determine the burrow density at randomly selected points. Again, in evaluating results, it is wise to be sceptical of the use of the term random – it is sometimes used to glorify a haphazard or non-systematic laying out of points. In fact it takes considerable time and trouble to lay out a random pattern. A map of the colony is made and a numbered grid superimposed on it (Fig. 10). Then the required points are selected using a table of random numbers. These points must then be found on the ground, for instance by measuring distances and angles from known points. A mean burrow density is then calculated from counts of burrows in quadrats placed at these points, regardless of whether or not there are any burrows, even if the whole area is bare rock. The size and shape of the quadrats are not important as long as the average quadrat contains some burrows. Circular quadrats of $30\,m^2$ have proved to be the most easily and quickly counted. Points can be staked and used in future years. The accuracy of the estimate depends on the number of quadrats and the uniformity of the burrow density. If there are obvious differences in burrow density (often indicated by differences in vegetation) greater accuracy is obtained by sub-dividing the colony and treating each part as a separate colony. This technique is unlikely to detect a change in burrow density if the birds leave or join the colony at the edge. Adequate monitoring needs both fixed transects and randomly placed quadrats.

The extrapolation of colony size from burrow density adds another inaccuracy – that involved in calculating the colony area. This is extremely difficult to measure due to the irregularities in the ground and the virtual impossibility of defining the edge of a colony with scattered outlying burrows. So far as I know, no method of population estimate of a burrow-nesting bird has taken adequate account of these potential inaccuracies.

THE ST KILDA POPULATION

The problems associated with counting Puffin burrows and the interpretation of old descriptive accounts are well illustrated by the study of the colonies on the St Kilda islands group. These islands, situated 66 km west of Harris in the Outer Hebrides, are among the most spectacular of British islands with towering cliffs rising sheer from the sea, their tops often shrouded in mist. The islands are Hirta (where the resident human population lived prior to its evacuation in 1930, and at present the site of an army camp), Dun, Soay and Boreray. Together they once had one of the world's largest concentrations of Puffins. By the time of the first detailed survey in 1969 the numbers were greatly reduced but even now there are probably 300,000 pairs.

The native St Kildans, and to a slightly lesser extent the birds, attracted much attention following the visit of Martin Martin in 1697. Most visitors accepted that Puffins were part of the scene and just remarked on the large numbers and how the islanders snared them. There are, however, the following dated accounts, which give some idea of the Puffin's numbers, distribution and changes of fortune. These admittedly sparse details, taken from a paper published by Harris and Murray in *British Birds* (1977), are far superior to those available for almost any other Puffin populations.

1758   Incredible flight of these Puffins . . . and sometimes while on the wing, involve everything below them in darkness, like a small cloud of locusts, in another country (Macaulay 1764).

1829–43   It is by far the most numerous of all the birds which frequent these islands. There is not a suitable spot anywhere which does not swarm with them. Everywhere you see them in thousands, while at the same time the air is full of them coming and going. I estimate that there cannot be fewer of them than three millions (Mackenzie 1905).

1876   Sands (1878) calculated that 89,600 Puffins were killed on the islands.

1894   By far the largest colonies of this bird are on Borrera and Soay, where they are said to be on the increase. They have destroyed the greater part of the pasture of these islands by burrowing and killing the grass around, owing to their immense numbers. They also breed in countless thousands on St Kilda (Hirta) and Doon as well. The factors receive about 200 stone [over 2,000 kg; 10 kg = one St Kilda stone] of feathers from these islands yearly. It takes about 450 Puffins to make a stone of feathers. The feathers of other birds are mixed with them, but Puffins are by far the greatest producers (Elliott 1895).

1902   It is difficult, without seeming exaggeration, to describe the immense multitudes of these birds . . . Plentiful as they are on the main islands, it is only when one visits the subsidiary islands that the full wealth of Puffin life becomes manifest. They occur in countless thousands on Dun, but on Boreray and Soay the vast hordes of birds baffle description . . . There seems no doubt that of late years they have considerably increased in numbers due to the fact that they are no longer secured for the sake of their feathers (Wiglesworth 1903).

1920s   Puffins were abundant around much of the coast of Hirta with the largest colonies at Carn Mor, where they nested in large numbers both in the boulders and turf, and at the back of Conachair. Up to 14 were killed with a single shot just south of the village, a place where now it is rare to see more than the occasional Puffin.

Puffins were all over Dun but there were rather fewer on the flatter areas down on the western end and probably none in the lazybed area (see Plate 2).

1931   David Lack's diary records the Puffin as being: By far the commonest bird on the island, nesting everywhere on the upper parts of the cliffs. The numbers on Hirta had left us totally unprepared for the simply incredible numbers of the species on Dun. The whole of the Bay side of the island was covered with the birds, the burrows being about a yard apart throughout an area half a mile long and about 200 feet broad.

1939   Undoubtedly the most numerous bird in the group ... Numbers may be safely estimated at above 100,000 pairs, and the actual total may be very much larger (Nicholson and Fisher 1940).

1947   James Fisher (1947) wrote: I judged each of the following six Puffin-slopes of St Kilda to contain more burrows than any colony I had seen elsewhere in Britain (even more than Garbh Eilean of the Shiant Isles, which we had explored in the previous week):- the north face of Conachair, the highest cliff in Britain, on the north side of Hirta; the island of Dun; the Carn Mor on Hirta's south-west aspect; the sides of the Cambir of Hirta; the island of Soay; the island of Boreray.

1948   James Ferguson-Lees's diary records: During the day the air above Dun continued to be a whirling twisting mass of these birds – uncountable thousands ... On Dun, the entire grassy slope was found to be one mass of burrows seemingly one every foot or two in all directions ... Adults flying round overhead and over the sea in hundreds and thousands, all forming one huge unbroken circle ... These slopes are so riddled by burrows that it is impossible to walk more than a few steps without raising a protesting groan from the inmate of some burrow, whose roof has been broken in.

1956   Major colonies of probably over 100,000 pairs were seen on the north-eastern slopes of Dun, eastern face of Soay, on south-western slopes of Boreray and Sunadal of Boreray (Boyd *et al.* 1957).

1960   Donald Baird pointed out that birds were deserting the mainland slopes overlooking Village Bay on Hirta. The numbers in the other colonies there were also by no means so large, and the birds had begun to leave the centre of the landward end of Dun, though vast numbers could still be seen visiting the far end and the slopes of Soay.

1969   Two estimates of the population were a half to three-quarters of a million burrows (but few seemed to be occupied) and 33,800 occupied burrows (Flegg 1972, Birnie 1972).

1970–71   In 1971, there were no more than 15,000 pairs on Hirta. Between 1969 and 1971, the numbers on Dun appeared to decline dramatically, and in the latter year the population was estimated at between 7,000 and 20,000 pairs (Flegg 1972).

1972   There was no evidence of a further decline and several areas appeared to have been recolonized since 1971 (Schofield 1975).

More recent changes

Dun

In 1975 Stuart Murray and I noted the extent of the main Puffin areas on an aerial photograph, measured their areas and sampled the density of occupied burrows in various parts of the colony. The area not occupied by Puffins was either solid rock or very eroded, bare earth slopes tenanted by Fulmars. The population was *c.* 40,000 burrows in 15 ha. We roughly checked this by a simple marking and recapture experiment. In 1975, 858 young were ringed in burrows on Dun and eight of these were found among 444 juvenile Puffins caught at fledging. Nesting success was about 80% that year. Extrapolation from these figures gives a population of 55,000–60,000 breeding pairs. In 1976, 422 fledglings caught included three out of 226 young ringed in burrows. Nesting success was 67% so about 47,000 eggs had probably been laid, though there were certainly other occupied burrows in which no eggs were laid. The accuracy of these estimates is unknown but the population was probably within the range of 40,000–60,000 pairs. Such estimates as these cannot be refined without an unreasonable effort. As it was, the estimate of the numbers of burrows took us both two weeks.

It is difficult to make comparison with past surveys because different observers have treated the problem in different ways and measured different things. It is imperative that techniques are standardized. We tried to do this each year by counting the numbers of occupied burrows in 12 permanent transects laid out across the colony. Counts (in the 5,000 m^2 covered) have been:

1974	1,367	1978	1,280
1975	1,460	1979	1,431
1976	1,551	1980	1,711
1977	1,345		

We also counted occupied burrows in 56 randomly placed quadrats which gave population estimates (and 95% confidence intervals) for the part of the colony sampled at:

1977	25,000	(21,000–29,000)
1978	17,000	(13,000–21,000)
1979	23,000	(18,000–27,000)
1980	22,000	(16,000–28,000)

Although the mean burrow densities in 1977, 1979 and 1980 were similar, that in 1978 was significantly lower. The apparent loss of 30% of pairs between 1977 and 1978 appears to have been due to these pairs not having bred rather than to birds having died, because the population returned to its normal level in 1979.

Obviously the population decline had halted. Although there had been a decline one wonders if it had been as dramatic as claimed. The statement that Puffins covered Dun from one end to the other must be viewed with suspicion, since, even in the 1920s, before there was any suggestion of a decline in numbers, Puffins were scarce or absent from the old lazybed (cultivated) areas at the west end and at a low density on the north-west part (Plate 2). Mike Hornung dug soil profiles in areas where there are now no Puffins and found no signs of the soil having been burrowed by birds, certainly not for 30 years and probably not for much longer. The effects of human activity in the lazybed area are still noticeable at least 100 years after their last cultivation. Agriculture and

Puffins hardly go together. I think that there has been no recent decline in numbers on Dun.

Hirta

In 1973–79 there were about 10,000 pairs of Puffins on Hirta whereas the older accounts leave no doubt that there were once many more. Very large numbers certainly occurred up to the late 1940s, but had gone by 1958. The most important reference is that of James Fisher, who remarked that there were more Puffins on the north face of Conachair in 1947 than on Garbh Eilean in the Shiant Islands. Even now, following its marked decline, the number of Puffins at the Garbh Eilean colony is as spectacular as anything on St Kilda. The Conachair colony has become a mere shadow of what it must have been, having lost most of its Puffins by 1956, and virtually all by 1958. Nothing that I have read or been told convinces me of any large change in Puffin numbers on Hirta since 1957 and the situation today is almost identical to that in 1968–69. Thus, it appears that the decline occurred in the late 1940s and early 1950s.

Soay and Boreray

The population on Soay has always been larger than that on Hirta or Dun but it has been poorly documented as the island is extremely difficult to land on. In 1971, Brooke (1972a) estimated 70,000–80,000 pairs on the main colony, whereas in 1977 we thought that there were double this number. Such discrepancies are to be expected given the difficult nature of the island.

The main colony on Boreray has some 40,000–60,000 occupied burrows (Duncan *et al* 1982). There are several other colonies and the total population is probably of the order of 100,000 pairs. A photograph taken at the Cleit Village in 1975 showed a similar number of Puffins to one taken by Richard Kearton 1905. Perhaps there has been no great change in numbers in recent years.

The total number of Puffins on St Kilda

The total population on St Kilda is now about 300,000 pairs. How does this compare with previous figures? Mackenzie who was the minister on the island 1829–43, was an acute observer of the habits of St Kildan birds, but it would be impossible to fit his calculated 50,000 Guillemots on to Stac Biorach, so there must be doubts about the accuracy of his estimate of three million Puffins (and a million Guillemots) on the islands then. There must, however, have been far more Puffins on Hirta in the nineteenth and early twentieth centuries than there now are and numbers probably decreased sometime between 1947 and 1957–60. However, over the last 10 years there is no evidence of a significant decline.

THE ISLE OF MAY COLONY

The fortunes of this population in the Firth of Forth are in sharp contrast to St Kilda, for the population is increasing at a spectacular rate. Also its history is

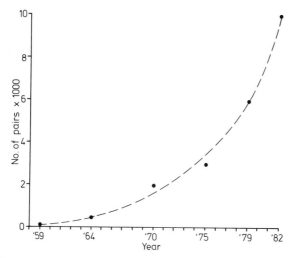

11 The increase in the number of Puffins on the Isle of May 1959–82.

well documented (details in Eggeling 1960, Harris 1977).

There were no very early records of Puffins on the Isle of May but in 1883 there were 30–40 pairs and Southern (1938) suggested maybe 50 pairs in 1936. The population was only 5–10 pairs in the early 1950s but in 1957–58 at least

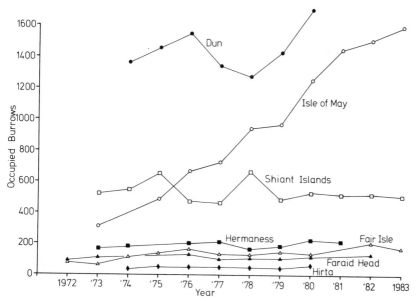

12 Recent changes in the numbers of occupied Puffin burrows in fixed transects across seven Scottish colonies.

50 pairs attempted to establish a colony. This attempt was brief and unsuccessful and in 1960 there were only a few pairs all breeding in cliff fissures. However, since then the population has rocketed with 2000 pairs in 1970 and maybe 10,000 in 1982 (Fig. 11). Between 1975 and 1982, the number of occupied burrows in my monitoring areas·increased from 489 to 1,511 and the overall area of the colony increased by 50%. The rate of increase since 1951, 22% per annum, was more than double that that the population could manage on its own and was due, in part, to immigration from the Farne Islands (later).

OTHER COLONIES

The occupied burrows in fixed transects were counted more or less annually at four other Scottish colonies: Garbh Eilean in the Shiant Islands, Fair Isle situated between the Orkney and the Shetland Islands, Faraid Head in Sutherland and Hermaness on Unst, in Shetland. The numbers on Fair Isle increased from 65 in 1973 to 181 in 1983, whereas the counts at the other colonies all remained at approximately the same level or increased only sightly (Fig. 12). All these populations appear to be flourishing.

A survey of the literature and a comparison of estimates of numbers made in 1969–70 during Operation Seafarer, and since, show that there have been some dramatic declines in numbers of British Puffins this century. However, the regular monitoring of numbers, a survey of changes up to 1975 and a further partial survey in 1979, suggests that the overall decline has probably halted, at least temporarily. The populations which are still declining are those on the fringe of the species' breeding range and it may well be that some of these are now too small to be viable.

SUMMARY

The historical record is difficult to interpret and changes in Puffin numbers are best followed by annual counts of occupied burrows in permanently marked areas.

Burrows should be counted early in the breeding season in transects crossing the colony and in randomly positioned quadrats.

There were once many more than the present 300,000 pairs of Puffins on St Kilda. Most of those on Hirta disappeared between 1947 and 1957 but it is impossible to determine the extent or timing of changes on the other islands. In contrast the population on the Isle of May has increased from 5–10 pairs in the 1950s to at least 10,000 pairs in 1982. Numbers of burrows at four other Scottish colonies have increased or remained constant in recent years.

CHAPTER 5

The Puffin outside Britain and Ireland

The main centre of the Puffin world is Iceland, where the population is several times greater than that of all other countries combined. Large numbers also nest in Canada, Norway and the Faeroe Islands. Colonies further north are very small and the population of the high arctic subspecies is probably less than 10,000 birds. The changes of fortune of most of these populations is undocumented but there are now many fewer pairs in France and America than there once were. The populations in Sweden (maybe 50 pairs at the start of this century) became extinct in about 1970 while that on Heligoland disappeared in about 1830.

The following accounts are based on information supplied by local ornithologists and in a few cases I may well have bullied or inveigled them into making rash or speculative assessments of colony size. Figures *must* be treated as order of magnitude and nothing more. Much of this information is incomplete; however, it is the best available. Details of sources are given in Appendix B.

FRANCE

The only French Puffins nest in Brittany (recent details from E. Pasquet). Both the range and numbers have greatly diminished and in 1982 there were less than 250 pairs. The only real colonies are on the two small islands of Rouzic and Malban in the Sept-Iles. Rouzic had 10,000 pairs of Puffins when it was made a reserve in 1912, and 6,000 in 1950. This decline has continued to

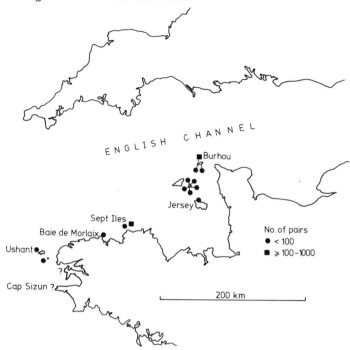

13   *Puffin colonies in France and Channel Islands.*

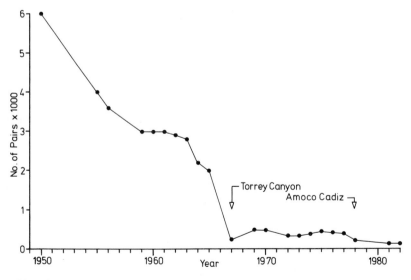

14   *The decline of the Puffin population on Rouzic, Sept-Iles. (Counts from Pénicaud 1979 and E. Pasquet.)*

the present (Fig. 14). Oil from the *Torrey Canyon* wrecked off England in 1967 removed 85% of the remaining pairs and further oil from the *Amoco Cadiz* in early 1978 further reduced the colony. There were 100–150 pairs in 1981–82. However, the earlier gradual decline, spead over 20 or more years, shows that these disasters only hastened but did not cause the decline of the population. The latest estimates for the population on Malban were 350 pairs in 1976 and 50–100 pairs in 1981–82.

The other colonies are minuscule with (in 1981–82) 10–15 pairs on the three islands in Baie de Morlaix, one pair on Banneg (archipel de Molène), Keller (possibly a few) and Ar Youc'h, Ushant (three pairs). There might still be a single pair on Ar Gest, near to Ile de Crozon. Two birds were seen throughout the 1979 season at Cap Sizun; these were the most southern Puffins in Europe. The species is now extinct on archipel de Glenan (last bred late 1950s) and archipel d'Houat (1969). Birds were seen on Cap Fréhel in the 1960s and early 1970s but they were not proved to nest.

CHANNEL ISLANDS

There are now less than 500 pairs in the Channel Islands. Great numbers bred on Burhou in 1878, though maybe fewer than there were in 1866, and in 1946 Lockley (1953) described how 'probably a hundred thousand Puffins were simultaneously on the wing, sweeping upwind in two parallel lines divided by the rocky back bone of the island, and swinging downwind over the sea. Endlessly the twin ellipses swung round, with a roar of wings like the thunder of the traffic of a distant city'. Lockley returned in 1949 and did not remark on any change. In 1966 there were 2,500 pairs whereas recent maximal annual counts of birds have been less than 500. The same story of decline holds for the smaller colonies on nearby islands, e.g., 200–300 pairs at Plémont and Grand Becquet, Jersey, in 1911–14 but only 20 in 1919. Numbers once bred in holes in soft soil and among stones on small islets spread from Les Amfroques off the northern end of Herm; Guernsey fishermen used to visit these colonies 'barbeloting', i.e. taking eggs. There are few pairs now. In 1946 there were 750 pairs on L'Etac de Serk but less than 30 pairs in the last few years.

Very small numbers nest on Sark (L'Etac, Moie de Brenière and Moie Fano), Jersey (Plémont), Alderney (Cocque Lihou and Hannaine Bay), Jethou, Crévichon, Herm and Les Amfroques (including Longue Pierre and Godin).

FAEROE ISLANDS

Some of the colonies here are extremely large, and are found on isolated stacks or very large cliffs. All are very difficult to count. The vast majority of birds nests on the coast but there are also small colonies up to 2 km inland on Fugloy, Svínoy, Streymoy, West-Vagar and Mykines, and young sometimes fledge by floating down the streams. Lights from villages attract young Puffins from these inland colonies and it is not uncommon to see confused fledglings

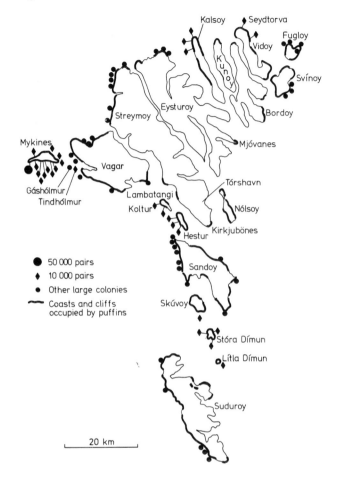

15   The main Puffin colonies in the Faeroe Islands (E. Mortensen). Smaller numbers nest on the marked coasts.

walking the streets. Many of the colonies have suffered from rats which are now numerous on the larger islands of Suduroy, Vagar, Streymoy, Eysturoy, Kunoy, Bordoy, and Vidoy. On some of these islands the populations are only a third to a fifth of their previous size. Most colonies appear to be holding their own in recent years, and declines have only been noticed in colonies close to villages, presumably due to persecution. The total population is now estimated at half to three-quarters of a million pairs but it may have been twice as large 100 years ago. The following account was supplied by E. Mortensen and refers to the population in 1982.

The rat free island of Mykines at the western tip of the Faeroes is now the Puffin's stronghold, with over 100,000 pairs scattered around the island. The largest numbers are on the slopes and among the boulders on the south side and the biggest concentration is between Mykineshólmur and the west of the village.

Although tens of thousands of pairs breed around Vagar, Puffins are now completely absent from several kilometres of once thriving, perhaps over-crowded colonies. Only in the west have Puffins survived in numbers in accessible places. Poisoning of rats has resulted in an increase in the numbers of Puffins in some boulder colonies which suggests that these animals caused the large reduction of the population size. There is a large colony on Tindhólmur, and small numbers on Gáshólmur, two small islands at the entrance to Sorvagsfjordur. Further south Puffins breed in large numbers on the north-west cliffs and on the north-east slopes and cliffs of Koltur, while there are three large colonies in earthy areas on the west side of nearby Hestur and smaller numbers on the eastern side.

Rat-free Sandoy has tens of thousands of pairs split between eight main colonies of 5,000–20,000 pairs. On the west side most burrows are in earth, elsewhere they are in slopes and boulders. The important bird island of Stóra Dímun has great numbers on the eastern slopes, on the western cliffs and along the cliff edge to the south-west. Skuvoy has very many Puffins on the slopes of the southern side and some thousands of pairs breed on the west. Considerable numbers breed on the slopes all around Lítla Dímun. Only about a fifth of the total which once occurred on Suduroy now survive but the population is still many thousands, breeding on stacks, among boulders and in earthy cliffs all along the west side. There are only some hundreds of pairs on the east.

Nólsoy, the island opposite the capital Thorshavn, has great numbers breeding among very large boulders and on the cliffs in the east but only small numbers on the west. Streymoy was once an important Puffin island, but the only dense concentrations now are in earthy burrows and on stacks off the enormous north-west cliffs. Small numbers occur on the south-east and south-west.

Some thousands breed on the cliffs and stacks of the northern coast of Eysturoy and in restricted areas near Mjóvanes at the eastern tip and at two small colonies in the south-east. The colony south-west of Kallur on Kalsoy is one of the largest in the Faeroe Islands; there are also small numbers on the long western shore, and the island total must be very high. Across the water, on Kunoy, Puffins survive only around the north tip on stacks and in earthy burrows in cliffs where there are some thousands of pairs. Bordoy has maybe 500 pairs on the northern and south-eastern points.

Vidoy was once an important Puffin island but the only large colonies remaining are in earthy slopes near the northern tip in Seydtorva and in boulders to the east of Villingadalsfjall. Very small numbers occur on the south-east coasts. The three main colonies on Svínoy (two in earth, one in boulders) are on the southern coast but there are small numbers in many other places. The population is of modest size. The easternmost of the Faeroes, Fugloy, has Puffins breeding all around the island; there are four main colonies, a large one in the north-west and two inland colonies in boulders, and an eastern colony in a cliff slope.

ICELAND

Although the majority of North Atlantic Puffins nest in Iceland their distribution is very imperfectly known. This is due to the large numbers of colonies scattered over hundreds, perhaps thousands, of islands and along large stretches of coast, and the lack of observations. Many colonies on islands or even mainland slopes in the north-east, north-west and east mainland will certainly have been overlooked, but probably most colonies on the south coast between Thorlakshöfn and Hornafjordur are plotted because the coast is mainly sandy and Puffins do not nest in such habitat. The marked areas at Breidafjördur and Myrar in Fig. 16 have 2,000–3,000 and hundreds of islands respectively, and many of these islands have Puffins nesting. Many colonies have never been visited by an ornithologist and some may now be extinct.

Lockley suggested that there were five million Puffins in Iceland in 1953, but F. Gudmundsson thought this conservative. Petersen (1982), the only person intensively to have studied auks in Iceland, and who supplied this account, suspects that there may now be 8–10 million Puffins in the country. The overall impression is that there has not been any recent general decline although the colonies at the Myrar islands do appear to be smaller now than they were several decades ago. In parts of Breidafjördur there may have been a slight increase since the Second World War, possibly because of less persecution and some small new colonies have been established on Tjörnes in the north-east.

About a third of the total population is on the Westman Islands off the southern coast, where Puffins burrow in the earthy tops of the high and precipitous islands. Between 1850 and 1870 numbers declined markedly due to the use of nets which were spread over the burrows to catch breeding birds. This practice was banned in about 1870 and around 1875 the 'fleygastrong' (háfur, meaning sack net, in Icelandic) was introduced from the Faeroes. This method of bird-fowling tends to catch immatures and not breeding birds at precipitous colonies such as these, and the population soon increased.

Many of the colonies on the Breidafjördur islands are in the grassy tops (and to a lesser extent in boulder screes) of small islands only a few metres above high-water mark. Most mainland colonies are in steep slopes or cliffs overlooking the sea but that at Vik is unusual in being about 1 km inland on a 70 m-high cliff. Puffins nesting here do so because there are few alternatives. They place themselves at risk from kleptoparasitic Arctic Skuas for a much longer time than if they nested on the coast.

The colonies on Grimsey in the north are large and the birds nest in grassy slopes and boulders, not only high up the slopes as in Britain, but at sea level. In contrast, the colonies at Hornstrandir, the north-west tip of Iceland, are small, ranging from less than a hundred to 5,000 pairs and are mainly located in scree slopes on inaccessible parts of the 500 m-high cliffs. Several of these small

1 *Upper:* Puffin landing with wings spread to give the lowest stalling speed. The worn primaries are clearly visible and note that the wear is most pronounced at the tips, areas which are not protected by the adjacent feather when the wing is closed. *(D and K Urry)*
Lower: The moth-flight display showing the crossed feet and the hunched appearance. *(D and K Urry)*

2 *Upper:* Dun (left) and Hirta, St Kilda. The ridges of the cultivated lazybeds are clearly visible and it
doubtful if Puffins ever bred in this area. The lower part of the slope is the area of low burrow density wher
Great Black-backed Gulls kill large numbers of Puffins.
Lower: Part of the high density study area on Dun, St Kilda with Hirta in background. The fleshy leaves i
the foreground are sorrel which is common in ungrazed Puffin colonies. Late in the season sorrel grow
waist-high and hides the Puffins.

Upper: Great Island, Newfoundland where Puffins breeding on the slope do better than Puffins on the
[fl]at because they can escape parasitic Herring Gulls by landing directly in their burrow entrances. *(S W*
ress)

[L]*ower:* Puffins and sheep co-exist on Boreray, St Kilda. Grazing keeps the grass short and the burrows are
[v]ery stable. *(K Taylor)*

4 *Upper:* The main Puffin colony on the Isle of May looking over the Low Light towards the Fife coast. This was taken on an April morning.
Lower: By the evening large numbers of Puffins were ashore at one of the study areas. Note the marked burrows, the rocks where Puffins stand, and Herring Gulls taking up territories.

5 *Upper:* The collapsed and deserted Puffin colony on Grassholm in about 1930. At the turn of the century there were hundreds of thousands of Puffins here. *(R M Lockley)*
Lower: A similarly defunct colony on Staple, Farne Islands in May 1974. *(M Hornung)*

6 *Upper:* A juvenile Puffin on its way to the sea at night. *(C M Perrins)*
Left: A first-year Puffin on the Isle of May in July with a small bill and a few black feathers in front of the eye. Note the immaculate freshly moulted primaries; by this date the feathers of adults are very bleached and abraded.
Right: A two-year-old Puffin with a larger bill and one ill-defined bill groove.

7 *Top:* A breeding adult Puffin with three well defined bill grooves.
Left: A two- or three-year-old Puffin with the typical 'kinked' beak of an immature.
Right: An unusual Puffin caught on the Isle of May in August which had a winter face and had lost some of the bill plates.

8 *Upper:* An adult Puffin in winter plumage about to go down a burrow on Great Island in July 1975. Puffins rarely breed in this plumage. *(S W Kress)*
Lower: A Puffin with a load of small sandeels in Shetland. Some Puffins have pale edges to their back feathers but this is not a sign of age. *(Bobby Tulloch)*

9   *Upper:* This Puffin was hatched on Great Island in Newfoundland but was artificially reared on Eastern Egg Rock in Maine. Three years later it returned to its foster home and was enticed ashore by some dummy Puffins. *(S W Kress)*

Lower: If given sufficient care and extremely good conditions Puffins can live in captivity. These birds were raised in captivity in Holland and later one pair laid an egg in the nest-box. *(P Duiven)*

10 *Upper:* A fixed transect in a Puffin colony at Røst, Lofoten Islands.
Lower: Puffins hovering in the updraught at the cliff-edge. It is these birds which are most easily caught by bird-fowlers. *(Bobby Tulloch)*

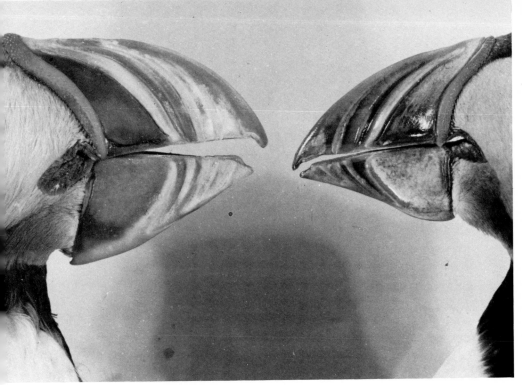

11 *Upper:* Bills of adult male Puffins from Spitzbergen (left) and Britain. There can be little doubt that the birds belong to different subspecies.
Left: Mist-netting Puffins and collecting fish which they had dropped. Puffins bite and scratch – notice the tears in the net.
Right: Puffins almost always mate on the sea where the female is all but drowned. Matings on land are usually unsuccessful. *(P Duiven)*

12 *Upper:* Puffins have small pointed wings well suited for use as paddles underwater. The colour of the underwing is very variable (compare Plate 6).
Lower: A load of many rockling. Such loads weigh little and the fish often fragment or are dropped before they reach the chick.

13 *Upper:* A Puffin landing with a super-load of sandeels. The characteristic sideways position of the inner toe is clearly visible. *(D and K Urry)*
Lower: Four loads of fish brought to young composed of one saithe and two very small sprats, five sandeels, four small sprats and two large sprats. Several of the fish show marks where they were caught just behind the gills.

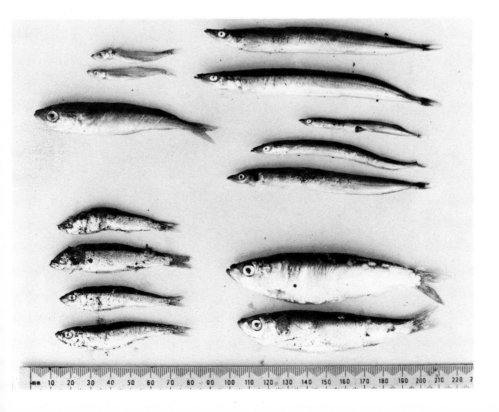

14 *Upper:* A Puffin trying to get to its chick on the Isle of May with a load of large sandeels is thwarted by a Herring Gull which will shortly try and steal the fish. *(K Taylor)*
Lower: Billing Puffins soon attract an audience. Notice the colour-ring which indicates at which colony the bird was ringed. *(K Taylor)*

15 *Top left and right:* Young Puffins can swallow surprisingly large sprats.
Lower: Young removed from a burrow always rush towards the darkest place available.

16 *Upper:* A young found dead at Røst, apparently of starvation, even though there were fish in the burrows. It may have been too weak to have swallowed such large fish. *(G Lid)*
Lower: Young Puffins found dead at Hernyken, Røst. Such mortality has occurred in 12 out of 14 recent summers. *(G Lid)*

17 *Upper:* Part of the colony at Hernyken with the precipitous slopes of Trenyken in the background.
Right: Puffins and modern man co-exist at Heimaey in the Westman Islands.
Lower: A Puffin on Hornøy, northern Norway still unable to get into its burrow in May because it is plugged with ice. A late spring delays breeding in the arctic.

19 *Left:* A flying Puffin caught in a fleyg in the Faeroe Islands. This technique catches mainly nonbreeders. (*C Perret*)   *Right:* A St Kildan catching Puffins using a long thin pole with a running noose at the end. Both adults and immatures are caught by this method. (*N Rankin*)

21   A Faeroese fleyger at work behind a bank with his decoys exposed, his net ready and his catch hidden. (*T Borch-Jacobsen*)

22 *Upper:* A Faeroese fowler returns with his catch in the 1930s. *(R M Lockley)*
Lower: The same still occurs although the economic status of the fowlers has improved considerably
(T Borch-Jacobsen)

23 Puffins are still killed on Røst by laying nets over the colony. This method catches mainly breeding adults and can cause severe damage to the population. *(E Aspegren)*

24 Puffin colony on Bleiksøya, Norway. In 1968 there were some 40,000 pairs nesting with about a pair per m². *(S Wanless)*

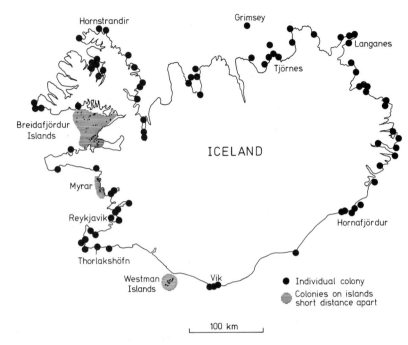

16 Puffin colonies in Iceland. There are many colonies in the cross-hatched areas. (Redrawn after Petersen 1982.) No attempt is made to indicate colony size.

northern colonies appear to have been much more extensive and the Puffins have destroyed the habitat just as has happened on the Breidafjördur islands.

NORWAY

Puffins are the most numerous seabird along the coast of the Norwegian mainland, but their numbers rapidly diminish further west on Jan Mayen, north on Bear Island and Spitzbergen, and east along the Russian coast. Brun (1979) estimated the Norwegian population to be well over one million pairs with the largest colonies and 94% of the population, being in the north of the country. Very little is known of changes in the Norwegian population. The following account of Norwegian, Russian and nearby colonies has been written by R. T. Barrett drawing on the results of Brun (1963–79), Norderhaug *et al* (1977), Haftorn (1971) and recent unpublished surveys.

Southern Norway

The southernmost colonies are extremely small. Breeding is known on Store Kjør and neighbouring Hengsøy. A few pairs nest on Imsen, Liknesoya and other Ferkingstadsøyene islands, and on Spannholmane (Utsira archipelago). There are colonies on several islands around Utvaer and in 1970 the population was 200 pairs. The majority of Puffins nest on an island south-west of the lighthouse where the thin soil layer is riddled with burrows; elsewhere nests are in crevices in rock or under boulders. Less than ten pairs breed on Husøy in the Ryggsteinen group. Maybe 1,000–2,000 pairs nest on Veststeinen and Nord-Vägsøy, Einevarden.

A much larger colony (30,000 pairs in 1974) occurs on Runde, with the most birds among large stones on the grassy slopes on the west side. Burrows are under large stones or dug out of the slopes and grassy shelves on the steep cliffs. There are 100 pairs in the grassy centre of Svinoy.

A few pairs breed under stones on several of the small, flat islands around Froan and on Saløy. These are the only colonies known along 450 km of coastline – a major gap in the Puffin's distribution. Further north there are 3,500 pairs in turf burrows on the side of Heimø, the biggest island of the Sklinna group, and a few pairs on neighbouring Hårholmen.

Nordland, Lofoten and Vesterålen Islands

The 60,000 pairs on Lovunden are concentrated in one large and several smaller screes totalling 13.5 ha on the north-west side of the island. Most nests are in deep cavities behind the stones but some are also dug out of the turf between the stones. The density of the nests in the scree varies from 0.2–0.5 /m². Puffins are the only breeding seabirds on Fugløy i Gildeskål; most nest in screes on the south and south-east side of the island up to 500 m above sea level. Earthy burrows in soil between the screes are now abandoned. There are now 5,000 to 8,000 pairs; Brun recorded 800 pairs in 1968.

The largest population in Norway (estimated total 700,000 pairs) is scattered on ten of the islands in the Røst Archipelago. The majority nest among screes of large stones on Storfjell, but colonies of 100,000 or more pairs occur in grassy slopes and ledges on the cliff faces of Vedøy and Trenyken (where density reaches 2.7 burrows/m²). Puffins at these colonies have reared few young the last 14 years and some breeding adults are killed by local people; the population must decline soon unless there is massive immigration from elsewhere. On Vedøy Puffins only nest in the higher regions of the island, perhaps due to rats which occur on this island but not in other colonies in the archipelago. Smaller colonies, but still with tens of thousands of pairs, are on Ellefsnyken and Hernyken; even smaller colonies occur on at least five other islands.

The main bird cliff on Vaerøy is on the 300 m-high peninsula round Maastadfjellet and Maahornet, but Puffins also nest on the slopes and cliffs south of Maatuen. The overall density of nests is low with 70,000 pairs in 2 km²; the largest part of the population being in a large scree on the west side of Maastadfjellet.

In 1967 there were 30,000 pairs breeding in holes in the turf on the steep sides of Fuglenyken and over 10,000 pairs on Måsnyken off the village of Nykvåg. Nearby Frugga had 5,000 pairs. Further north, 20,000–25,000 pairs breed on Anda north of Langøy – a recent large increase. On Bleiksøya, the

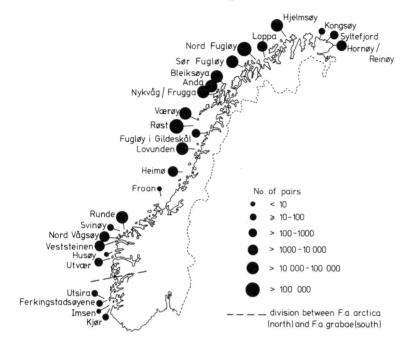

Hjelmsøy
Kongsøy
Loppa
Syltefjord
Nord Fugløy
Hornøy /
Sør Fugløy
Reinøy
Bleiksøya
Anda
Nykvåg / Frugga
Værøy
Røst
Fugløy i Gildeskål
Lovunden
Heimø
Froan

No. of pairs
•   < 10
•   ≥ 10–100
●   > 100 –1000
●   > 1000 –10 000
●   > 10 000 –100 000
●   > 100 000

Runde
Svinøy
Nord Vågsøy
Veststeinen
Husøy
Utvær

Utsira
Ferkingstadsøyene
Imsen
Kjør

— — — — division between F. a. arctica
(north) and F. a. grabae (south)

17   Puffin colonies in Norway (R. T. Barrett).

40,000 pairs are concentrated on the steep grassy slopes with about a pair every square metre throughout 5 ha (Plate 24).

Troms and Finnmark

Puffins nest on steep slopes all round Sør-Fugløy with the majority of the 40,000 pairs nesting under and behind stones on the south and west sides. The colony on Nord-Fugløy, the second largest in Norway, is spread along 11 km of near-vertical cliff, up to 500 m-high on the west side of the island. The majority of the 200,000 pairs nest in burrows in the grassy slopes on the cliff, the rest in crevices and behind stones in the top third of the cliff.

In 1968 Brun found only 180 pairs on Loppa, but more recent visits have shown that there are several thousand pairs. A 2 km stretch of coast at the northern tip of Hjelmsøy has the largest seabird population in west Finnmark, including 20,000 pairs of Puffins in the less steep slopes along the top of cliffs and on the 100 m-high cliff itself.

About 20,000 pairs breed on Storstappen, the biggest and outermost of the Gjesvaerstappene group, mainly in earthy burrows which riddle the steeply-sloping sides of the whole island. Nearby Kirkestappen and grass-covered Kongsøy east of the North Cape in Kongsfjord have small colonies. Further east there are 100–200 pairs on the 3 km-long, 150 m-high cliff of Syltefjord.

The remaining two Norwegian colonies are at Hornøy and Reinøy which have 6,000 pairs between them. These colonies have increased greatly in recent years.

RUSSIA

Compared to the other areas of the Barents Sea, the Kola Peninsula has relatively few and small seabird colonies, perhaps due to low plankton production off the coast and to a lack of suitable breeding sites. Kittiwakes are the commonest seabird, and guillemots (two species) and Puffins are found in near equal numbers, although not necessarily in the same colonies. Eleven Puffin colonies are documented (Norderhaug *et al* 1977), the largest being on O. Bol'soj Ainov (3,000–4,000 pairs) and O. Malyj Ainov (8,000 pairs). Only two other colonies O. Bol'soj Zeleneckij and O. Malyj Zeleneckij, have over 1,000 pairs. A few auk colonies occur further east but no details are available.

The seabird colonies on Novaya Zemlya are along the west coast, which is ice-free in summer. They include some of the largest concentrations of seabirds in the northern hemisphere, a result of the extremely high primary production immediately off the coast where a branch of the Gulf Stream meets cold polar water. Brünnich's Guillemot dominates but there are smaller numbers of Common Guillemots, Kittiwakes, Little Auks and Puffins. Puffins nest on the Oranskiye Islands, in the Archangel Gulf, in Gribovaya Bay, on the Karpinksi peninsula and in Pukhovy Bay. The largest colony at Gribovaya, had 64 pairs in 1950. Isolated pairs also occur, generally in association with other species. The total population is a few hundred pairs. Burrows are most frequent in a thin layer of peat or shale, less often in cracks and gaps between rocks, and are usually on the edge or slope of a cliff. The burrows are rarely more than 15–20 cm below the surface of the peat and only 0.5–1.5 m long due to the slow melting of the ice which plugs them during the winter.

Franz Josef Land has large colonies of Little Auks, Brünnich's Guillemots and Kittiwakes but Puffins are not known to nest.

SPITZBERGEN

The great majority of seabirds breed along the west coast, which is generally ice-free in summer. The Puffin is nowhere very numerous and Løvenskiold (1964) did not know a colony with more than 100 pairs. Puffins nest in holes and crevices on mountain sides and on rock-strewn slopes. This may be due to permafrost preventing burrowing, but the numerous arctic foxes would certainly soon dig out any burrow. Puffins here belong to the large-billed race *F.a. naumanni*.

BEAR ISLAND

A few colonies of rarely over 100 pairs occur around the north end and there

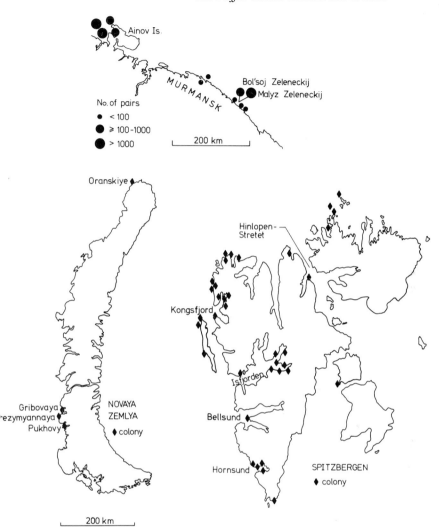

18 Puffin colonies in north Europe. (Redrawn after Norderhaug et al. 1977, and Løvenskiold 1964.) No attempt is made to indicate the size of colonies in Novaya Zemlya and Spitzbergen but all colonies are small.

is another colony of 100 pairs on the north-eastern side of Miseryfjellet. At least 600 pairs were reported in 1980 (Luttik and van Franaker in Cramp *et al* in press).

JAN MAYEN

A few hundred Puffins breed in deep crevices in the cliffs.

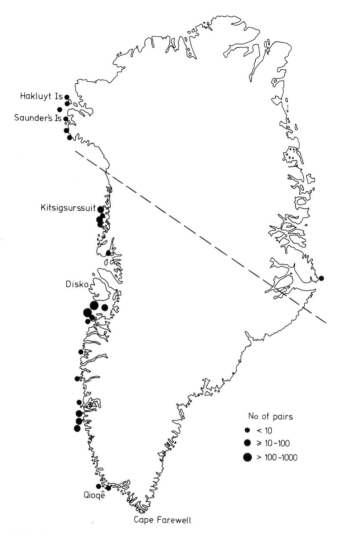

19 *Puffin colonies in Greenland (F. Salomonsen). Colonies north of the dashed line contain birds of the race* F.a. naumanni, *those to the south* F.a. arctica.

GREENLAND

The colonies are all very small and divided between two subspecies. Details are from Salmonsen (1950) and Brown *et al* (1975). The nominate race *F.a. arctica* nests on the west coast from Qioqê Island and Outer Kitsigsut Island to Kitsigsurssuit at 74° N. The total population can only be a few thousand pairs. Two colonies near Disko each have between a hundred and a thousand pairs;

the other 20–25 colonies have less than a hundred pairs each. Most pairs nest in earthy burrows dug by the birds themselves on small islands and skerries, sometimes in ledges on cliffs. Colonies are very obvious because the droppings enrich the soil so that there is a great flush of vegetation in otherwise barren areas. Lesser numbers nest among fragmented rock, alongside Razorbills or, less commonly, Little Auks and Black Guillemots. More Puffins were found in the Upernavik district in 1965 than had been recorded in 1936 but this was because more islands were visited (Joensen and Preuss 1972).

Six colonies north from 76°N to 77°25′N are inhabited by the large-billed *F.a. naumanni*. Extremely little is known of these colonies; Salomonsen (1950) reported two small colonies totalling maybe 30 pairs on Saunder's Island, and all other information is pre-1919. There are probably 100–200 pairs in all, breeding in cracks in the high, steep cliffs, often near Little Auks or Brünnich's Guillemots. This subspecies has bred on the east coast on Raffles Island near Scoresby Sound, but recent visitors have found none there and only a few birds elsewhere, e.g. Kap Hodgson and Kap Brewster (Salomonsen 1950, Korte 1972).

Puffins have never been numerous in Greenland but several colonies have been wrecked by Greenlanders digging up nesting burrows and some are now deserted. Recent legislation to prevent this may help the species recover but enforcement is difficult. Indeed, the visitor to Greenland despairs for its wildlife.

CANADA AND UNITED STATES OF AMERICA

At least 60% of Puffins here nest on islands in Witless Bay, Newfoundland, but there are also colonies scattered from Coburg Island in the north (76°N) to Matinicus Rock (43°N) in Maine (Fig. 20). The most recent survey (summarized here by D. N. Nettleship) found 52 colonies and a total population of some 338,000 pairs. The vast majority of these birds nests in burrows dug in the soil or turf on relatively low islands. The little earlier information suggests that the populations in the Gulf of St Lawrence, Nova Scotia, New Brunswick and Maine certainly declined considerably in the last century, and probably continue to do so.

United States

The initial declines were certainly due to persecution. Serious shooting of Puffins started in the early 1800s and there were far less birds at several colonies by the time the artist Audubon visited them in 1833. The history of the most southern colonies is a depressing catalogue of man's greed and insensitivity to the conservation of living things. The population on Matinicus Seal Island, the main colony in Maine, had been wiped out by 1887. That on Western Egg Rock suffered a similar fate. The species was exterminated on Eastern Egg Rock in 1908 but has recently been re-introduced and 11 pairs bred in 1982 (Kress 1977–82). Puffins managed to hang on at Matinicus Rock

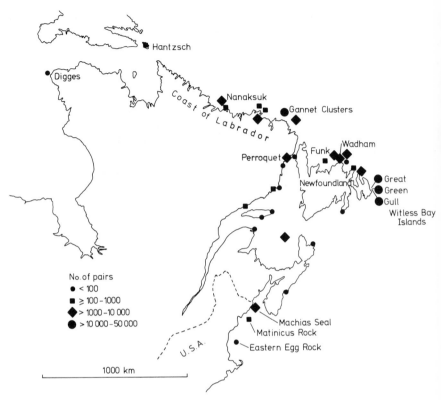

20   *Puffin colonies in eastern North America.*

(a single pair in 1902) but with protection the population has very slowly increased to 125 pairs. The same happened at Machias Seal Island, but here the recovery has been much better, as shown by counts made in 1883 (60 birds), 1902 and 1911 (300 birds), 1932 and 1935 (400 pairs), 1937 (500 pairs) and 1974 (900 pairs). Puffins, apparently, also once bred on other islands near here.

Gulf of St Lawrence

Colonies in Nova Scotia and the north part of the Gulf are all small, but those off the north shore are larger and well documented as they are mostly sanctuaries. The numbers of birds has been assessed about every five years since 1925. Counts have been made in a variety of ways and so are often not strictly comparable, but overall there has been a marked decline in numbers. This decline was most evident on Perroquet and Greenly Islands in Bradore Bay which so impressed Audubon in 1833. The population here increased from a few thousand in 1908 to 50,000 birds in 1925, and 62,000 in 1935, then declined slightly until the mid 1950s. It then crashed to 10,000–20,000 birds in 1960–65; numbers have now stabilized at about 14,000 birds (Nettleship and Lock 1973, Chapdelaine 1980). Most of these remaining pairs nest in or near rocks whereas, before, the bulk of the population was in the earthy ground at the centre of the island.

Newfoundland
This is the main area of Puffin distribution in the New World with some three-quarters of all the nesting birds. D. N. Nettleship estimates the population at 250,000 pairs. The largest colonies are on Great, Gull and Green Islands within 3 km of each other in Witless Bay. In 1973 the former had 148,000 pairs (44% of North American Puffins), the second 60,000 pairs, the third 17,000 pairs. Since then, these colonies appear to have decreased, perhaps by a third. Other colonies along this coast are mainly small, although Small and Coleman Islands, both in the Wadham Group, had 10,000 in 1979 and 3,000 pairs in 1973 respectively, and Baccalieu Island 10,000 pairs in 1979. Many other colonies, also, have declined in recent years, the small colony on South Cabot Island was deserted in 1973. A much needed survey of these colonies is being made by the Canadian Wildlife Service.

Labrador
The 17 colonies have about 77,000 pairs, about half on Gannet Clusters and Herring Island. The most northern colonies are small and it is not until one comes south to Kidlit and Nunarsuk Islands that colony size increases. These islands are at 56°N – the latitude of southern Scotland – well south of the majority of the large east Atlantic colonies. Cold water reaches further south on the west side of the Atlantic than it does on the east, and it is water temperature which appears to influence Puffins and not latitude.

Puffins have been seen carrying fish to an islet off Western Digges Island in north-eastern Hudson Bay (Gaston and Malone 1980). This was thought to be a range extension of some 1,300 km but Bureau (1879) published a map showing possible breeding near here. It is now known that a few pairs breed on Hantzsch Island, off Resolution. In 1982 Puffins were also seen carrying fish on Coburg Island at the entrance to Lancaster Sound (D. Orienti). This is far to the north of other Canadian colonies but relatively close to those on the Greenland coast. These appear to be recent colonizations. Puffins are occasionally seen elsewhere in the Canadian Arctic, for instance a bird at Bylot Island in 1978 and 1979, and there could well be small undiscovered colonies in the far north.

Seabird populations in the west Atlantic are threatened by oil pollution, possibly offshore drilling for oil and exploitation of minerals, a large industrial fishery for the small capelin (the main food of Puffins here), fishing nets and an increasing gull population. Brown and Nettleship (1983) considered that the recent declines in the numbers of Canadian Puffins may have been due to a change in the availability of food (partly because of man's increasing harvest of capelin) and other even less understood factors operating at sea. Again these might be linked to man, e.g. oil pollution. The future of many of the seabird populations appears uncertain.

WORLD POPULATION

In Chapter 3, I suggested figures, with some trepidation, for the total British and Irish population; here I am probably guilty of reckless speculation by putting forward the following 'guestimates' (in the only units available) for the world population:

Iceland	8–10 million birds
Norway	1 million pairs
Britain and Ireland	0.7 million pairs
Faeroe Islands	0.5–0.7 million pairs
West Atlantic	0.3 million pairs
Russia	20 thousand pairs
Spitzbergen	5–10 thousand birds
Greenland	a few thousand pairs
Elsewhere	a thousand pairs

These 'guestimates' *suggest* a world population of the order of 5 million pairs or 15 million birds, allowing for the very many immature Puffins in the population. This compares to 6–8 million individual Tufted Puffins, 2–4 million Horned Puffins and less than a million Rhinoceros Auklets (Wehle 1980). The bulk of these Common Puffins belong to the subspecies *F.a. arctica* and the high-arctic form *F.a. naumanni* is a rare bird with only a few thousand pairs.

CHAPTER 6

Breeding biology

Although the breeding of Puffins is similar throughout their range, there are some fascinating differences even within a single country. This chapter follows the Puffins' summer and seeks to combine and compare information gathered from various studies. Growth and behaviour are discussed later.

RETURN TO THE COLONIES

Birds come to the colonies in the early spring immediately after their flightless period. It is not known when they arrive offshore but they may come directly to the nesting area from their winter quarters as the first records of the spring are of birds on the water close inshore under the colonies. Birds then come and go with an irregular cycle of presence and absence but numbers gradually increase. During the first visits the birds do little but float around in small groups, all heading into wind and waves. After a couple of days they swim about in pairs, or perhaps one should say couples, and courtship starts with birds circling each other and indulging in a little billing. Puffins normally retain their mates from one year to the next so presumably the birds know each other as individuals and it is tempting to suppose that these activities are the pairs reforming. However, I doubt whether each can recognize its mate from the thousands of others on the sea after an interval of five or six months. It also seems unlikely that they will have wintered together as it would be virtually impossible for them to remain in touch for such a long a period. In most

75

seabirds the territory or nest site acts as the link to re-unite a pair and the same probably holds for the Puffin, in which case these twosomes on the water are perhaps birds engaging in casual flirtations.

The best series of dates of return comes from Skokholm, where visitors to the bird observatory record the Puffins' arrival annually. The average date when Puffins were seen on the water over a period of 40 years was 23rd March, with the extremes being 4th March and 3rd April (Table 4). Over 27 years the average date of the first visit to land was 4th April with a range from 22nd March to 13th April. There has been no change in this timetable during the last 50 years. Information from further north is less complete because most ornithologists visit the islands in summer but on Fair Isle, Shetland the mean dates of first sighting and first ashore are 28th March and 1st April.

The return to the colonies and laying are each several weeks earlier in eastern Scotland than elsewhere in Britain, although air and sea temperatures in the early spring are much lower than those at the Atlantic colonies. The reasons for this early return are unknown. Between 1974 and 1982 birds were on land or flying in front of mainland cliffs between 14th and 24th February (Table 5). The only earlier records of Puffins at or near colonies are 6th January at Dunnet Head, Caithness and 9th February at Bempton, Humberside. This early return is new. Presumably there has been some change in food or other sea conditions in recent winters which allows these birds to spend more of the year visiting the colonies. Razorbills have recently taken to coming to these colonies with Guillemots in October, whereas until a few years ago they were never recorded until February.

The few dates from North American colonies indicate return in the second half of April. As might be expected, birds from the more northerly part of the species' range arrive much later. In the Faeroes, Puffins traditionally return on 14th April, the first day of summer, which is known as *summarmaladagur* (return of the puffin) (Williamson 1970). In Iceland, movement inshore occurs in the middle of April and birds start visiting the colonies at the end of the month or the start of May (Gudmundsson 1953); further north in Russia birds have sometimes been seen at the same time but most do not arrive until the second or third week of May (Belopols'kii 1961). The northernmost Puffins in Greenland and Spitzbergen start landing in mid and late May respectively.

CLAIMING OF BURROWS

As days pass the birds spend more and more time both on the water below the colonies, and on land. During the first landings they tend to stay on the exposed rocks but gradually they gain confidence and scatter over the colonies to the holes where they bred in the previous years. A Puffin usually remains faithful both to its mate and its burrow from one season to the next, if each survives the winter. If the burrow is still intact the pair attempt to repossess it. Usually they succeed. If one bird does not return the other usually keeps the burrow and attracts a new mate, though it may revert to its ex-partner if the original bird returns later. At this time many birds are house-hunting and an owner has to protect its burrow. A threat by the owner, who puffs himself or herself up and opens the beak and wings slightly, is often sufficient to send off an intruder, but fights are common early in the season. Although usually short and sharp, they are sometimes prolonged when birds get a good hold of each other and neither will let go. Occasionally a toe nail gets hooked into the skin, or even into an eye, and cannot be withdrawn. Birds then tumble over and over and roll down the slope, sometimes even over a cliff and into the sea. There is often a great shortage of burrows and a Puffin is prepared to risk injury to get one. Surprisingly, predators seldom take advantage of such fights, although the birds are sometimes so completely engrossed that a man can catch them by hand. Once the birds' confidence has returned, they go down their burrows and start to clean them out and repair the damages of winter.

THE COLONY

The majority of Puffins nest in earthy burrows. New burrows are constantly being dug, existing ones enlarged and old ones eroding and collapsing. Colonies are, therefore, a dynamic rather than a static environment and careful study is needed to understand the interaction of soil and birds. This has been done by Mike Hornung (1976, 1982), and I am grateful to him for supplying details of the structure and digging of burrows, his interpretation of why the Grassholm colony collapsed and his work on the Farne Islands.

NESTING SITES

Puffins usually choose to nest in colonies on small, rocky islands or on steep sea cliffs. The actual nest site is a burrow dug into the soil or a crevice between boulders, or a crack or cleft in the cliff face. Burrow-nesting predominates in the southern part of the range, including North America, Iceland and the Faeroe Islands, but further north there are some very large colonies among rocks and in crevices, for instance on Røst and Lovunden in Norway. This latitudinal difference is partly because soils in some northerly colonies remain frozen or snow covered until mid-summer thus preventing burrow excavation. However, even in Murmansk and Novaya Zemlya many birds still manage to excavate their own earth burrows – though doubtless with extreme difficulty. In the southern colonies a small proportion of birds also choose to nest in crevices. Thus, in some sites, the use of crevices is a response to climatic factors whereas elsewhere it is merely a utilization of the best available sites. Given an option Puffins nest near to the cliff-edge and burrow density is almost always highest here. However, this rule breaks down in flat colonies, such as the Farne Islands, where soil depth limits the distribution of burrows. Where there is a shortage of nest sites bizarre locations may be used. Two or three pairs nest each year among the timbers of a wrecked ship washed up on the Farne Islands, and a pair have nested in the basement of a house built in the middle of a colony on

Skomer. The Pacific Tufted Puffin has been recorded nesting in low banks in estuaries (Gill and Sanger 1979). The nearest our species comes to this is among boulders on storm beaches.

Burrows are usually in peat-like soils, or in the humus-rich surface layers of mineral soils, which are common on steep maritime slopes and small uncultivated islands favoured by the Puffins. Burrow excavation is easy in these soils and the resulting tunnels are surprisingly stable provided that a thick enough roof exists and there are few heavy mammals such as sheep and man.

Digging

The bill is often used for making the initial cuts into the soil surface, with the feet shovelling away the loosened material. Once a burrow has been started in soft peaty soil the feet are used for digging and shovelling, the soil being ejected by alternate kicks. In harder material the bill remains the main tool for loosening the soil. The repeated scratching and kicking produces two parallel furrows on the floor of the burrow. The characteristic ridge between becomes worn down and less obvious during the breeding season. Although excavated soil may be scattered a metre or more from the digging, the vast bulk of it remains close by. Much is packed into one end of a channel which extends for a short distance out from the entrance – evidence of a gradual cutting back of the entrance. In other burrows a mass of excavated soil is packed into a ramp leading into the tunnel mouth.

On slopes the tunnel is driven in horizontally, but on level areas it is dug parallel to the general ground surface after the initial entry which is usually in the side of a hummock or other irregularity. The burrow floor remains horizontal unless a stone or other obstruction is encountered or the floor collapses into an underlying tunnel. A downward sloping burrow is difficult to dig because earth falls back down it and an upward sloping burrow is risky because it increases the chances of an egg rolling out.

On the Farne Islands a large number of new holes is started each year but rarely if ever is a completely new burrow used for breeding the first year. Some parts of the Farne Islands are unusual in that burrows rarely last for more than one breeding season. These burrows are all in sandy soil. Elsewhere, burrows last for many years and there are remarkably few records of Puffins starting new burrows. Either there are enough burrows in relatively stable soil to satisfy the needs of the breeding population or the hardness of the surface soil or the fibrous, spongy root mat formed by grasses hinders digging. Rabbits occur in many southern colonies and Puffins commandeer the shallower holes whereas the deeper warrens are retained by the rabbits.

Nests placed in crevices are usually amongst rocks or boulders below vertical rock faces. The holes most commonly used by pairs breeding in rock cliffs are near horizontal ledges formed by the differential erosion of narrow layers of softer rock or by the widening of joints or bedding planes. Sites in irregular cracks are less common.

THE BURROW

The burrows vary in length from inadequate burrows just long enough to shelter a bird, to those several metres long, but most are 70–110 cm long. The nest itself is a slight hollow, usually at the innermost end, which may have a lining of plant material or feathers, but the egg often rests directly on the earth or rocks. A latrine or 'guano pit' is usually present, often in a blind side tunnel or just where the light reaches in the main tunnel. On the Ainov Islands most burrows were about 150 cm long, curved and with a latrine sited on the curve, but the same colony also contained burrows up to 15 m long. These very long burrows are in fact complex systems of interconnecting tunnels. Skokova (1967) referred to these labyrinths as 'towns' and one had 33 burrow entrances in 25 m² of ground; most of the entrances led to interconnected burrows but the system contained 26 nest chambers, nine of which were occupied in one season. One can envisage the burrow system being expanded, new tunnels added and existing ones linked as the birds are forced to re-route their burrows due to a lingering mass of ice or because meltwater flow has caused a roof collapse. Considering that there is little, if any, light below ground it is a wonder that the birds do not get lost.

Burrow systems are found in other Puffin colonies but are usually of a rather less complex nature. On steep slopes tunnels can collapse into underlying levels thus producing vertically linked systems. Puffins on the Farne Islands some-times excavate into low hummocks 1–2 m across and a gradual merging of the tunnels can result in the hummock being hollowed out. The resulting cavern, with up to ten entrances, serves as a nest chamber for just one pair. Thus many pairs are displaced and counts of burrow entrances can give inflated estimates of colony size.

DAMAGE TO COLONIES

Most Puffin colonies have areas of bare ground, and erosion resulting from burrowing can lead to the destruction of the habitat and the colony. Darling (1947) talks of Puffins 'destroying their habitat by so far tunnelling it that the bank slips away' and suggests that 'this must be responsible for several mass disappearances of Puffins from places where they formerly bred'. Lockley (1953) expressed a similar view 'It seems to be a habit of Puffins to colonize a turfy island, work it to ruin, and, perforce, depart for new territory.'

GRASSHOLM

A good example of the rapid decline of a colony as an apparent consequence of habitat destruction by burrowing is the small (8.9 ha) Welsh island of Grassholm. In 1890 there were 'over half a million' Puffins and two to three pairs to every square metre (Lockley 1938). There was hardly a plant of grass left and the Puffins had so ruined the shallow soil that it gave way at every step.

Drane (1894) calculated a total of 689,638 (!) birds standing on the land at one time in 1893 but this total was too high as the area of the island was wrongly calculated. In fact, there could have been no more than 200,000 birds (Williams 1978). Whatever the actual figure, this very large colony was reduced to only 200 birds by 1928. In 1940 there were 25 pairs and none in the mid 1940s, although a few returned in 1948 (Lockley 1953). Thus the population had suffered a total collapse over a maximum period of some 40 years. The burrows were excavated in a shallow layer of peat formed from the red fescue grass *Festuca rubra*, mixed with disintegrated fragments of rock. The suggestion that when burrowing began there would have been a bed of turf or dried hay up to a metre thick is probably an over-estimate as in 1894 there was no more than a foot or so of dry, friable, peaty soil. In 1928 all that remained was a maze of isolated pillars and tussocks (Plate 5). The remnant peat hummocks are now 30–45 cm high so the initial layer of soil was probably only 30–60 cm thick. This is just adequate for burrowing but the burrow roofs would be very thin. Such peaty soils commonly have two distinct layers, a surface fibrous mat of dead stems and roots up to 20 cm thick, and a lower, dark-coloured layer of well humified organic material. Once broken the surface layer is readily eroded by wind and rain, particularly if the surface vegetation dies back. The lower material is soft and readily burrowed but the organic fraction of it is easily blown away after excavation.

At the end of the last century there were possibly several burrows per square metre and the pressure for burrowing sites must have been very high. Burrowing in friable soil on almost level ground could soon lead to severe erosion, especially on such an exposed and windswept site. However, at present, Grassholm could still support a population of a few thousand pairs and so one wonders why the colony became extinct. Erosion was an important factor but probably not the only one involved in the decline. Other colonies in essentially similar peaty soils have not suffered such severe erosion and have remained in existence over long periods.

FARNE ISLANDS

These are a group of small, low-lying, rocky islands a few kilometres off the coast of Northumberland. Burrows are dug in shallow peaty soils over bedrock or in the highly organic surface layers of mineral soils. There is a definite limit to the depth of soil available for burrowing due to the bedrock, or, in the mineral soils, naturally-cemented or highly-compacted layers. The cementing material is a complex phosphate, probably from bird droppings.

Large areas of bare ground and subsequent soil erosion developed in the mid 1960s and this escalated until parts of the islands had the most severe erosion of any Puffin colony in Britain. During the 1970s the erosion was studied in detail (Hornung 1976–81). Initial work confirmed rapid erosion by wind and rain from the bare areas but, as expected, virtually no soil loss where vegetation remained. On the islands of West Wideopen and Brownsman, where there are large colonies of Puffins and other seabirds, but no seals, most soil was lost between May and September. Nearby Staple Island, which is intensively used both by Puffins (summer) and grey seals (autumn), lost soil during May–August and November–December, the latter being the seal breeding period. In the bare areas the annual cycle of erosion started in the spring when burrows were being cleaned and excavated and large amounts of freshly dug soil were spread on the surface. Little of the soil was actually lost at that time; loss occurred in June and July when the lumps of excavated soil had become broken down, by rain and the trampling of birds, into small particles which were easily washed or blown away. In some years the soil surface was also eroded and on gentle slopes on West Wideopen rainwater run-off in September was important in causing erosion. Thereafter, the soil surface stabilized as it became thoroughly wet in autumn, and there was almost no soil loss until the following spring (unless there was disturbance by seals). The algae *Praseola* commonly developed on the wet soil surface and provided a stabilizing influence, but each June or July the mat dried and cracked, and pieces were often blown away, carrying attached soil, so adding to the soil loss.

Evidently, much of the soil lost had been excavated during burrowing. The amount of fresh burrowing each year on the Farne Islands was far greater than at many other colonies because burrows often became blocked with eroded soil or as a result of seal activity and so required re-excavation. The actual amount of material excavated was significantly correlated with the degree of vegetation cover. In bare areas with organic soil some 850 g per burrow was excavated compared to only 300 g per burrow in vegetated ground. In sandier soils the weights were 2,800 g (that is a tonne of soil per 350 pairs) and 550 g respectively. The excavated material in the bare areas was soil, whilst amongst vegetation it was mainly plant debris and old nest lining.

Between breeding seasons, up to 90% of burrow entrances in bare areas became filled in, whereas most burrows in vegetated ground remained open. Where the infilling was by eroded soil it generally happened soon after the breeding season, but where it was caused by seals it took place in November–December. The amount of excavation each spring was far more than would be required to re-open the burrow. The entrance was often cut back by the birds as it was cleaned out and the tunnels were frequently lengthened. Pairs often ignored infilled entrances and excavated new burrows, although these some-times intercepted an existing one. Thus, although the total number of burrows in bare areas remained relatively constant, only 35% of burrows remained in use for three breeding seasons, compared to 90% of burrows among vegeta-tion. Erosion, therefore, led to further excavation which resulted in more erosion and, once into this cycle, destruction of an area was almost inevitable.

Colony destruction on the Farne Islands seems to take place as follows. Initially, burrows are scattered and relatively widely spaced with only small areas of bare ground at the burrow entrance. Soon, groups of burrows are formed with entrances opening off a common bare, hollow. The hollow is then gradually enlarged as burrow entrances are modified and cut back. Coalescence of these hollows become the foci for entrances of burrows which are dug under the mound. Eventually the mound becomes hollowed out or dissected, and collapses leaving many homeless Puffins (Plate 5). Several areas which now have few burrows were once thriving colonies which have been almost completely dug over. Such areas can be identified by a characteristic soil profile in which the old tunnelled layer can be recognized by shell fragments, feathers, etc, long after the tunnels have collapsed. Past accounts indicate that the colony was previously centred on different islands and it seems that the process of colonization, increase in burrow density, erosion and burrow collapse has gone on for at least the last 200 years. The time needed for one complete cycle from colonization to evacuation on any given site will vary with soil depth and type but is probably in the region of 50–100 years.

Although some Puffin colonies soon become unstable due to burrowing, others remain stable for long periods. Soil type, depth and structure, all influence the physical stability of a colony but the most important factor is the slope. On very steep slopes the soil will be liable to slumping but on stable slopes, between 20° and 40°, burrowing results in much less disturbance to soil and vegetation than on level ground. On level ground burrowing is restricted to one level, the tunnels running parallel to the ground surface at a depth which gives an adequate thickness of roof, whereas on steep slopes the burrows can be driven in horizontally. The amount of soil disturbed on level ground is a proportion of the surface area while on the steep slope it is a proportion of the total volume of soil. A density of 3 burrows/m^2 in soil 50 cm deep will affect 48% of a level site, but only 12% of a 30° slope. The relatively thin wall of soil remaining between burrows in level ground makes linking of burrows almost inevitable. The proportion of the vegetation which has its rooting zone directly affected by burrowing will also be much less on the steep slope than on the level site. On the slope the greater distances between burrows, the thicker roofs and less effective disturbance to soil and vegetation, ensures greater stability.

These differences between the level ground and slope sites will be crucial, given similar soil conditions. Densities of 3 burrows/m^2 have been reported from a number of colonies on sloping sites which are apparently stable. Densities of this order were probably reached in the gently sloping Grassholm colony prior to its collapse. On the Farne Islands, densities at any one time rarely exceed 1.2 burrows/m^2 over large areas but in the badly eroding parts they commonly exceed 2 burrows/m^2 and reach 4 burrows/m^2 in some particular instances. Such densities plus the rapid turnover of burrows result in devastation of the local area. However, the destruction can be halted. Hornung suggested covering parts of the badly eroding colony on one of the Farne Islands with a thatch of one or two layers of small, overlapping tree branches. In addition seed collected from vegetation growing on the islands was sown below the thatch which eliminated the trampling by birds and greatly reduced the activity of gulls which pluck vegetation for nests and display. Stabilization of the soil surface was almost immediate and a complete vegetation cover was achieved in one growing season where seed had been sown, and in 3–5 years without added seed. At first the Puffin numbers declined in the treated areas but after two years they started to increase and in three or four years they were close to or above the former levels.

MATING

The behaviour of the birds gradually changes until, when disturbed, they dive down their burrows rather than flee to the sea. Now there is much billing, both near the burrows and on the sea. Sometimes the male gets especially enthusiastic and solicits the female by much exaggerated head-tossing and occasional rapid vibration of the wings. Rarely, he gets carried away and attempts to mate. During such matings the female lies breast down on the ground while the male balances on top with rapidly vibrating wings. The bulk of these copulations appear to be unsuccessful and most matings presumably occur on the water well away from human eyes (Plate 11). Mating might occur in the burrow but this seems unlikely, if only because there is hardly enough room. A 'hoarse cry at the moment of pairing' has been reported (Kaftanovskii 1941), but this I have never head.

NEST BUILDING

Many Puffins line their nest chamber. This behaviour is very different from that of a bird playing with a piece of grass for a few minutes and then dropping it. A Puffin collecting nest lining does it with a vengeance, spending up to half an hour rushing from one grass clump to the next tugging and heaving out dead leaves and roots. Once it has a beakful it runs earnestly across the colony and dives down its burrow. The nest is made of dry materials. Dead ragwort stems, feathers, pieces of paper and string are in great demand and birds will try and take down any sticks lying around the colony, regardless of their length. When they have an egg or a chick, birds also take in snippets of green mayweed, campion or other nearby plants. Less commonly Puffins bring back seaweed, and some pairs make nests with off-cuts of braided nylon or fishing net, but these are always pale blue or very pale green. Perhaps the incubating bird wants to be reminded of fish! The quantity of nest lining is extremely variable, large amounts of plant material are common amongst boulders in Norway and in burrows on the Isle of May but there is almost no lining in the Russian colonies. On the Farne Islands it varies widely, even on one island. A major factor may be the availability of suitable, easily plucked vegetation adjacent to the burrow, as birds only rarely carry material from any distance. The largest nests would do justice to a passerine; they are found among boulders and the linings presumably help to prevent the egg being dented.

So far we have assumed that a bird already has both a mate and a nest burrow. Many birds arriving at the colony in March or April have neither. A few will have lost their mates during the winter, some will have had their burrow destroyed by rabbits or other animals, or badly damaged by soil erosion, and others will not have bred before. Mates are probably easier to acquire than burrows, as nest sites are in extremely short supply in many colonies, but permanent pairs do not form unless the birds have a burrow. Homeless Puffins investigate every crack and potential burrow and try to enlarge them. Some manage to usurp a burrow for a day or two but are evicted by the returning owner. Although Puffins often take over holes started by rabbits, they can and must dig their own holes where these do not occur. It is rare for a pair to dig a new burrow and to breed in it during the same season, although one pair bred in a concrete nest box the first year it was in place. Puffins occasionally lay in very open or short burrows, but they are rarely successful if they have to incubate in direct light.

LAYING

Puffins are among the earliest seabirds to lay, virtually throughout their range. In Britain only Shags lay earlier. The early laying is probably because the Puffin's incubation and chick period are so long that early laying is essential if the young are to be fed when food is abundant. With the staggered laying of seabird species and the different incubation periods, young of all species at any colony are being fed at approximately the same time.

Examination of burrows daily for four or six weeks is time consuming and also risky as a Puffin will frequently desert its egg if disturbed. Therefore, most information on the timing of breeding comes from the hatching dates of chicks, calculating back from chicks measured soon after hatching. Laying is always earliest in east Britain. In extremely early years on the Isle of May a few eggs are laid in the closing days of March but the normal first-egg date is between 4th and 9th April. The latest eggs are laid in the third week of June. On St Kilda, on the western side of Scotland, the earliest recorded laying is 22nd April, the latest 20th June. However, in some years eggs must be laid in July as juveniles have been caught fledging in mid September. The mean annual dates of hatching were 9–17 days later than on the Isle of May (Fig. 21). In 1973 most young had hatched on the Isle of May before many eggs had been laid on St Kilda. This is a remarkable difference between colonies only 400 km apart. At Welsh colonies, egg laying starts in the last week of April and lasts about a month. The peak is usually at the start of May but, rarely, as late as the third week (Ashcroft 1976).

Laying is much later in northern colonies, starting in mid May in central Norway and Iceland, late May in Murmansk and early June in Greenland. In Spitzbergen the few eggs collected suggest laying in early July but birds have been seen taking food to burrows on 5th July, so some eggs must be laid in May (Løvenskiold 1964). In arctic colonies snow and ice accumulate in depressions in the ground and, after a snowy winter, many burrows remain blocked until mid June. Annual first-egg dates on the Ainov Islands varied from 11th May to 7th June (Belopol'skii 1961), a spread of 26 days compared with 19 days on the Isle of May and 13 days on St Kilda. On the Kharlov Islands nesting usually

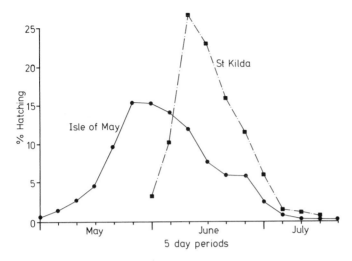

21 The distribution of hatching dates of Puffin eggs on St Kilda and the Isle of May in 1974–75. Some young had hatched on the Isle of May before the peak of laying on St Kilda.

starts in the first third of June but an early thaw will sometimes allow laying in mid May.

Variation of laying dates within a colony
We have considered a colony or a whole island as a single unit as regards the time of breeding but this is far from true. Groups of birds behaving as distinct units within a single colony have been discovered in many colonial seabirds, including species which nest in the open (gulls, Gannets, boobies, albatrosses), on cliffs (Kittiwakes) or in burrows (Manx Shearwaters). Puffins are no exception and, in several colonies which have been studied in detail, pairs in some areas always lay earlier than pairs elsewhere in the colony. There may well be no single or simple explanation, but nest density, weather and soil drainage all appear to have influence.

Seabirds breeding in large concentrations and at high density often lay earlier in the season, or more synchronously, than individuals nesting in the same general area but at a lower density. On Dun, Puffin pairs nesting in areas of relatively high burrow density (0.5 burrows/m²) laid on average 1–5 days earlier than nearby pairs breeding at about a sixth of the density. But there was no difference in the synchrony of breeding (Harris 1980). Guillemots are just as social as Puffins and when they occur in very dense concentrations their laying is very much more synchronized than the laying of birds at a lower density. This synchrony gives protection against predatory gulls which can steal an egg or young from scattered pairs but not from a dense group behaving in the same way (Birkhead 1977). Nest density is remarkably uniform in a Gannet colony, but large groups of Gannets lay earlier and more synchronously than small groups (Nelson 1978). This appears to be a social phenomenon as Gannets do not lose eggs or chicks to predators unless they are disturbed by man.

Snow and ice also influence the pattern of laying. In one year, the southern part of one of the Kharlov Islands was clear of snow and the ground was unfrozen down to a depth of 40 cm by 9th June, enabling the Puffins to nest. In the northern part of the island, Puffins had to wait several weeks more before nesting because there were still snowdrifts over the colonies with the ground frozen below 10 cm and 40% of the burrows still blocked by ice. Here there was typically a 10–15 day difference between laying on the two sides of the island (Kaftanovskii 1941).

The cause of these differences in laying dates is not always easy to discover because we know little of what happens underground. Hornung and Harris (1976) found marked differences in the timing of breeding on the Farne Islands. There were differences within West Wideopen and Staple Island whereas on Brownsman, the pattern of laying was uniform. These nesting differences were found to be associated with soil conditions: burrows in dry areas had young while those in wet areas still had eggs. On Staple Island the burrows in the early nesting area were dug into a steep, well-drained slope, whereas the areas of late nesting were in low ground where the soil water level was high enough to flood burrows for many days in April and May. Also, in the winter, the low area was occupied by large numbers of grey seals which transformed the low-lying ground into water-filled wallows, some of which still held water in mid May. In contrast, the soil water level rarely reached the burrow level on Brownsman, so laying was unlikely to have been delayed. The influence of soil conditions on breeding dates and synchrony is probably widespread among Puffins, as flooding of burrows has been recorded in many other colonies. However, even in what appears to be a uniform colony there is local clumping of laying dates, with neighbouring birds tending to lay at more or less the same time. Presumably this is a social effect but we are ignorant of how it is brought about.

AGE OF FIRST BREEDING

Puffins sometimes breed in their third year of life, but most seem not to breed until about the fifth year (Table 6). However, the available information is subject to two severe, and conflicting, biases. First, the birds may have bred a year or more before they were recorded breeding. Second, the studies which produced the ages were mostly of such brief duration that many of the late-developers would not have started to breed. The apparent earlier breeding in west Atlantic colonies may be an artefact due to the second point. However, these study birds (from an introduction) were recolonizing an area with an abundance of nest-sites so could well breed early in the absence of more experienced competitors.

A Puffin caught in a burrow cannot be assumed to be sexually mature as I have caught two- and three-year-olds in burrows where they were certainly not breeding. Probably they were just prospecting the entrances of burrows and were frightened into the burrow when I appeared between them and access to the sea. However, a pair reared in captivity in Holland bred, though unsuccessfully, when the birds were two years old (C. Swennen), showing that sexual maturity comes earlier than might be thought from field observations (Plate 9). Twenty-eight out of 32 ringed females aged three to five years killed on the Westman Islands had straight oviducts, indicating that they had definitely not bred. The remaining four had slightly convoluted oviducts which suggested that they might have laid, but this was by no means certain. Another four females aged six to eight years had highly convoluted oviducts and had certainly laid (Petersen 1976a).

THE EGG

A Puffin has two brood patches, so could theoretically incubate two eggs although the normal clutch is one egg. It is probably always one but, in some colonies, about one burrow in a hundred has two eggs. In most cases these are certainly not a single clutch; some are a result of an egg rolling downhill from one burrow into a second, others are due to the wall separating two nest chambers breaking down and one pair taking over both eggs. The usual cause is a pair either deserting an egg (possibly due to human disturbance) or the egg rolling out of reach into a crack or side-hole and the female then laying again. Pairs defend their burrow and entrance so fiercely that it is difficult to imagine that two females could share a burrow by nesting in different branches. Whatmough (1949) inspected large numbers of eggs from a Shetland colony and collected two similarly marked, sized and unusually elongated eggs from a single burrow. Both the eggs were about five days incubated. He thought that they must have been produced by the same female, but if so one would have lain unincubated in the burrow for at least a week while the female formed another egg. Whether or not a female Puffin ever lays two eggs as a single clutch, the two eggs never hatch and an adult has not been found with two chicks.

The egg is rounded elliptical (as compared to that of Guillemot which is pear-shaped) and is about 14% of the female's weight. Eggs from northern populations are larger (Table 7) but so are the adults, so the proportionate weight remains the same (Fig. 22). Eggs laid early in the season are larger than those laid later and so may give rise to larger young at hatching. On St Kilda the size of the egg had no effect on the likelihood of it resulting in a fledged young.

The fresh laid egg is whitish and its fairly rough surface is often streaked with blood. Some eggs have feint lilac markings or blotches but these soon disappear and the egg is often stained or covered with mud. Rarely, eggs have black speckling, or a large cap of lilac, or are a pinkish stone colour heavily spotted with purple. Even apparently white eggs show markings if the shell is viewed against the light. Strikingly marked eggs are important to species like Guillemots, which nest in crowded colonies, since they allow birds to recognize their

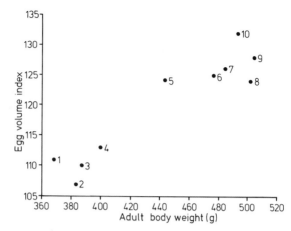

22   *The relationship of egg size (as indicated by length × breadth²) and adult body weight at St Kilda (1), Skomer (2), Shetland (3), Isle of May (4), Lovunden (5), Gulf of St Lawrence (6), Iceland (7), Novaya Zemyla (8, but only 6 eggs), Murmansk (9), Iceland (10).*

eggs, but they are of little use to birds which nest underground. Puffins cannot recognize their own egg or even their young and will readily adopt another egg or chick if given one in place of, or even in addition to, their own. The colouring of a Puffin's egg may be left-over from a time when the ancestral Puffin (may have) nested in the open.

The shells of eggs of Puffin and Black Guillemot are of uniform thickness, whereas those of Razorbills and Guillemots, which usually lay on rocky ledges, have the shell thickened where the egg is in contact with the rock and at the pointed end – places where the egg is likely to be damaged (Kaftanovskii 1941). Puffins protect their eggs by laying them on the soil or by making nests of grass, while Black Guillemots make a rudimentary nest or a bed of small stones. In wet burrows, Puffin eggs may become completely covered in mud and some embryos suffocate. A Guillemot egg is often covered in sticky guano and the shell has many more pores than, for example, a Puffin egg, and presumably these pores help the embryo respire (Kaftanovskii 1941). The Puffin tries to make up for this low density of shell pores by keeping the egg clean (hence the substantial nest lining which helps to prevent soiling and the flurry of nest lining after heavy rain).

If the egg is lost a replacement may be laid two to three weeks later. Extremely rarely, even replacement eggs may be replaced if lost and the exceptional, very late young may come from such eggs. Overall about 10% of lost eggs are replaced, and these are usually eggs lost soon after laying. Well incubated eggs tend not to be replaced, possibly because the follicles in the ovary which give rise to the egg have by then been re-absorbed.

INCUBATION

Each adult incubates the egg in turn by tucking it against the bare, heavily vascularized skin of one of the two lateral brood patches and holding it there with a slightly drooped wing. Feathers are lost from the brood patches just prior to the egg being laid and grow again when the chick is a week or so old. Non-breeding adults (but not immatures) also have brood patches but these do not have an enhanced blood supply.

Incubation stints are variable and often last more than a day, but a Puffin incubates intermittently and often comes out of the burrow, and even goes to sea for a short time, leavings its egg safe and warm in the burrow. Incubation usually takes from 39 to 43 days, including the three to five days between the egg chipping and the chick emerging. The egg might well hatch a few days earlier if incubation was continuous, certainly it is prolonged if the birds are disturbed frequently. However, supposed incubations of over seven weeks probably involve a lost egg and its subsequent replacement.

THE CHICK

One of the highlights of summer on a seabird island is the first Puffin carrying fish ashore, indicating that its young has hatched. Once it has dried, the young resembles a dark fluffy ball with a stubby pale-tipped bill poking out. The pale tip is the egg 'tooth' which the young used to force its way out of the egg. It persists for several weeks before dropping off. The chick is covered with soft, long, slaty-black down over most of the body but with a shorter, white down on the ventral side. The legs, feet and bare skin around the eye are black. The luxuriant down is slightly unexpected in a young bird living in a hole but in this respect the young Puffin is similar to young shearwaters and storm petrels.

The young bird cannot maintain its own body temperature until it is six or seven days old and it is usually brooded during the first few days of life, though it can survive alone. Even then the ability to survive is soon lost if it receives insufficient food and the body temperature drops too low. If removed from the burrow it hesitates briefly, sometimes *peeps* quietly, and then dashes towards the nearest dark area (Plate 15). This negative phototropic response remains strong until near fledging and has obvious survival value since a chick venturing to the burrow entrance is likely to get eaten by the gulls which are always stalking the colony. Only extreme hunger will cause a chick to move into the daylight. The young is well house-trained, which is as well since the long down could easily become fouled. It uses a latrine either near the entrance, where the burrow often bends, or a side chamber. The natal down is retained until near fledging, and even then some wisps still adhere to the head, nape, rump or under the tail. The main wing feathers show through after about 10–12 days and the tail feathers appear about a week later.

Corkhill (1973) replaced the side of a nest chamber with a glass panel and watched an adult feed its young. The returning adult stood in the centre of the nest chamber and uttered a soft clicking call. The young appeared from the back of the burrow and pecked at, and then took, a few of the fish dangling from the parent's bill. The adult then dropped the remaining fish and the young picked them up from the floor. Chicks often call when being fed and also give plaintive peeps when hungry. Adults do not feed older young directly but just rush into the burrow, drop the fish on the floor of the burrow and rush away again.

Young are extremely pugnacious and will attack a strange chick entering the burrow, and it is quite impossible to keep two young in a single box. Adult Puffins do not recognize their chick but will feed any young in the burrow, so the chick must protect it against intruders in order to keep its food supply to itself. In contrast, Guillemot chicks are quite happy together. In this species groups of adults and young are better able to protect themselves against predatory gulls than single birds, and so aggression between the young is not an advantage. Guillemots recognize their young by voice.

The young receives several feeds a day (Chapter 9) and grows rapidly, reaching a peak of 70–80% of adult weight at four or five weeks of age. Although the young is not deserted by the adults it receives fewer feeds and loses weight for a few days before fledging. Just before this the behaviour of the young changes and it becomes extremely active. Hand-reared young at this time make repeated efforts to get out of boxes where they had previously remained quiet. A chick near to fledging occasionally comes out of the burrow to flap its wings. By day this is usually when its parents (which may bill with it or preen it) are present. Such young sometimes become disorientated, or are attacked by adults, and go down the wrong burrow or, exceptionally, fledge to the sea by day. Most young normally fly from the colonies but some walk, especially if the ground is flat. Virtually all leave at night (Plate 6) and are well away from land by dawn.

The normal fledging period, at least in Britain, is 38–44 days (Table 8) and a shorter period is open to doubt as the chick may not have fledged but have wandered to another burrow or have been eaten by a gull. Similarly, the exceptional, very long periods occur when young are so sick or weak that they are unlikely to fledge successfully. If food is short, the fledging of whole groups may be delayed. When gulls stole much food on Great Island in 1968 the mean fledging period of Puffin chicks was 59 days, with extremes of 45 and 83 days (Nettleship 1972). The fledging period is very variable and the chick is fed by the parent birds for as long as is necessary.

Even the normal fledging period seems inordinately long when compared to the three weeks that young Razorbills and Guillemots are fed at the colony. But whereas the Puffin chick is safely tucked away in the burrow, with both adults free to spend time ferrying food back to it, Razorbill and Guillemot chicks are exposed on their ledges and have always to be protected. Males of these species take the chick away to be fed at sea when it is only about a third grown; the females remain at the colony, presumably to retain ownership of the nest-site.

The Puffin chick grows slowly because it takes the adults a long time to find and return with food.

NESTING SUCCESS

Hatching success is usually high, and fledging success extremely high, but verification is difficult because a Puffin will often desert its egg if disturbed. Even infrequent checks by human observers can cause considerable reduction in nesting success. Some burrows on the Isle of May were checked every few days. Eggs were laid in 87, which were then left undisturbed for a month, and thereafter checked every few days until the young had hatched. Only 51 eggs (59%) hatched, but 48 of these young fledged, giving a chick success of 94% and an overall production of 0.55 young per pair. In burrows checked only once, to see that an egg had been laid, and then not again until the young was a week or so old, 43 young fledged from 58 eggs (0.74 young/burrow). In general in Britain about 65–90% of occupied burrows fledge young (Table 9).

Desertion is the commonest cause of failure to hatch, even when burrows have not been disturbed by humans. A few eggs get cracked on rocks, buried in mud if the burrow gets wet, or are ejected, either accidentally or by other Puffins trying to gain possession of the burrow. Where they are present, rats and Jackdaws eat some eggs, almost certainly when the adult is away, and Manx Shearwaters caused the loss of 5–10% of eggs each year on Skomer (Ashcroft 1976). Infertility is unusual, but some few young die during hatching. An incubating Puffin trapped in a burrow will usually retreat to the back of the burrow, face away from the entrance and expose the egg. This has given rise to the myth that it will give its egg to a predator in order to escape itself. This was reported from Skye in 1792 (Martin 1792) and is still believed by fishermen there today.

The majority of young which hatch, fledge; the few which do not, usually perish in their first ten days of life, probably because the adults do not care for them adequately. However, older young occasionally suffer from lack of food, either because the adults cannot find enough fish or because it is stolen by gulls. The effect of such gulls can be devastating. On Great Island, Newfoundland, Nettleship (1972) found that the nesting success of pairs breeding on flat ground was only 10% and 24% in two years and even those pairs with burrows in steep slopes reared young only from 28% and 51% of the eggs laid. In the second year, 87% and 93% of eggs laid in two gull-free colonies in the same province gave rise to fledglings.

Despite the high, general breeding success, failures do occur and these are discussed under food shortage below.

BURROW DENSITY AND BREEDING

Puffins appear most at ease and breed most successfully when they are present in large numbers. I studied this matter in detail on St Kilda by comparing the breeding performance of birds nesting in a dense area of burrows (0.5–0.6 occupied burrows/m^2) with those in a sparse area, 500 m away, where there were only 0.1 burrows/m^2. Superficially there was little to choose between the two areas as places for Puffins to nest (Harris 1980).

Birds in the Dense burrow area laid, on average, a few days earlier each year than those in the Sparse area although there was no tendency for greater synchrony of hatching. The Dense area birds were also more successful; more occupied burrows had eggs laid in them, more eggs hatched, and a higher proportion of the young fledged. Significantly more eggs were deserted in the Sparse burrow area and fewer lost eggs were replaced. Chicks reared in the Dense area reached higher peak and fledging weights than those in the Sparse area. There was obviously a great advantage in breeding where there were many other Puffins. On Great Island, Nettleship attributed a higher success among pairs nesting on the slope to their being better able to cope with parasitic gulls. However, on Great Island the density of burrows was closely correlated with the slope, so density might also have been affecting the breeding.

Birds nesting at low density did badly because of the presence of predatory Great Black-backed Gulls. These gulls killed 4% of the Puffins breeding in the Sparse area each year, but less than 1% of those in the Dense area. However, only about 1 in 25 nests would have been affected by the loss of an adult, which is insufficient to explain the poor breeding. Photographs and direct observations showed that birds nesting in the Sparse area spent little time on land or circling in front of the colonies, in marked contrast to those in the Dense area. Presumably they were obliged instead to sit on the water where they were safe from gulls. There were also many fewer immatures in the Sparse area than in the Dense area, probably because immatures were attracted to the flourishing Dense area. Also, adults in the Sparse area had more bill grooves showing that they were, on average, older than those in the Dense area, which again suggests that few immatures were coming to that area.

The effect of the gulls on the Puffins was far greater than the actual numbers killed, in that many Puffins were scared off. The resulting low density of birds flying at the colonies made the Puffins in the Sparse area even more vulnerable to predation, there being too few of them to form the circular displays called 'wheels' which probably help reduce predation (p. 111). Unless there was a great surplus of immatures in the colony, and this seemed unlikely, it is possible that the Sparse area is doomed. It may be anthropomorphic to say that Puffins breeding at a high density are 'happy', but they certainly survive and breed better.

ROLE OF THE SEXES

The sex ratio is approximately even and males and females are equally represented among the first birds to come ashore at the start of the season and among the last birds to leave. Both sexes incubate: of 65 known-sexed birds I found incubating eggs, 40 were male and 25 were females. Although this

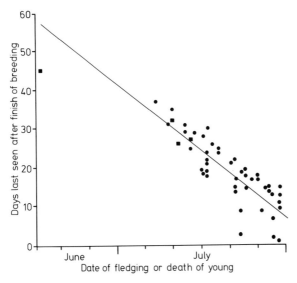

23 The relationship between the time spent at the colony by Isle of May Puffins after completion of breeding and the date that their young fledged (circles) or died (squares). The correlation is highly significant (r = −0.87, P < 0.001). (Redrawn after Harris 1982a).

suggests that males takes a larger share of the duties, the figures are not significantly different from equality. Both on Skomer and the Isle of May the females fed the young far more frequently than did males, but overall the sexes probably take fairly equal shares in rearing the young.

END OF SEASON

This period is difficult to define as there is a variable cycle of a day or two when large numbers of Puffins are present, interspersed with a few days when the only birds seen are a few adults still bringing fish to young. The true end of season happens when most of the birds do not turn up when they might have been expected! On the Isle of May, the only place for which there are data, the length of time an adult spent at the colony after breeding ended was negatively correlated with the date when it lost its egg or fledged its chick (Fig. 23). This caused the marked synchronization of birds leaving the colony. Even then, a few hundred birds may return and sit on the sea, sometimes coming ashore for a few hours, sometimes not. The latest chicks are sometimes fed for a month after most birds have gone.

In Britain, most Puffins have left by the middle third of August (Tables 4 and 5); only stragglers are seen later but these may visit young into mid September. On the Isle of May the majority of Puffins leave between 1st and 10th August, but birds have been seen ashore or carrying fish on 12th and 15th September in different years. On Skokholm for 40 years the mean last date was 20th August, with the extremes 11th and 28th August. Although Puffins on St Kilda breed several weeks later than those on the Isle of May, they usually leave the colonies at about the same date and it is extremely rare that congregations are seen, either on land or under the cliffs, even in early August. However, in 1958, numbers of adults were present up to the first week of September and juveniles were seen in mid September, almost two months after the first young had fledged.

Clarke (1912) recorded the species as very numerous on the sea around Boreray, St Kilda, in October 1910 and October 1911. These are intriguing records, for if these birds belonged to the large breeding colonies there, breeding was exceptionally late; if they did come from elsewhere it is one of the very few records of flocks of Puffins seen outside the breeding season.

Further north, the end of the season is a week or so later, with birds from Greenland, Iceland and Russia leaving from mid August to early September. However, Faeroese birds sometimes leave towards the end of September. The few records from Spitzbergen and Novaya Zemlya suggest adults depart in mid September. In Newfoundland the earliest young fledge about 10th August; most breeders leave in late August but a few young do not fledge until the end of September.

The end of the breeding season is more synchronized throughout the species range than is the return to the colonies, which extends from mid February in north-east Scotland to the second week of May in Greenland. Belopolskii (1962) suggested that the length of the breeding cycle, from laying to fledging, was reduced the further north one went, giving (correctly) 86 days for the period in England, 78 days in eastern Murmansk but only 60 days in Novaya Zemlya. This last figure allows only 30 days for both the incubation and fledging periods; either is unrealistically short compared to about 40 days for each elsewhere in the range. The variation in the time that birds in different parts of the range spend ashore is due to a reduction in the length of the prelaying period, with greater synchronization and less repeat layings in the far north.

SUMMARY

The date of return to the breeding colonies varies from place to place: late February in east Scotland, mid March in Wales, early to mid April in the rest of Scotland, Faeroes, Newfoundland, mid to late April in Iceland and May in the most northern colonies.

Most Puffins nest in earth burrows or amongst rocks. Burrows are dug using the bill and feet. Digging sometimes results in severe soil erosion and even collapse of the colony. Eroding colonies can be stabilized by suitable management.

Laying follows the same pattern, being earliest (sometimes even late March) in east Scotland and latest (late May or June) in Greenland and Spitzbergen.

Within a colony laying may be prevented by snow, ice, or flooded burrows.

A bird usually retains the same mate and burrow from one season to the next. The pair clean out the burrow and line the nest chamber with dry grass, feathers, etc.

Puffins sometimes breed when three years old but most do not do so until they are five or six. One captive pair bred when both birds were two years old.

The single whitish egg is incubated by each adult in turn for 39–43 days, and normally the chick fledges aged 38–44 days.

Nesting success is usually high; 70–80% of eggs giving fledged young. The main cause of failure is desertion of the egg.

Birds leave the colonies in August and September.

CHAPTER 7

Puffin behaviour

by K. Taylor

Puffins use a variety of displays and postures in their social life at the colony. While some displays, such as those associated with mating and pair bonding, are quite obvious to the human observer, others are more subtle. A catalogue of Puffin behaviour is given here to serve as a brief guide to Puffin society. The descriptions are based on observations of individually colour-ringed Puffins of known breeding status and sex on the Isle of May. Some of these displays have previously been described by Perry (1946), Lockley (1953) and Myrberget (1962b).

COURTSHIP

Head flicking with wing flutter
This behaviour is performed by the male near a female as a precursor to copulation. At first the head is thrown sharply up, back and down again with mechanical regularity at the rate of at least one throw per second. As he approaches the female, the male raises his chest and begins to flutter his wings in short bursts, still head-flicking. If the female allows a close approach, his wing fluttering becomes continuous, and he mounts the female for a few seconds to copulate. This display is seen most often in rafts of Puffins on the sea prior to egg laying. Often, the female dives or takes off and the male may then approach and repeat the display to another female. A single male once

displayed to seven different females in 20 minutes (Myrberget 1962b). When mated, paired Puffins may swim closer together in the rafts than un-paired birds (Conder 1950).

Head flicking/wing flutter is sometimes seen on land, but although the male may succeed in mounting the female briefly, copulation is not usually successful. Wing fluttering with occasional head flicking is also used by the male to coax a female to a burrow. The female Puffin has no special mating display. She merely tolerates or rejects the advances of the male. In the Guillemot, head throwing is a female behaviour seen before copulation.

Billing

Billing (Fig. 24) is a very obvious and noisy Puffin activity, mainly associated with pair bonding, occurring both on sea and land throughout the breeding season. At the start of a bout of billing on land a Puffin of either sex makes a low profile approach (see later) to another, often its mate. The approaching bird swings its bill from side to side, and may nuzzle or nibble under the other's bill. The two birds then begin to knock their bills broadside together, for from a few seconds to a minute or more. During the billing one bird often adopts a high profile posture with neck and head feathers raised and the bill angled down, while its partner maintains a lower profile with more sleeked feathers. Both birds cock their tails and pad slowly round on the spot with toes splayed. On the sea, billing birds tend to pirouette in the water as the bills meet near the sea surface.

The noise of clashing bills can be heard several metres away, and billing often attracts the attention of other Puffins in the vicinity, which rush over and stand close to the displaying pair. A prolonged bout of billing may draw an audience of ten or more Puffins encircling the billing pair. The onlookers are not always content to be passive spectators, but may themselves attempt to

24   Billing is mainly, but not entirely, associated with pair-bonding.

nibble the beaks or feathers of the billing birds, and some bouts end in a fight between a displayer and a spectator. Sometimes one of the initial pair breaks off billing but immediately starts again with one of the onlookers. As well as stimulating the interest of bystanders, billing often has a contagious effect on other pairs in the vicinity, so that it is not uncommon to see several pairs with associated bystanders, billing simultaneously. At the end of a billing bout, one Puffin often keeps swinging its head from side to side for several seconds after its partner has lost interest. Some nibbling of the fleshy yellow gape rosettes may occur at this point. This is reminiscent of the mutual allopreening often seen in the Razorbill following billing, but absent from Puffin behaviour.

Billing is stimulated by a variety of events, such as the landing of a bird near its mate, a fight near a pair, or another Puffin just passing by. Although it is a characteristic interaction between Puffins in a mated pair, some features of billing, such as its attractiveness to onlookers and its often 'promiscuous' nature, suggest that it may have a wider significance than just a pair-bonding behaviour.

Bowing

Though it is seldom seen, bowing is performed by both sexes. In one form it appears to be an invitation to start billing, whereas without head movement it may be a threat display (Myrberget 1962b). On land a bowing Puffin bends its head downwards almost to ground level, as though it is trying to look backwards through its own legs. The head and neck feathers are raised, and the head turned slowly from side to side, the posture being held for up to a minute. On the sea, the beak is bowed downwards to the water surface, and the posture is usually associated with the male's pre-copulation display.

THREAT AND FIGHTING BEHAVIOUR

Gape

Gaping is a threat used by both sexes, and has a range of intensities. The bill is held slightly open, the tongue may be raised and the neck feathers erected with increasing threat intensity. A brief gape, where the head is angled towards the bird being threatened, is frequently seen in communal grouping areas, directed at a bird which has landed nearby and is often followed by a swift bite at the lander. In this situation, the threatened Puffin usually moves off, but in burrow areas the threatened bird may return the gape. The two birds then face each other, gaping and turning their heads in a gape contest, a high-intensity mutual threat display.

Gape contest

The contestant's beaks are angled up slightly, opening and closing slowly, and often synchronously. Head and neck feathers are erected, tongues raised, and a low 'creaking' call is uttered (Lockley 1953). The birds avoid eye-to-eye contact by turning their heads in such a way that each bird turns to its left and right in unison with the other. The whole performance has a slow motion appearance, and the yellow mouth lining is vividly displayed during each gape. One bird in a gape contest usually stops gaping after a while and hurriedly moves or flies off, but if not a full fight can develop.

Fight

Classically, the assailants face each other with feathers stiffly raised and wings outstretched. They interlock beaks and wrestle with twisting head movements. The outstretched wings are alternately pressed to the ground for balance and used as flails to buffet the opponent, and the feet claw upwards like grappling irons. One bird may grab the other by the scruff of the neck or by the wing. The bitten Puffin then usually tries to break free and the fight becomes not so much a contest as a one-sided struggle to escape. A loud growling call is given by fighting Puffins, and is often the first indication of aggression noticed by the human observer. Fighting Puffins often become so intertwined that they tumble as a single furious ball of feathers down the burrow slope, occasionally even overshooting the cliff edge still locked in combat. Fights can end many metres away from their point of origin with one bird rapidly breaking from the tussle and flying off. If the victor is far from its burrow it may become involved in further threatening or fighting while walking back to its own burrow.

Fighting is a popular spectator sport among Puffins, groups of a dozen or more forming around prolonged contests. Despite being noisy and sometimes prolonged, fights probably never result in severe injury as happens with some other seabirds, although some contestants leave fights with a bleeding gape. Fights are often associated with burrow defence, and even a shallow scrape being excavated by a young pair in the season before they breed will be defended vigorously. The frequency of fights is highest in the evening, partly because there are more birds ashore at this time but, more importantly, because of the increased ranging behaviour of individual Puffins around dusk (see below).

STYLIZED WALKING

The great development of chest and leg muscles for swimming and digging are the probable cause of the Puffin's rather 'rolling' gait in any situation. The normal walk, in which the body position is neither stiffly upright nor depressed, is used most often when the density of standing birds on rocks and between burrows is low. When the density of standing birds is higher, two other forms of walk are frequently used, both as a means of locomotion and as a display.

Low profile walk

In the low profile walk the body is held horizontal, close to the ground (Fig. 25), and the head held more in line with the back than is the case in the normal walk. The carpal joints are raised, giving the body a slightly hunchbacked appearance. Birds tend to move rapidly, in brief spurts, stopping to rise up and

25   A Puffin using the low profile walk usually moves rapidly in brief spurts.

look around before moving on. The low profile walk is used at all times of the day by birds moving outside their own burrow territory, but there is a dramatic increase in its frequency around dusk as more and more birds investigate burrows in their part of the colony. The low profile walk posture, which is the antithesis of the upright gape or fight posture, and the context in which the walk is used, suggest that it serves to reduce aggression while birds are moving outside their own burrow territory. To burrow owners standing nearby the walk might signal 'I'm just passing by and mean no harm'.

Pelican walk

In contrast to the low profile walk, the pelican walk posture is stiffly erect with the head lowered to touch the puffed breast feathers and the tail is often raised (Fig. 26). Foot movements are slow and stylized, each foot being raised and lowered in turn in an exaggerated manner, as if the bird were treading on hot coals. This walk is most frequently used by a bird near its burrow, where it may

26   During the pelican walk, foot movements are slow and stylized.

take a few pelican walk steps, often circling the burrow entrance, after its own landing or after another Puffin has passed or landed nearby. It is also used sometimes by a Puffin approaching another prior to billing. It is a site-ownership display which may serve as a mild threat to near, passing low-profile walkers. It is intriguing to think that Puffins can conduct silent locomotion dialogues, where the *status quo* is maintained by each walker adopting a body posture appropriate to its position relative to its home burrow.

Spot-stomp

Although not actually a locomotory behaviour, the spot-stomp may have been ritualized from moving postures during evolution. In spot stomping, the Puffin raises and lowers alternate feet with the webs spread, several times in succession while remaining on the one spot. It is a frequent response to a landing nearby and is also used by burrow owners on the near passage of another bird. Again it signals site ownership – either of a burrow or of space on a grouping area. Stylized foot movements, as in the pelican walk and spot stomp, may have led to the evolution of the Puffin's bright orange–red foot colour due to selection for good visibility of display signals.

DISPLACEMENT BEHAVIOUR

Rise-up/wing-shake is normally used on land and sea to settle the feathers. The Puffin raises its chest, fluffs its body feathers, beats its wings briefly, shakes its tail, then settles down again. On the sea, the chest rises well clear of the water surface. In head dip there is a brief submersion of the head, often repeated many times in quick succession. These movements are also used as 'displacement' behaviour – a kind of redirection of nervous energy – signifying that the Puffin is anxious to take flight, but unwilling to do so alone. The frequency of these behaviour patterns increases greatly when birds in a water raft are about to take off and move to land. Bill dipping in the Black Guillemot is also a displacement activity which indicates nervousness (Asbirk 1979).

HEAD MOVEMENTS

Head shake

The rapid side-to-side head movement which is used to shake water from the bill, also indicates site ownership: a higher proportion of Puffins landing at their burrow head shake soon after landing than birds landing on other areas.

Head jerk

In head jerking, the body is stretched upright and the feathers may be sleeked while the Puffin head jerks. The head is thrown back at a shallower angle than in male head flicking, and there may be some lateral head movement (Fig. 27). Head jerks are performed at the rate of one per second, or slower, in bouts which may last several minutes. The behaviour can be performed by static or

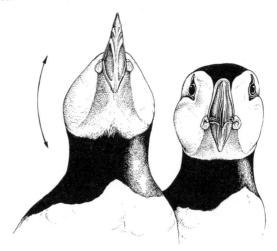

27   Head-jerking is performed at about, or less than, one movement a minute.

moving birds, by singletons or by large groups simultaneously. A monosyllabic call – 'uh . . . uh . . . uh' – is uttered once for each backward jerk of the head. Whilst head flicking as part of the male's pre-copulatory display is usually seen on the sea in the spring, head jerking is performed on land by both sexes throughout the breeding season.

Although head jerking can be seen from time to time throughout the day, the frequency and intensity of the behaviour increases around dusk. Then it is not unusual to see every Puffin on a burrow slope doing it, and at this time the behaviour is frequently associated with low profile walking. My interpretation of this display is that in part it signals the readiness of a bird to leave for the sea. It may stimulate similar excitement in other Puffins nearby which culminates in mass head jerking and eventually in the more or less synchronized departure to the sea of Puffins from one small part of a colony. The call must be audible underground as it is also used by the adults to encourage their chick out of the burrow to exercise its wings in evenings prior to fledging. At dusk, groaning calls by birds underground increase, perhaps stimulated in part by head jerking calls from above ground. Head jerking may be interspersed with brief bouts of gaping, and in some periods is performed more by males than females. As with billing, head jerking is a complex social behaviour which deserves further study.

OTHER BEHAVIOUR

Looking down a burrow is a distinct behaviour which can be used as a social signal. The bird stands at a burrow entrance and peers down the hole, periodically raising its head to look around before looking down again.

When performed by one bird near its mate or prospective partner, this behaviour signals the bird's readiness to go down the burrow and is used to encourage the partner to join it. The behaviour is used more generally, at dusk, in conjunction with head jerking and low profile walking as part of the wider evening reconnaissance of several burrows. A breeder looking down a neighbour's burrow may receive a sharp jabbing attack from the burrow owner. This partly explains the increase in fighting around dusk. Immature Puffins without mates investigate many burrows in this way throughout the day, and are often attacked as a result.

POST-LANDING POSTURE

When a Puffin lands near other Puffins, the body is kept horizontal, the legs partly bent, the wings held above the back, and the feathers slightly sleeked (Fig. 28). The head is often angled up, and one foot may be placed prominently in front of the other. A Puffin landing away from other Puffins folds its wings immediately. A Puffin landing close to a bunch of others may keep its wings raised for three seconds or more, even though it has space to fold them. In general, the closer a Puffin alights to another Puffin, the longer it maintains the post-landing posture. This is an appeasement display – that is, it functions to reduce or inhibit attack in conditions where escape is disadvantageous. A Puffin may gain advantages from joining a group, such as increased protection from predators, but it would lose these advantages if it were forced to take off again by an attack from a group member. The post-landing posture helps the lander to stay in a group without disruptive aggression. Since this was first written, Danchin (1983) has also described this behaviour.

MOTH FLIGHT

In moth flight a Puffin takes off from the colony and angles its wings more upwards from the body than in normal flight, movement being powered by rapid fluttering of the wing tips and by gravity. The body is arched with the head angled down, and the feet often crossed (Plate 1). Moth flight, which cuts the Puffin's airspeed to about half normal flight speed, is used by both sexes, and is a final signal of a bird's readiness to depart for the sea.

It is sometimes the main flight seen over the burrow slopes at dusk. At this time singleton moth flyers which are not joined by other birds in the air tend to track in a wide circuit around the burrow slopes and land at the colony again. The bird repeats this performance until it is joined in the air by one or more other Puffins. They then head out to sea together and in most cases do not return to the colony that night. I have seen members of known breeding pairs synchronize their evening departure to the sea in this way. The Razorbill, but not normally the Guillemot, also uses a moth flight, but this is used throughout the day.

GROUP BEHAVIOUR

Milling

Milling is an erratic to-and-fro swimming movement, usually performed by small groups of neighbouring birds in dense water rafts close inshore. The head is held high and the back sunk low in the water, giving the participating birds the appearance of stretching their necks upwards.

Flocks on the water often drift near the shore shortly before the raft birds take off to occupy the land. Milling may indicate pre-flight excitement before birds move to the land during the day, or fly farther out to sea in the evening. Myrberget, who called this behaviour the 'water-dance', saw it most commonly at dusk in Norway.

Wheeling

Wheeling is a very noticeable behaviour. The wheel flight is in a broad elliptical track above a small area of the breeding colony. It is most obvious when performed simultaneously by large numbers of birds. The birds fly into the wind over land, turn sharply at the end of a few hundred metres, then fly with the wind offshore or on the outer wheel track before turning in again to complete the circuit. Wheel turning-points are often above geological features, such as gullies, which demarcate sub-areas of the Puffin colony. Each sub-colony has a distinct wheel track which varies little from year to year. In moderate to strong wind most wheeling birds follow a figure of eight air path at one or both turn points. Each wheeling Puffin flies in a land track roughly over its own part of the burrow slope, so that for example a bird flying high in the wheel will tend to land at a high burrow area. Individuals normally make only a few wheeling circuits before landing or heading out to sea. At large colonies the heavy traffic of birds to and from wheels maintains numbers in the air, and can give the impression of incessant roundabout flying. Wheeling is a virtually constant feature of some large colonies. The number of birds in a wheel tends to be greatest in the evening, when individuals, often using the moth flight before joining a wheel, make repeated circuits and landings at the colony before flying out to sea.

Wheeling is used for reconnaissance of a burrow area before a bird lands. It allows reasonably synchronous occupation of small areas of burrows, since each Puffin in the wheel is often flying near its close colony neighbours and can quickly follow any landings at its own part of the burrow slope. Wheeling also signals a bird's readiness to land, and may encourage birds in nearby water flocks to join it, again helping to synchronize colony occupation.

PUFFIN-WATCHING

The descriptions above indicate the main features of Puffin behaviour which can be observed at the breeding colonies, but some comments on the tempo of Puffin social life may help Puffin-watchers.

In the incubation period, the birds spend more time ashore, but the extent of colony visitation is variable, both within and between days. Even on a day when many Puffins are ashore there may be long periods of inactivity on the burrow slopes, with most birds merely sitting, preening or sleeping. More exciting behaviour tends to occur in bursts – a pair begins billing, some spectators rush over, a fight breaks out, a gull flies over and panics the slope to flight, the Puffins land again and settle down, to sit, to preen, to sleep.

After the chick has hatched, the adult Puffins spend much of the day flying to and from the fishing grounds, but by then the summer influx of immatures has occurred and there will usually be at least a few birds ashore at the colony. Immatures spend much of their time loafing, but are also inquisitive and eager to try out their social skills, so many behaviour patterns can be seen throughout the day. In general, though, the best time to watch Puffin behaviour is in the evening during the chick-rearing period. At this time, many of the breeders will have finished fishing, and on a good landfall day the immature birds will swell the ranks on the burrow slopes. An observer sitting quietly in a good vantage point before sunset can see many behaviour patterns and watch the suite of head-jerking/fighting/low profile walking/burrow visiting and moth flying behaviour gradually unfold as areas of the slope begin to be abandoned in the fading light.

Despite the inevitable waiting, cold limbs, and eye strain, the experience of watching this feverish colonial activity more than compensates for the discomfort.

CHAPTER 8

Puffins at the colonies

Puffins are highly social birds and tend to do things in groups. Except where pairs nest in isolated cracks in cliffs it is unusual to see a single Puffin standing at a colony. Two aspects of Puffin life are discussed here – fluctuating numbers and the spectacular fly-arounds or 'wheels'.

The number of Puffins at a colony varies greatly. On some days thousands or tens of thousands of birds will be on land, or floating in 'rafts' on the sea, while on other days few will be present. Sometimes such changes occur during a single day. These violent fluctuations make it impossible to estimate the size of the colonies from the numbers of birds present. There are three quite distinct types of fluctuations: a daily cycle, a cycle of a few days and a seasonal cycle partly caused by the return of immatures to the colonies.

DAILY CYCLE

This seems to be directly related to the intensity of light and several studies at widely different latitudes have found the same patterns of behaviour.

Usually few Puffins stand around at the colony in the middle of the day, even though many may be underground and some on the water. Birds gather in groups or rafts on the sea during the afternoon and evening and gradually come ashore, so that peak numbers on land occur in the late evening. Most birds leave at dusk and it is extremely rare (I have seen it only three times) for adult Puffins to be on the surface of the colonies in the dark. Immatures have, however, been recorded roosting ashore. At dawn there are few Puffins loafing on land and sea, but occasionally many come ashore just after first light and spend a few hours standing around. These occurrences are usually early or late in the season and often follow an evening when very large numbers were ashore. Feeding conditions are probably good and the food is close to the colony, so birds can afford the luxury of a morning visit. Myrberget (1959a) counted the birds standing around on an area of boulder scree at Lovunden every 20 minutes for eight days, spread through the breeding season, and found that the pattern of attendance changed during the season. Before egg laying, birds were only present in the late afternoon and evening, with some remaining later and later as the evenings lengthened. There is almost no night in late June and July at that latitude, and birds stood around at all times of the day, but still there was a noticeable peak in numbers at 2200–2400 hours. Late in the season there was also a tendency towards an evening peak and I have seen it in other arctic colonies. This seasonal pattern also occurs in colonies elsewhere.

CYCLE OF A FEW DAYS

This cyclic attendance at colonies has been known for centuries and various factors, such as weather and availability of food, have been suggested as having some control over the rhythm (Lockley 1953, Williamson 1945). At the start of the season, large numbers of Puffins suddenly return to land for an evening or two and then just as suddenly disappear for a few days. After a few such visits, an ill-defined cycle arises with numbers each evening increasing day by day to a peak and then declining again. This is very obvious early in the season when days with large numbers of birds alternate with periods of almost complete or complete absence (Fig. 29). Once laying starts some birds are always present but a cycle persists and again becomes very obvious once the immatures start coming ashore. The cycle continues until the bulk of the birds leave. The periodicity varies somewhat, being 4–7 days on Skomer and Great Island

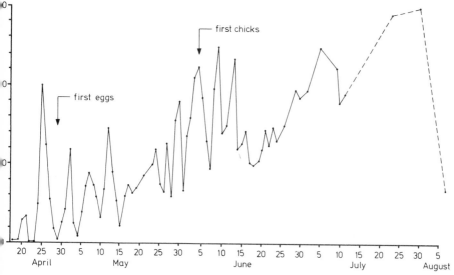

29   The total number of Puffins at North Haven, Skomer on evenings in 1973. Although Puffins were present from 4 April they were not regularly counted until 15 April. Only scattered counts were made after 11 July. (Redrawn from Ashcroft 1976.)

(Ashcroft 1976, Nettleship 1972), 4–11 days on Lovunden (Myrberget 1959a), and 4–6 days on the Isle of May; and also it may be upset by very rough weather. There would seem to be something significant in the minimum of four days, but I have no idea what it is. Peaks of high and low numbers sometimes occur on the same days on neighbouring islands, e.g. Skokholm and Skomer (Lloyd 1972), but various subcolonies on the Isle of May are usually completely out of phase. I am at a loss to explain these differences.

Many earlier puffin-watchers were puzzled by this periodicity but the general consensus was that the weather was the likely cause. However, opinions varied as to what aspect was likely to be important. Some people thought that periods of absence followed a change of wind, others detected a fall-off in numbers after heavy rain, while yet others speculated that birds left to avoid approaching storms as they disliked rough seas and a heavy swell. Lockley (1934) tried in vain to relate his observations to changes in the weather and concluded that food was likely to be the controlling factor. Ashcroft (1976) made a statistical regression analysis of the numbers of birds she counted on Skomer with windspeed, rainfall, sunshine, date and the numbers present one to six days previously. This showed that the main relationship was between the number present one day and the number which had been present on the previous day; that is, there was cycle!

Razorbills and Guillemots have similar patterns of colony attendance prior to laying (though they usually return several months before Puffins). On Skokholm and Skomer, peaks in their numbers coincided with these for Puffins (Lloyd 1972). This suggests that some common factor influences the colony attendance of these birds. The availability of food is a possible (to my mind the most probable) factor but there is no direct evidence for or against this. Also it is difficult to see how or why the food should fluctuate with such regular periodicity. Also how does an individual auk know when to come back to the colony as the flocks form close to the island and not on the feeding grounds? Possibly they have some innate cycle which tells them when to return, although this is modified by local conditions. We have not progressed at all in understanding this phenomenon since Lockley first considered it 35 years ago.

SEASONAL CYCLE

Large numbers of Puffins are present the few weeks before laying, but numbers decrease during the laying period. About the time the young fledge there is a gradual but very marked increase in numbers as more and more immatures come to the colonies in mid June (in southern colonies) and July (further north). The maximum attendance is followed by a rapid decline as the birds leave at the end of the season.

Puffins ashore in the early spring are all old enough to be breeding; and must come back early to have any chance of getting a burrow. The few four-year-olds which breed come ashore at this time, but most birds of this age do not appear until the peak of laying. As the season progresses, younger and younger birds

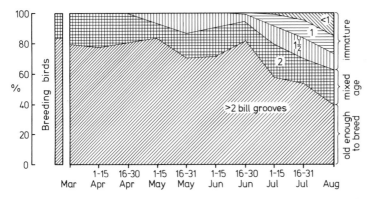

30   The proportions of immature and adults among Puffins caught on the Isle of May every two weeks through the season. The number of bill grooves is a good indication of age.

appear at the colonies until the peak of numbers is reached in July. The few evenings when all these immatures are ashore at the same time as the adults are impressive and it is such occasions that were described in the literature by phrases such as 'the sky was darkened by the birds'.

On the Isle of May the first three-year-olds, colour-ringed as young, so their ages are definitely known, are seen at the end of April and in early May, while two-year-olds arrive in late May or, more usually, in June (Table 10). Only a few birds return to the island in the year following hatching and these arrive at the end of the breeding season. In late July these yearlings form up to 15% of the birds in rafts, but, although some fly over the colony, few actually land. The occasional report of recently fledged birds on the sea near the colonies (e.g. Kornayeva 1967) probably refer to these one-year-olds. The build up of the numbers of immatures in the population is shown by looking at the bill grooves of birds caught at the colonies (Fig. 30). In April all birds have at least two grooves and are capable of breeding; however, by August almost half of the birds caught have fewer than two grooves and so are immatures. On Skomer immatures return about a month later than similarly-aged birds on the Isle of May; for instance, three-year-olds are normally seen in June (once on 16th May), two-year-olds in late June or July (Ashcroft 1976). This difference between colonies is presumably because Puffins arrive on the Isle of May in late February, which is earlier than those on Skomer. In turn, this is presumably because the Isle of May birds stay relatively nearby in winter, whereas Skomer birds migrate far to the south.

END OF SEASON

The end of the breeding season is abrupt and most Puffins depart within a few days of each other, leaving behind the few adults still with chicks. This synchronized departure is brought about by successful and failed breeders, and immatures of all ages (Table 11) continuing to visit the colony until about the same date. I followed both the nesting success and the colony-visiting of 163 individually marked Puffins on the Isle of May. The mean dates when successful and unsuccessful breeders were last seen were 7th August (n = 52) and 8th August (n = 4), which are hardly different from those of birds which did not breed because they had no burrow (5th August, n = 95), or because the female did not lay (5th August, n = 12). Successful breeders on the Isle of May remained near their burrows for two to three weeks (rarely four) after the young had fledged, and the length of time the adults remained was negatively correlated with the date that the bird lost its egg or fledged its chick (Fig. 23); this resulted in the marked synchrony of departure. In other colonies many, or perhaps most, birds depart as soon as their parental duties are completed. Korneyeva (1967), observing Puffins on the Ainov Islands, remarked that their departure at the end of the season was more protracted than was their appearance at the beginning. This is, perhaps, true if one includes the few extremely late breeders, but otherwise the fall in numbers at the end is far more abrupt than the build-up of birds at the start of the season. Puffins do not like to be on their own. Little is known about the factors influencing why birds do not lay later than they do. It is often stated that food becomes scarce, but there is little direct evidence of this.

WHEELS

One of the most impressive sights in a Puffin colony is the large numbers of Puffins circling high over the sea in front of the breeding area (Plate 18). These flights have given rise to the frequent analogies to 'bees around a honeypot'. These 'wheels', 'roundabouts', or 'carousels' are not just birds flying around at random but are well structured displays where all the birds fly in the same direction and follow the same general track (Chapter 7). Wheels may occur when the birds are disturbed, for example by a gull or a human, or may arise spontaneously. In the first situation most birds leave an area, circle a few times, or for as long as the disturbance remains, and then begin to land so that there are fewer birds in the wheels each time it goes around. If the disturbance continues, the birds may land on the sea, so such a wheel lasts only a few minutes. In the second situation birds may circle for hours although it is probable that no individual stays for long. There may be a single or several such spontaneous wheels at a colony. The frequency of wheels varies greatly but they are most noticeable at colonies where there are many avian predators.

Behaviour during the wheel

One of the best descriptions (vivid even in translation) of a wheel concerns a Russian colony, observed by Skokova (1962):

> A typical feature of the daily rhythm of Puffin activity is the 'roundabout', a mass circular flight between the nesting colony and the feeding area on the water. These flights occur several times each day and last from 15 to 20 minutes. We recorded a

'roundabout' lasting from 18.10 to 18.25 by a colony in the western part of Ainov (Major). Some 200 birds simultaneously left the water-feeding-area and flew towards the colony. They all flew in a clockwise path descending to 1.0–1.5 m above the colony and rising to 30 m outside the colony area. Some birds hovered above the colony with wings and claws spread as if about to land, but then joined in the circular flight once more. When they had circled above the colony several times the Puffins flew down to the burrows and were replaced in the 'roundabout' by other birds leaving the burrows. During this time some 3–5 birds at a time left the main circling flock and descended to the feeding area, until the majority had settled on the water and the 'roundabout' came to an end.

Apparently this circular flight does not end until a complete exchange has taken place in the 'roundabout' between birds in the air and birds from the burrow. This phenomenon can easily be observed at mass feeding times when large shoals of capelin, pollock and herring approach the island. At these times most of the birds flying in from the sea have a fish in their beaks. Gradually the number of Puffins with fish decreases until eventually there are birds in the 'roundabout' without fish (i.e. from the burrows).

In periods of calm or light winds Puffins fly in a circle or an ellipse in clockwise and anti-clockwise directions. When the winds are strong, the circle tends to break up and birds follow a figure-of-eight flight pattern. Birds generally go against the wind or glide with the body-axis perpendicular to the wind-direction.

In 1967, Skokova suggested that each colony on the island had its own feeding ground and circular flight territory linking it to the adjacent breeding grounds. As this is the only record of Puffins regularly feeding close to the colonies. I wonder if these so-called 'feeding grounds' were the places where the Puffins gathered before starting the wheel. Disturbance would prevent fish-carrying Puffins getting to their burrows and they would either join the wheel or land on the sea, giving the impression that they were feeding there.

PURPOSE OF WHEELS

Puffins spend so much time and effort in these displays that presumably they serve an important purpose. Wheels are commoner, more obvious and last longer at colonies where there is much gull predation which suggests a link between the display and predation. Skokova thought that wheels were disadvantageous in that they facilitated attacks by gulls when the wheels passed close to cliffs or large boulders behind which gulls could hide. However, far from having a negative function, these wheels probably allow the Puffins to come and go from the colony, or simply look at the land, with a reduced chance of being killed. The display allows the more or less synchronous occupation of a colony which seems to be socially important to Puffins even where there are no predators. Taylor (1982) studied wheels on St Kilda and found that Great Black-backed Gulls had difficulty in catching a Puffin in a flock and preferred to attack solitary birds. The density of Puffins in the wheels is difficult to measure objectively but the gulls on St Kilda hunted mainly when there were moderate numbers of Puffins in flight. When there were few or very many Puffins in the wheel the gulls usually remained on the ground, suggesting that a high density of potential prey may reduce the gull's effectiveness by confusing or swamping it. At the same time I monitored the mortality of Puffins at this colony and noted that a smaller proportion of Puffins nesting in a high density part of a colony were killed by gulls compared to those nesting in a low density area. There were so few Puffins in the low density part that an efficient wheel could not be formed. Wheels are probably primarily an anti-predator strategy.

The possibility that birds are able to tell each other about the location or abundance of food at communal displays, or at roosts and colonies, has been discussed by several authors (e.g. Ward and Zahavi 1973). It cannot be discounted just because we cannot imagine the mechanism involved in the communication. If bees can pass information, why not Puffins? The clumped nesting of Puffins, and their gatherings on the water under the colonies may be associated with their feeding in groups. Puffins sometimes depart to the open sea in groups, and often return in groups, but it is not known whether they remain and feed in the same groups. Probably they do not; Taylor (1982) found that groups coming back to St Kilda and the Faeroes split up some way from the colonies and the fish-carrying birds went to widely scattered burrows. After feeding the young, adults may remain in the burrows for some time, may come out and stand nearby, or fly down to join the rafts or may fly directly out to sea. It is difficult to see how they could form the same groups again, or even how neighbouring birds could manage to fish together. A more serious drawback is that there is no evidence that birds gain any advantage from fishing in groups. If there is no advantage then it would not pay a successful Puffin to divulge where the fish were. More probably, coming ashore in groups simply reduces the chance of a bird being killed or losing fish.

Wynne-Edwards' (1962) theory that animals can in some way assess their own numbers and regulate their breeding so that they do not wastefully over-exploit their food resources is appealing. The appeal remains even though it is difficult to envisage how it could have evolved by natural selection. However, there is no suggestion that anything but shortage of nest sites prevents all Puffins from at least trying to breed every year.

INTRODUCTIONS

The pronounced tendency for seabirds to return to the natal colony and the fact that the location of the colony is not genetically fixed but learnt at fledging, have been put to use in re-introducing Puffins to Eastern Egg Rock, Maine (Kress 1977–82). Since 1973, Puffin chicks have been taken from burrows on Great Island and transported 1,000 km to their foster island. A total of 728 Puffins have fledged, a success rate of 96% which is probably better than their own parents could have managed. In 1981, five pairs were seen feeding young. Seven of these adults were four-year-old, transplanted birds, another was five years, and both members of the last pair were unringed and so were presumably 'normal' birds attracted to the rock (Plate 9). In 1982, these five pairs were joined by nine more, and 42 other Puffins were seen. These must be some of the most expensive and pampered Puffins in existence, but the detailed studies by Stephen Kress and his Audubon Society team are producing much needed information on their biology.

These techniques should not be used uncritically, for example to boost a very small population, unless it can be shown convincingly that the reasons for the decline have been removed. It would be completely futile to introduce young birds to southern British populations until they start to increase naturally if, as seems likely, the decline was caused by natural circumstances. An introduction has been made of Faeroese Puffins to the Breton colonies (Duncombe and Reille 1980) but this is, to my mind, a mistake until the oil menace is under control, and there seems little likelihood of that in the near future.

SUMMARY

The largest numbers of Puffins are seen at the colonies in the late afternoon and evening. Early and late in the season there is a marked cycle of attendance, with peak numbers occurring about every 4–6 days.

Only birds old enough to breed come ashore in the early spring. As the season progresses younger Puffins return to the colonies, and the annual maximum number present occurs about the time that the young fledge. Some one-year-old Puffins come and sit on the sea near the colonies but few come ashore.

Large numbers of Puffins often spend time circling in 'wheels' in front of the colonies. The 'wheels' are primarily an anti-predator strategy and allow the Puffins to come and go from, and just look at, the colony in safety.

CHAPTER 9

Food and feeding

FOOD OF THE YOUNG

The Puffin, Common and Brünnich's Guillemots, Razorbill and Black Guillemot all carry fish back to their young, held in the bill. There are, however, marked differences, for Puffins carry several or many fish at a time, Razorbills usually two or three, and Guillemots and Black Guillemot just one.

Although most of the food of young Puffins is comprised of sandeels, sprats, herring and capelin, the list of fish recorded is quite long:

TYPICAL FOOD SPECIES

Sandeel *Ammodytes* spp.
Sprat *Sprattus sprattus*
Capelin *Mollotus villosus*
Whiting *Merlangius merlangus*
Saithe *Pollarchius virens*
Red-Fish *Sebastes marinus*

Haddock *Melanogrammus aeglefinus*
Herring *Clupea harengus*
Five-bearded Rockling *Ciliata mustela*
Northern Rockling *Ciliata septentrionalis*
Three-bearded Rockling *Gaidropsarus vulgaris*

UNCOMMON FOOD

Mackerel *Scomber scombrus*
Cod *Gadus morhua*
Witch Sole *Glypotcephalus cynoglossus*
Long-rough Dab *Hippoglossoides platessoides*
Norway Pout *Trisopterus esmarkii*
Arctic Cod *Boreogadus saida*
Catfish *Anarhichas lupus*
Jelly Cat *Lycichthys denticulatus*
Snake Blenny *Lumpenus lampretaeformis*
Morid *Halargyreus* sp.
Atlantic Poacher *Leptagonus decagorus*
Angler *Lophius piscatorius*
Sculpin *Triglops* sp.

Blue Whiting *Micromesistius poutassou*
Grey Gurnard *Eutrigla gurnadus*
Crystal Goby *Crystallogobius linearis*
Lumpsucker *Cyclopterus lumpus*
Fifteen-spined Stickleback *Spinachia spinachia*
Pearlsides *Maurolicus muelleri*
Lesser-Weever *Echiichthys vivipera*
Torsk *Brosme brosme*
Sea Scorpion *Myoxocephalus scorpius*
Yarrell's Blenny *Chirolophis ascanii*
Ling *Molva* sp.
Butterfish *Pholis gunnellus*

The commonest and most widespread fish is the sandeel, an elongated silvery eel-like fish with long dorsal and anal fins, a forked tail and a protruding lower jaw. Sandeels do spend time buried in sand but they also occur in vast shoals in mid-water, or near the surface, where they are eaten in vast numbers by fish and birds. Equally vast numbers of sandeels are now caught by trawlers and processed into fishmeal for animal food and fertilizer. The impact of this 'industrial' fishery on other fish and seabirds has yet to be demonstrated but might well be severe as the catch of sandeels in Shetland and elsewhere is doubling each year. Five species of sandeels occur in the north-eastern Atlantic but all species collected from Puffins have been identified as *Ammodytes marinus*. Most sandeels eaten by seabirds are in the first year of life (the O-group of fisheries biologists) when they grow from transparent larvae into recognizable fish. They reach a length of 80–90 mm at six months and 110 mm when one year old. Larger sandeels (up to 130 mm) are probably in their second year of life. Puffins can handle the latter but nothing larger. Shags and other larger seabirds eat these and older sandeels up to the maximum length of 320 mm. Sometimes Puffins are seen holding large numbers of minute transparent fish – these are usually larval sandeels.

The other main foods in Britain and Scandinavia are sprats and small herring. These green–blue-backed and silvery-sided fish can be distinguished by running a finger along the belly from tail to head; sprats have large backwardly pointing scales which give the belly a diagnostic, very rough feel; herrings are smooth. Further north and in the west Atlantic their place is taken by capelin – small pelagic salmon-like fish which are eaten by many birds, fish and marine mammals when they come inshore to spawn.

Occasionally, Puffins bring in great numbers of juvenile rockling (Plate 12) which are sometimes so abundant at the surface of the sea as to be known as mackerel-midges. These surface rockling are always minute and will migrate to the sea-bottom when about 60 mm long.

Other fish brought to young Puffins include the immature stages of well-known food fish, mostly in the cod family. The commonest is the whiting, but only first-year individuals are taken; they grow rapidly to a length of 150 mm in one year and are then safe from Puffins. These young whiting often shelter among the stinging tentacles of large jelly-fish where, perhaps, they are safe from birds, or maybe birds then know where to find them. Young haddock, cod, saithe and red-fish (though the last not in Britain) are sometimes eaten in numbers, but all other species are so infrequent that they can be ignored. In the far north, crustacea and pelagic worms are sometimes brought in but I have only six records of British young receiving anything but fish – small squid (five) and a small shrimp.

THE DIET

The diet is sampled by mist-netting the Puffins (Plate 11) to make fish-carrying individuals drop their loads. The numbers of the various fish species are easily counted but they can give a biased impression of the diet since one large sprat weighs as much as a hundred or more rockling or larval sandeels. Even when the lengths of the fish are taken into account, biases still remain as the weight of a fish increases in proportion to the approximate cube of the length. The best comparison is between the total weights of different species, achieved by weighing the fish or by calculation, using formulae relating weight to body length (in Harris and Hislop 1978).

There are marked differences in the diet at different places and in different years (Table 12). Between 1973 and 1979, on the Isle of May, sprats, herring, and sandeels made up 92% of the numbers of fish brought in and 94% of the biomass. Only in 1976 was any other species important; then saithe made up 9% of the biomass. The proportion of sprats varied 3–73% (biomass 7–86%) and sandeels 21–93% (13–90%). In later years, herring have become increasingly important until, in 1982, they comprised 33% of the number and 29% of the biomass (Fig. 31). Young Puffins in the Irish Sea get only sprats and sandeels, with sandeels predominating in 14 out of the 16 years for which I have records, while those on Fair Isle have sandeels only. The situation on St Kilda is very different and only in one year in seven did sprats and sandeels combined make up more than 80% of the numbers or biomass, and in two years only about 25% of the biomass came from these fish. The shortfall was made up by rockling, whiting and an assortment of other species.

Sandeels, herring and sprats are the most important food species for Puffins throughout the eastern Atlantic and the Barents Sea, but in eastern Canada and sometimes in north Norway and Russia their place is taken by capelin. Other species eaten in small quantities include arctic cod (Spitzbergen), red-fish (Norway), and in northern areas small numbers of crustacea (especially *Calanus* and the euphausids *Thysanoessa* and *Meganyctiphanes norvegica*), and polychaete worms and squid. Puffin chicks grow less rapidly when fed on these less common fish so they can be assumed to be poor food. Crustacea seem to be fed when nothing else is available.

One must be careful not to be too general about the diet as this can change dramatically within a season. On St Kilda in late June, 50–60% of the fish were rockling but the proportion had declined to 10% a month later. In late July of another year, 88% of the fish were sprats and whiting but three weeks later these accounted for only 2%; their place being taken by small sandeels. The species composition also varies between nearby colonies. Once, when sprats were the dominant prey on St Kilda, two-thirds of the fish at the Flannan Islands only 80 km away were sandeels. Presumably birds from these colonies were feeding in different areas.

SIZE OF FISH

The lengths of fish brought ashore to any one colony tend to be uniform within a season except for a slight increase as the season advances and the fish grow. However, occasionally the mean length decreases with date – perhaps

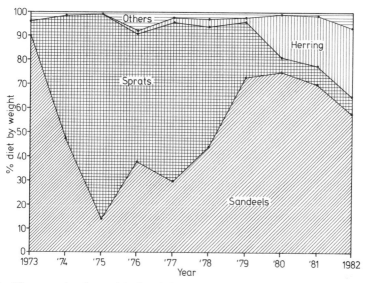

31   The proportion (by weight) of sandeels, sprats and herring in the diet of young on the Isle of May.

because the larger fish move to deeper water or further from the colonies. There are significant differences in the lengths of the fish in loads taken from different Puffins at the same time and place, indicating that individual adults feed on different fish shoals and take a full load at a single school. It has been suggested that small young are fed on minute fish and only later graduate to large sandeels and sprats. Although this seems reasonable, and might well be true for young newly-hatched, I have failed to detect any tendency for Puffins to select larger fish for older young. Young Puffins can swallow fish that are so long or large as to seem well beyond their capabilities (Plate 15). A three-quarter grown young I reared, swallowed a sprat weighing 25 g and followed it with two others totalling the same weight with hardly a pause for breath. Another young, itself only about 150 mm long, swallowed four sandeels which laid end to end measured 500 mm. Lid (1981) thought that saithe brought back to starving young in Norway were too large to be swallowed (Plate 16). I suspect that healthy young could probably have coped with these but agree that weak young might well have been defeated.

Although Razorbills, Guillemots and Puffins feed their young on the same fish species they bring back different sized fish. The mean lengths (and range) of these fish collected at Welsh colonies over five seasons were:

	SANDEELS		SPRATS	
	no.	*mean length* (mm)	*no.*	*mean length* (mm)
Puffin	594	61 (36–90)	312	46 (25–86)
Razorbill	27	73 (55–158)	7	54 (30–105)
Guillemot	3	122 (115–130)	58	102 (73–130)

The most marked difference is between the size of fish carried by Guillemots and Puffins, presumably because Guillemots invariably carry a single large fish whereas Puffins usually have several small ones. The Razorbill is intermediate both in number and size of fish. The above measurements were of fish in seasons when food was abundant, suggesting that there may have been little competition for food. In times of shortage these differences might be even greater. However, the main factor bringing about ecological separation need not be what each bird eats but how, where and when the various birds catch their prey, and we know very little of the differences in feeding ecology of these auks.

NUMBERS CARRIED

Although many seabirds carry food for their young in the beak, most bring back just a single item, but Puffins carry back several items at a time. On the Isle of May the average number of fish per load is five, on Skomer and St Kilda it is 10–11. However, the number of fish varies greatly from year to year; on St Kilda there was a mean of 22 fish per load in 1971, but only 4 in 1978.

The fish are carried between the series of spines (denticles or *hornae papillae*) on the upper palate and the fleshy tongue, the distal third of which is enclosed in a horny covering (Bédard 1969). This cornification gives the Puffin a tongue that is intermediate between the larger, slender, rigid tongue of the Guillemot (which gives great leverage for holding a single large prey) and the fleshy tongue

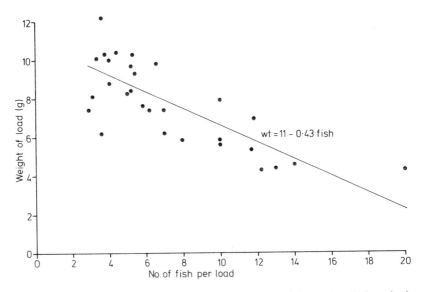

32   *The relationship between the weights of loads of fish and the number of fish per load. Each point represents an annual mean. The correlation is highly significant (r = −0.8, P < 0.001). (Data from Harris and Hislop 1978 and Table 14.)*

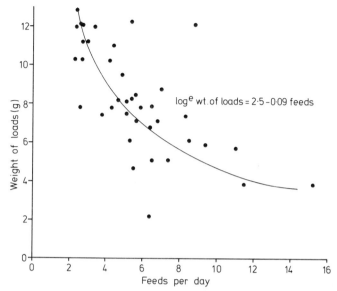

$\log^e$ wt. of loads = 2·5 - 0·09 feeds

33 The relationship between the weights of loads of fish and the frequency of feeds at various colonies. Each point represents a single feeding frequency plotted against the weight of loads collected either at the same time or within a few days. The correlation is highly significant (r = −0.6, P < 0.001). (Data from Harris and Hislop 1978 and Table 14.)

of a plankton eater, e.g., Little Auk, (which has to manipulate small organisms). This intermediate tongue allows the Puffin to eat both fish and invertebrates (mainly in the winter). The beak's enlarged size is for display and not primarily for carrying large numbers of fish.

However simple the mechanism for holding the fish, it is still remarkable that a bird can carry several fish, and chase, catch and hold another. The record is held by a Puffin which had 61 sandeels and a rockling clamped in its beak. These 62 fish weighed only 5 g. Perhaps surprisingly, the weight of a load is reduced as the number of fish increases (Fig. 32) because the size of the fish declines dramatically. These multi-fish loads are also of low food value as the fish often are transparent larval forms which dry out and sometimes fragment as the bird flies back to the colony. A few large fish are a better return for effort expended. However, extremely large loads (maximum of 29 g in Britain, 37 g in Norway), or very long fish (maximum 210 mm), are also disadvantageous. Puffins grab the fish just behind the gills and cannot adjust their grip without risking the loss of other fish already held. This is not the centre of gravity of a fish, so that a long fish flaps and swings wildly, impairing flight and making the bird obvious to piratical gulls and skuas. Perhaps this is why Puffins rarely bring in very large fish although such fish would provide the best value as food.

There is a popular idea that the fish are arranged neatly in the beak with heads and tails alternating on each side. Perry (1946) reported this as happening 90 times out of 100 due to the zig-zag course steered by the Puffin when underwater – 'Progressing thus he will first take a fish to the left, then right, then left'. This nice story is, unfortunately, quite untrue and the fish are arranged haphazardly.

WEIGHTS OF LOADS

The weights of loads vary far less than the numbers of fish. The annual mean weights for 12 years on the Isle of May ranged 8.2–10.4 g, and for seven years on St Kilda 4.3–10.0 g. The weights are similar elsewhere in Britain. The heaviest recorded load was 7% of the adult's weight. Outside Britain loads are slightly heavier – 10.3 g at Lovunden (Myrberget 1962) and 12.3–13.3 g in Canada (Nettleship 1972), probably because the adults are larger. Birds either bring in a few, heavy loads of fish each day, or several lighter ones. Figure 33 shows how the weight of loads declines significantly as the feeding frequency increases. Or perhaps we should say that birds can compensate for being able to find only small quantities of food by going fishing more often.

FOOD VALUE OF FISH

The energy values of different species of fish vary greatly. The calorific values (ranked in decreasing order) of fish dropped by Puffins (taken from Harris and Hislop 1978) are:

fish	length	kJ/g wet weight
Sprat	over 100 mm	10.9
Rockling	30 mm	7.1
Sprat	40–90 mm	6.7
Sandeel	over 60 mm	6.5
Sandeel	larval	5.8
Sprat	larval	5.6
Saithe	40 mm	5.1
Whiting	50 mm	4.1

Rockling are good value but are so small that many have to be collected to make a single meal for the chick. Crustacea have low calorific value (the shrimp *Crangon* is only 4.2 kJ/g wet weight; Jones and Hislop 1978) which probably explains why Puffins only bring them ashore when times are hard.

The calorific value (kJ/g wet weight) of sprats and sandeels increases with the length of the fish (in mm) because the proportion of fat in the body increases as the fish get larger. The increases are:

$$\text{Calorific value of sprat} = 3.215 + 0.063 \text{ length}$$
$$\text{Calorific value of sandeel} = 4.908 + 0.022 \text{ length}$$

The overall weight of a fish increases, approximately, as the cube of the length and combining these equations results in a striking increase in the calorific

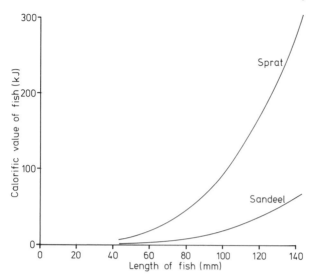

34 The calculated increase of calorific value of a sprat and a sandeel as the length of the fish increases.

value of an individual fish as it gets longer (Fig. 34). For instance, a sprat 60 mm long contains about 10 kJ of energy, a sprat 140 mm long about 200–300 kJ. The more fish in a load, the lower is its calorific value due to the inverse relationship between numbers of fish and weight of the load. A few large sprats, herring or other oil-rich fish offer by far the best return for effort.

Young Puffins fed on oil-rich fish grow best. In years when whiting made up over half of the biomass fed to the young, fledgling Puffins on St Kilda were significantly lighter than when sprats were the most important food (Harris 1982b). The general ranking of breeding performance, based on weights of young and nesting success, was 1980 (least successful), 1974, 1976, 1975, 1977 (most); the ranking of proportion of sprats was 1980 (least), 1974, 1976, 1977 and 1975 (most). In 1980, juveniles had a mean fledging weight of 225 g, compared to 266 g in 1975. The only significant annual difference between fledging weights on the Isle of May was in 1979, the year with the lowest proportions of sprats, when fledging weights were low. Sprats were obviously the best food for young Puffins.

There is no information as to which proteins are required by growing Puffins, nor indeed on the amounts of various proteins in small fish. It is conceivable that the protein quality of the diet is more important than the calorific value, but in gross terms all these fish should supply enough protein. Fish such as blue whiting have 2–3% of their body weight as fat, sandeels 7% and sprats 4–14% depending on the size and the time of year (Murray and Burt 1969). The high concentration of fat in sprats is in the nature of a bonus in that fat replaces water in the tissues. Puffins fed on non-oily fish may have to utilize some of their protein intake for metabolic energy, leaving less for growth or fat reserves. My attempts to rear young Puffins on whiting when I could not get sprats all resulted in failure. Not surprisingly adult Puffins feed their young the most nourishing food available at the time.

FISH AVAILABLE TO PUFFINS

Do Puffins select certain fish for their young or do these fish happen to be the most abundant? It is difficult to determine the relative densities of the various fish living in mid-water but some data are available for the North Sea, taken from mid-water trawl surveys of small fish by fisheries biologists of the Department of Agriculture and Fisheries for Scotland (Harris and Hislop 1978).

Species caught in mid-water trawls in the North Sea 1973–79 (mean catch per hour):

North of 59° N	*South of 59° N*
Sandeel (4,961)	Sandeel (3,503)
Norway Pout (2,786)	Sprat (432)
Haddock (360)	Herring (57)
Whiting (109)	Whiting (36)
Sprat (76)	Long-rough Dab (22)
Cod (27)	Cod (12)
Saithe (23)	Haddock (10)
Long-rough Dab (12)	Norway Pout (6)
Witch Sole (3)	Grey Gurnard (2)
Herring (3)	Crystal Goby (2)
Pearlsides (3)	Rockling (2)
Blue Whiting (2)	Saithe (2)
Lemon Sole (2)	Witch Sole (2)
Crystal Goby (1)	Pearlsides (1)
Grey Gurnard (1)	
13 other species (< 1)	13 other species (< 1)

Puffins in these areas mainly took the commonest species but there were some interesting exceptions. Sandeels were 10 times as numerous as sprats in the trawl catches in the North Sea off north-east Scotland, but only 1.8 times so among the Puffins' fish. Around Shetland the corresponding figures were 65 and 16. These results suggest that Puffins select sprats. The species that are not taken by Puffins are just as interesting. Norway pout were extremely common in the trawls yet were virtually never brought ashore. This is probably because young pout make extensive daily vertical migrations and only occur near the surface of the sea by night, when Puffins do not feed. There were also numbers of young dabs and soles in the trawl catches but trivial numbers were fed to young Puffins, probably because they are so small and so fragile that they would be likely to break up in a Puffin's beak.

Young rockling are much more common than the fishery results suggest as they live at the surface, a habitat not adequately sampled by the trawls. The few trawls made near St Kilda suggest that there were few sandeels, and Puffins there were forced sometimes to eat less desirable species, such as whiting and haddock, because of the lack of anything better. Other gadoids are less at risk because they occur further offshore or have shorter pelagic phases and so spend less time in mid-water. Although the trawl data are not really suitable for comparisons between years, young saithe, haddock and cod were far more numerous in the trawls than normal in 1974, 1976 and 1979. They were the only years in which these species were commonly brought to young Puffins. Since 1977, Puffins on the Isle of May have eaten herring in increasing numbers; possibly the cessation of commercial fishing for this species is allowing the stocks to recover from near-extinction due to overfishing (Hislop and Harris 1984). It is, however, possible that the change was a result of a decline in the numbers of sprats, forcing Puffins to herring.

TIMING AND FREQUENCY OF FEEDS

How often the chick is fed may be determined by all-day watches made at marked burrows. This is a time-consuming and demanding procedure since Puffins coming to the chicks usually dive straight down burrows and feeds can easily be missed. Recorded feeding frequencies may, therefore, be slight under-estimates.

Young have been recorded as being fed 24 times per day but the usual daily average varies from four to ten feeds. The number of feeds varies with the age of the chick (Fig. 35), with young in the middle third of their development

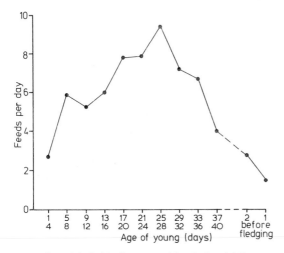

35   *The mean number of feeds per day received by chicks of different ages on Skomer. (Redrawn after Ashcroft 1976.)*

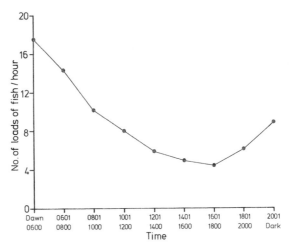

36   The diurnal variations in the number of loads of fish brought to part of the colony on the Isle of May. This is the mean of ten day's observations.

receiving most. This pattern is, however, sometimes upset, as on St Kilda in mid July 1976 when chicks received so little food (a mean of 6.4 feeds of 2.1 g per day) that many young aged between 20 and 32 days died. Younger chicks, which needed less food, survived and fledged successfully. Most feeds are brought in the early morning (Fig. 36), but although the adults usually spend the night at sea, the first food brought to the young is not at dawn but 30–60 minutes later. Adults presumably start fishing at dawn, satisfy their own needs and then collect food for the chick. Usually, few feeds are given in the middle of the day; presumably food is unavailable as adults rarely try to get food at that time even when their young are starving. Often there is a slight resurgence of feeding during the evening and the last feed is brought just before dark. Puffins appear to sleep at night.

As the young near fledging the adults bring them fewer feeds. This change could either be due to an inbuilt timing mechanism, with some internal factor telling the adults that it is time to reduce their effort, or to some feedback mechanism whereby the chick indicates that it needs less food. The latter seems more likely because captive young near fledging voluntarily reduce their food even when offered an excess (Fig. 37). Also adults can be tricked into bringing significantly more feeds to large young if a chick-begging call is played to them from a tape recorder every time they enter the burrow, presumably they think the chick is still hungry (Harris 1983b).

WHERE PUFFINS FEED

There are many generalized statements but few facts on where Puffins obtain food for their young. In Russia they are thought to feed closer inshore than other auks, but it is difficult to credit the reports that they feed within 300–400 m of some colonies, whereas birds from others go 8–10 km (Gerasimova 1961, Kozlova 1957). In Spitzbergen, Løvenskiold (1964) reported the species as feeding close inshore and rarely going to feed even as far as the centre of the bays, contrasting it with the Norwegian Puffin which (he said) obtains most of its food from the high seas. In Britain, Puffins feed fairly near to the colonies, although not inshore like the Black Guillemot and it is unusual to see them fishing within sight of land. Ashcroft (1977) and Corkhill (1973) counted numbers of Puffins carrying fish up to 15 km offshore from the colonies on Skomer and found the bulk were within 7 km of the colonies.

The time interval between alternate feeds (to allow for the fact that both adults feed the young) gives some idea of how far away the birds are feeding. This is especially useful in the early morning when the adults are feeding most intensely. On St Kilda the interval is about 1½ hours, on Skomer, the Isle of May and Hermaness it is 2–2½ hours (Harris and Hislop 1978, Corkhill 1973). The intervals include the time needed to fly to the feeding grounds, find a fish shoal, catch a beakful of food and perhaps something for the adult itself, and then fly back, so they can only give a maximum feeding range. Puffins fly at 50–80 km/hr so the feeding range is potentially very large even if each adult returns every 1½–2 hr. However, birds sometimes return within 15–20 mins, with fish which may be still alive showing that birds had fed very close to the colonies.

Puffins with fish do not arrive at random but are clumped, i.e., two or three

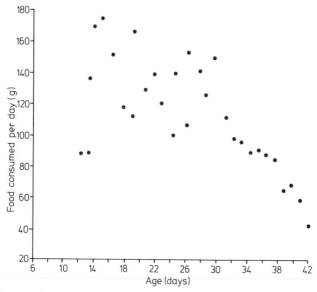

37   The mean daily food consumption of five young Puffins reared in captivity in relation to their age. The young had access to unlimited food. (Redrawn after Harris 1978.)

come back in quick succession, followed by a longer-than-expected gap before the next arrivals. This indicates either that the birds were feeding together, or that some had waited until others were flying in to minimize their own chances of being caught by a gull or skua.

FOOD SHORTAGE

Sometimes Puffins rear few or no young, apparently because the adults cannot find sufficient food. The best documented cases have been in the Lofoten Islands, Norway where nesting success at Hernyken (Røst) was assessed by Lid (1980, pers. comm.).

1970	Moderate	1977	Virtually zero
1971	Low	1978	Virtually zero
1972	Low to Moderate	1979	Virtually zero
1973	Low to Moderate	1980	Zero
1974	Good	1981	Virtually zero
1975	Virtually zero	1982	Virtually zero
1976	Moderate	1983	Good

In 1979, on Hernyken, about half of the eggs laid hatched but most of the young died. By early August only 200–300 pairs were feeding young, although the most recent (1966) estimate of the colony size was about 20,000 pairs. Lid and his co-workers took four of the few surviving young into captivity; all were emaciated (only 40–55% of the weight they should have been for their age) and although they soon gained weight when fed on herring and mackerel, all of them died. The weight of loads of fish brought by adults increased from 3.3 g at the end of June to 13.7 g in mid August, but still that year's mean weight was only 7.4 g compared to an expected 10–11 g (Myrberget 1962). The food changed from capelin, with some sandeels and a few krill, at the start of the season, to haddock, whiting and red-fish at the end. That is from high to low calorific value fish, which would have partly offset, perhaps even halved, the apparent improvement in the food value due to the heavier loads. The interval between feeds ranged 2–7 hours and the young soon lost the ability to regulate their body temperature and, not surprisingly, gained little weight and soon died. Birds dying in 1979 were 10–11 days old whereas in 1975 and 1978 they were only 4–5 days old, and in 1970 near fledging.

This strongly suggests a chronic shortage of food but it is conceivable that the young were diseased, especially as the captive young all died, even after gaining weight. Three factors argue against disease. First, post-mortem examinations showed no signs of disease. Second, young died at different ages in different years. Third, the breeding success of Guillemots on nearby Vedøy in the 1970s paralleled that of the Puffins (Tschanz and Barth 1979). It is unlikely that disease would occur in these two species on different islands in the same years. Food shortage or poor availability is a far more probable explanation. The Guillemot population on Vedøy declined from 11,900 pairs in 1960–63 to

2,380 pairs in 1978. The Puffin population on Røst must decline unless there is considerable immigration but, as yet, there has been no sign of a decline. These failures of breeding have been attributed to man's over-exploitation of local herring stocks.

In late July 1959, over 8,000 young Puffins died on St Kilda; post-mortem examinations again showed no evidence of disease or parasites, but the young were emaciated and starvation was the most likely cause of death (Boddington 1960). In 1976 about 10% of the young died of starvation and in other years Puffins there have had difficulty in rearing young, nesting success being often low and chicks growing better if given additional food (Chapter 10). Young on Great Island, in two years, grew slowly and fledged while still below normal weight (Nettleship 1972); this may have been due to gulls stealing food but the proportion of loads lost was small. Large numbers of dead young have also been found on Burhou, Channel Islands; Lockley (1953) thought they might have been killed by excessive numbers of mites, but starvation was also a possibility.

Other species of Puffins also have trouble rearing young (Vermeer *et al* 1979). Tufted Puffins in British Columbia fledged about 0.46 young per pair in 1975, but had almost total breeding failures in 1976 and 1977. In 1976 most pairs deserted their eggs, whereas in 1977 losses were divided between eggs being deserted near hatching and chicks dying. Even though these Tufted Puffins fed close to the colonies in 1977, the young received only about two feeds (of mainly sandeels) a day and the average weight of each feed declined from 19 to 10 g during the chick period. (A Tufted Puffin is about 70% heavier than an Atlantic Puffin, so proportionately these meals were not as large as they seem.) This quantity of food was insufficient to maintain the chick's growth. Guillemots also had a disastrous breeding season; only ten chicks were seen among 3,000 adults. On the other hand, Rhinoceros Auklets bred successfully, apparently because they managed to change from sandeels to sauries *Cololabis saira* when the former became scarce. Tufted Puffins did not and probably could not. Such is the price of specialization.

FOOD OF ADULTS

The diet of adults is difficult to determine because Puffins seem to digest fish very quickly. Even if birds are killed as soon as they come to the colonies about two-thirds have empty stomachs. However, the bulk of the food is fish. In Britain the commonest species are sandeels with a few saithe and whiting, while further north and west these are replaced by arctic cod, capelin and herring. In the winter, adults also eat numbers of pelagic polychaete worms (whose chitinous pharyngeal 'teeth' are often found in stomachs), pelagic shrimps, gammarids and other crustacea and a few pelagic molluscs.

Puffins can swallow surprisingly large fish. Swennen and Duiven (1977) offered captive but free-swimming Puffins, Razorbills and Guillemots a choice of different sized (dead) herring, sandeels and Norway pout. Small fish were always swallowed underwater, sometimes several during a single dive, but larger fish were brought to the surface. Rarely did a bird even touch a fish too large to swallow, which suggests that the choice of suitable prey was made by sight. Up to the maximum length of fish given (220 mm to Guillemots, 180 mm to Puffins and Razorbills), the length did not influence the choice of fish, but the depth did. A high proportion of the shallow-bodied fish offered were always eaten. Birds obviously found it easier to swallow long, thin sandeels than bulkier herring or other fish. Guillemots took fish up to 40 mm in depth, Razorbills and Puffins normally took only those under 22 mm. The maximum weights of herring and pout eaten by the Puffins both corresponded to fish 150 mm in length, and young can easily swallow fish this long.

Any marine bird excretes large quantities of salt. The kidneys of a Puffin are twice as heavy as those of a duck that drinks isotonic sea water, but most salt is removed by the nasal salt glands which secrete saline solution at 0.29 ml/min/kg of bodyweight (Hughes 1970). This is among the highest rates known in birds. A Puffin eliminated 75% of 4 ml of injected normal salt solution within 20 minutes. Such a capacity for salt excretion is theoretically not needed by a bird living on fish but would be essential if, as seems likely, large quantities of sea water were swallowed with the fish or plankton. Perhaps this capacity is needed in the winter when crustacea and worms may be eaten more frequently.

WRECKS

Occasionally large numbers of seabirds are washed ashore in what have come to be called wrecks. Rarely, these include numbers of Puffins; records include Norfolk in May 1856 and September 1858, Cornwall in 1858, west Scotland 1859 (Holdgate 1971), Brittany in winter 1873 (Bureau 1877), Sicily in January 1874 (Moltoni 1973), Malta in 1910 and 1912 (Bannerman and Vella-Gaffiero 1976), and east Scotland in December 1914 and February–March 1916 (Rintoul and Baxter 1917). These were all before large quantities of oil polluted the oceans. More recent kills of Puffins have often involved oil, as in the *Amoco Cadiz* incident in Brittany in 1978. Even so, 'normal' wrecks still occur, such as that in east Scotland during the extremely cold weather of early 1947 (Dacker 1948), on the Murmansk coast in the winter of 1962 (where a large mortality was followed by a halving of the number of pairs breeding in the Ainov Islands) (Skokova 1967), in the south-east corner of the Bay of Biscay in early 1978 and 1979, and in the North Sea in February 1983. Most of the Puffins involved were very thin, and doubtless died of starvation. It is impossible to know if this was due to food shortage *per se* or to severe storms driving birds away from their normal feeding area. In December 1979, 31 dead Puffins were found on a relatively small area of beach on Porto Santo, Madeira, where the Puffin is a very rare bird. There was no unusual weather at the time, but practically no tunny or bonito were caught at Madeira or the Selvagens in 1979, and Cory's Shearwaters left their nests 10–15 days later than normal, which suggests a shortage of food (D. D. Camara, A. Zino). Because Puffins winter so far from land we shall probably never know how close they are to starvation, but food is unlikely to be superabundant in the open ocean.

SUMMARY

Young Puffins are usually fed sandeels, herring and sprats (in the eastern Atlantic) or capelin (western Atlantic). The proportion of various fish species in the diet varies greatly from colony to colony, from year to year, and even within a single season at one colony.

Although a Puffin can carry many fish in its beak, the normal load is 4–20. Large sprats are by far the best food, whiting and crustacea the worst; young fledge heavier in years when they are fed on sprats. There is some evidence that adult Puffins deliberately select sprats for their young.

Young receive 4–10 feeds per day. Feeding frequency is highest in the early morning. Young in the middle third of their development receive more feeds than other young. Prior to fledging chicks voluntarily restrict their food intake. Most fish are caught near the colonies.

Sandeels and other small fish are the staple foods of adult Puffins augmented by pelagic worms and crustacea in the winter.

CHAPTER 10

Growth of young

The young Puffin is readily weighed, confined as it is to the burrow where it can be caught as required. The development of the chick is a good indication of feeding conditions in the sea, and although it is obviously impossible to alter the amount of food in the sea, the effect of additional food on growth can be assessed. Hatching and fledging dates are often mentioned below. This is because in some seabirds the maximum weights and fledging weights of chicks decline as the season progresses and chicks fledging earlier in the season have a much higher chance of returning to the colonies in later years than young fledging late. During my own studies I anticipated that the same would happen in the Puffin. I was mistaken.

WEIGHING YOUNG

At hatching the chick is little more than a dark-grey powder-puff weighing 35–45 g. Although it is usually brooded by its parents for several days, it is often not fed during the first day as it still has the remnants of the egg yolk inside it. Soon the chick shows its hunger by insistent and incessant 'peeping'. On being fed, it gains weight rapidly and typically reaches a peak of 250–350 g when four to five weeks old. It then loses some weight and fledges when 38–44 days old.

Disturbance of the incubating or brooding adult near hatching time sometimes results in temporary or even permanent desertion of the egg or chick, so nests are not disturbed at this time except if it is critical to determine the exact date of hatching. Usually it is sufficient to know the date to ± one or two days, which can be ascertained either from the bill length or the wing length of the chick. Both lengths are approximately linearly correlated with age during the period the young is in the burrow and growing fast. Either can confidently be used to tell the age of young if a development curve for a sample (say, 20) of young of known hatching date is available. Like many other aspects of Puffin biology such relationships must be found for each colony. The slight differences between years can safely be ignored in most circumstances. Weight is no use as an indicator of age.

GROWTH CURVES

There is tremendous variation in weight among Puffin chicks of the same age. This is partly genetic – that is, there are large and small Puffins – but the weight of a young Puffin is chiefly affected by the amount of food it receives. Young fed identical quantities of food show far less variation in weight than do 'normal' young. The pattern of growth, as shown by the shape of the growth curve, of an individual young is also very variable and young may have similar fledging weights but very different peak weights. Chicks which grow slowly but steadily to a peak weight at or near fledging are receiving less food than those which reach a large mid-period peak.

In a Puffin chick, growth (as expressed by weight) is not a slow, gradual process but occurs by a few, large daily increases interspersed in zigzag fashion with days when the young loses up to a quarter of its weight. The number of feeds a young receives obviously influences its increase in weight on any one day, but the relationship is not clear-cut. Some chicks receive ten feeds in a day but still lose weight, while others gain weight with only two feeds. Ashcroft (1976) and Hudson (1983) found that on Skomer there were 'good' days and 'bad' days when many or few young gained weight. This synchronization of 'good' and 'bad' days for weight increases of the young appears not to be due to chicks receiving many or few feeds on the same day (which would be related to the ease or otherwise the adults had in getting food), because captive young fed very different amounts of food all showed a typical zigzag pattern of growth. Captive young fed the most food had the largest fluctuations but, remarkably, the fluctuations in the weight changes tended to be synchronized between the groups, effectively removing the possibility that it was availability or quality of food which caused the synchronizations of weight increases in wild young. These changes were not related to meteorological conditions nor to the temperature of the young or its burrow. The whole subject is perplexing and obviously would repay detailed physiological study.

CONVERSION RATES

During the first few days of life the chick increases its body weight by 1 g for every 2 g of fish it eats. The conversion ratio steadily declines as the chick becomes older. This is because the chick is no longer brooded and needs more energy to maintain its body temperature, and as the body gets larger it needs extra food for maintenance. Figures calculated for wild young vary greatly, but a young at its peak weight needs to eat between 7 and 19 g of food to put on 1 g of body weight. Captive young sometimes eat 60 g of fish for every 1 g increase in body weight which suggests that they are not utilizing all the food they consume. Just before fledging, when they are losing weight, young still eat 50–100 g per day to maintain themselves, complete their feather growth and take a little exercise. Five young I kept for 8–10 days after they would normally have flown consumed 45 g of sprats per day. This compares with a captive moulting adult which ate 56 g of sprats per day and maintained its body weight, while Puffins kept in a large aviary where they could swim consumed about 130 g of herring or 165 g of pout per day (C. Swennen).

DIFFERENCES IN GROWTH

Although different individuals grow at markedly different rates, it is possible to construct generalized growth curves for different colonies by taking the mean weights of young of similar ages. These curves can be used to compare patterns of growth at different colonies. If the weights are expressed as a proportion of the adult weight at these different colonies we can compare growth in different areas or in different years. Figure 38 shows that chicks on Skomer grow fastest, followed by those on the Isle of May and eastern Murmansk. Chicks on St Kilda and Lovunden grow far less well. More detailed comparisons can be made by comparing four easily measured parameters of growth for individual young: the peak weights and fledging weights, the age when peak weight is reached and the age of fledging. The first and second pairs of measurements are correlated, i.e. if a chick reaches a high peak it will be heavy at fledging, and if it reaches a peak early it will fledge younger.

In most studies the date of hatching had little influence on peak weights or fledging weights. However, there was a seasonal decline in the weights of juveniles caught shortly after they had fledged on St Kilda in the years 1977–79, but was not in the years 1973–76. In two out of four years on St Kilda, and one out of five on the Isle of May, birds hatched late in the season reached a peak quicker and fledged younger than those hatched early; perhaps feeding conditions were better late in the season. Fledging weights of chicks reared in the same burrow in different years are more similar to each other than are the weights of young reared in different burrows (Ashcroft 1976). As pairs usually retain the same burrow from year to year, and as most adults survive from one year to the next, this suggests that pairs tend to rear consistently big, heavy chicks or small, light chicks: this is due either to genetic differences or because some pairs are more efficient. In two different studies, burrow habitat and burrow density influenced fledging weights; on Great Island this was because gulls stole more fish from pairs nesting in flat areas; on St Kilda this was because gulls killed more adult Puffins where the burrows were at low density (Nettleship 1972, Harris 1980). The food fed to young also affects fledging weights. On St Kilda, young from three years in which sprats were the

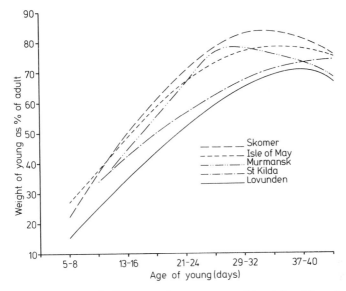

38 The growth of young Puffins expressed as a percentage of the adult weight at the same colonies – Skomer (adult 372 g), Isle of May (390 g), St Kilda (368 g), Lovunden (440 g) and eastern Murmansk (490 g). (Data from Ashcroft 1976, Corkhill 1972, 1973, Kartashew 1960, Myrberget 1962, and personal observations.)

commonest food fledged heavier (annual means 254–270 g) than young in three years when they were fed whiting (225–251 g).

IS THE YOUNG PUFFIN DESERTED?

Most Puffin young lose some 30 gm in weight (8–10% of the peak weight) in the six to ten days prior to fledging, mainly due to the utilization of fat with the increased activity prior to departure. Some water is also lost as tissues mature. Exceptional birds lose up to 140 g (40% of peak weight) but these are probably ill as they remain in the burrow far longer than normal. In his pioneer studies on the Puffin, Lockley (1934) described, apparently for the first time, how Puffins fledged at night. He also noted that matchsticks stuck in the soil in the mouths of burrows where chicks were near fledging were not knocked, indicating that the adults were not visiting the burrows. Lockley had just discovered that young Manx Shearwaters are deserted by their parents and complete their development on their fat reserves, so his conclusion that Puffins also deserted their young was immediately and widely accepted. However, Perry (1948), the only other person to have studied Puffins at that time, noted that large numbers of adults were still visiting the colony at Noss ten days after most of them had ceased bringing in fish. He saw two possible explanations, either that the previous findings on the fledging periods of Puffins on Skokholm (Lockley) and Lundy (his own) were wrong, or that adult Puffins did not desert their young after ceasing to feed them. Later he saw juveniles, ready to go to sea, come out of the burrows and stand with the adults. This hardly agreed with Lockley's writings that 'like the young shearwater, the young Puffin remains alone fasting in the burrow for several days. During this period, day and night, it sits close to the mouth of the burrow as if too timid to venture out.' Perry finally concluded that Puffins did not desert their young, but that they did stop feeding them. These observations of Perry's were overlooked or ignored. Years ago I realized that Puffins did not desert their young but it was not until I started studying them that I discovered that the rest of the world was still under this misconception and I had to clarify the situation.

Evidence came from several sources. First, young near fledging that were weighed every two hours day and night all showed weight increases the day before they fledged, indicating that all had been fed. The frequency of feeding did decline, probably as a result of less begging by the chick, but most young did get some food the day before fledging. Second, some young grew slowly but steadily from hatching to fledging and even fledged at their maximum weight. These could not have been deserted. Third, parents of chicks brought fish to the burrows the day after their young fledged. They appeared to be 'surprised' at the departure of the young. Finally, adults often spent several weeks, sometimes even a month, at the colonies after their young had fledged. Adult Tufted Puffins and Rhinoceros Auklets bring food to their burrows after their young fledge, and it now seems that no auk has a desertion period (Wehle 1980, Richardson 1961). Although some young seabirds are deserted, for instance Manx Shearwaters, as correctly described by Lockley, the many generalized statements that desertion periods are common in seabirds are in error.

Since I first wrote this, Tatarinkova (1982), working on the Ainov Islands, has suggested that the length of a fasting period, or even whether or not there is one, may depend on when nesting begins. This is determined by spring conditions and/or the geographic position. In 1967, hatching started at the Ainov Islands on 29th June and fledging on 12th August, and 28% of nests had fish brought to them after the young had fledged. In the cold year of 1968, fledging did not start until 19th August and there was a mean interval of six days (range 1–15) between the last feed brought to chick and it leaving. However, many of the chicks were weak and some even died of starvation, so this may have been an enforced fast. Obviously, the development of chicks in far northern colonies would repay detailed study.

WEIGHT RECESSION

What then is the significance of this peak of weight during growth and the loss of weight before fledging? The most pronounced post-fledging reduction in weight occurs in Manx Shearwaters, where the young reach up to twice the adult weight and then lose a third of it during the eight to nine days before fledging. During this time the adult shearwater has set off on its transequatorial migration to Brazil. The young shearwater's fat reserves allow it to complete its development and probably also help it survive even a severe food shortage earlier in its development. Audubon's Shearwater often suffers prolonged famines and any fat its young has is then critically important (Harris 1969). In the Puffin the peak weight is not much higher than the fledging weight, but the difference is still important to a bird which has to dive for its food. The fledging weight is probably a compromise between having fat reserves to carry the young over the difficulties which it must surely face when learning to fly, swim, find and catch fish for itself, and having to dive.

THE EFFECT OF FOOD ON GROWTH

Much has been written, including some of the foregoing, on the tacit assumption that food is in some way limiting the growth of young seabirds. It is difficult to manipulate the food supply of seabirds, but some attempts have been made in the case of young Puffins by adding food to burrows and rearing young in captivity. Some observations have been made on pairs rearing twins and on the growth of young when one of their parents was thought to have died (Table 16).

In 1973 and 1974, I found that Puffins on St Kilda were having difficulty in supplying enough food for their young, which were thin and continually begged for food. So in 1975, 50 g of sprats were put daily into 11 burrows which had small young to test the idea that young Puffins there could gain weight faster

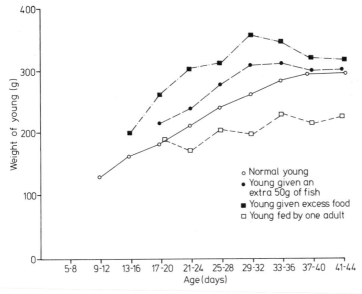

39 *Mean weights of young Puffins on St Kilda given access to excess food (5 young), wild young with (11) and without (17) an extra 50 g a day supplied, and young being reared by a single adult (3). (Redrawn from Harris 1978.)*

and attain heavier weights if given the chance (Harris 1978). The young ate all these fish as well as the food supplied by their parents. As a control, this was also done on the Isle of May where Puffins seemed to have enough food. In addition, five captive young from St Kilda and six from the Isle of May were given as many sprats as they would eat. On St Kilda all the captive young, all the 11 additionally-fed young, and 37 of a sample of 39 normal young, fledged. On the Isle of May, too, all the captive and supplementary-fed birds, and 65 out of 70 normal young, safely reached fledging age.

The captive young grew best (Fig. 39), followed by wild young given additional food, and then normal young. A few young thought to have been fed by only a single parent did poorly. On St Kilda the difference in weights was significant; that is, the young could grow better if they had more food. On the Isle of May the addition of food had less impact; it did not significantly increase the peak weight though it did increase the fledging weight.

A rather different technique was used on Skomer where Hudson (1979) fed five captive young 120 g of sprats per day, five other young 80 g per day and five more young the quantity that normal young received, about 60 g per day. The birds given most food reached significantly higher peak weights than either the young given 80 g of food or the control young, and also reached their peak weights at a younger age. Young receiving the most food also fledged heavier, but the differences were not statistically significant.

Thus, Puffins in some areas are sometimes short of food for their young even though they usually succeed in rearing them. A pair does not normally rear more than a single young at a time. However, a few Puffin pairs given an extra chick, as on Skomer (Corkhill 1973, Ashcroft 1976), have managed to rear both, so it can be done. Similarly, an adult which loses its mate sometimes manages to rear the chick alone (e.g. on the Isle of May). However, the chick's growth is always stunted (Table 16), and it frequently dies. Obviously the single egg is the best clutch for a Puffin, even though it has two brood patches.

POST-FLEDGING SURVIVAL

In some seabirds, such as Manx Shearwater, it has been shown that a high proportion of young which are heavy at fledging survive to return to the colony in later life, whereas fewer of the lightweight young are seen again. This is reasonable, as some fat will obviously help the young over the difficult time when it learns to fend for itself. However, too much fat will be a disadvantage as it will make the young buoyant and so will make diving difficult. Also, young Manx Shearwater fledging early in the season tend to survive better than those fledging late, presumably because early young are learning to look after themselves when food is still plentiful. The effects of date and weight on survival are confounded as the early young tend to be heavy and the late young to be light.

The situation in the Puffin may be slightly different. Peter Rothery and I have analysed the survival of young weighed on the Isle of May each year, 1973–79.

We found no differences between either the peak weights or the fledging weights of 57 chicks which were known to have survived their first winter, and 257 which were not recorded again (although of course some of these doubtless survived unseen). The age at which the young attained its peak weight, and its age at fledging, had no influence on survival. Nor did young fledging early survive better than those fledging late. Thus growth had no obvious influence on later survival. However, it must be stressed that the Isle of May population is increasing very rapidly and chicks are obviously well fed so that conditions must be approaching, or may have reached, optimum. Consequently, there may be so little selection acting against Puffins that even the weakest, or lightest, survive.

There are few data from elsewhere. Of St Kilda juveniles ringed at fledging, for a period of seven years, and known to have survived at least nine months, 18 fledged before the median fledging date in their respective years, 14 fledged later and five did so on the median date. This is again consistent with the hypothesis that fledging date has little effect on post-fledging survival, and this in a population which is certainly not expanding. However, eight of the 14 later birds were reared in 1975 so perhaps early young had some advantage in other years. Thirteen of these surviving young were heavier than the mean weight of young fledging that night, 21 were lighter, two were the same weight and the other was not weighed. Comparing these weights with the respective annual means, nine were heavier and 25 were lighter. One weighed only 205 g, a full 24% lower than the mean weight in some years. Weight and hatching date would seem to have little influence on later survival but more data are needed, especially from stable or declining populations.

SUMMARY

There is great variation in the weights of chicks of the same age but most young reach a peak weight of about 70–80% adult weight and then lose weight before fledging.

Growth occurs in zigzag fashion and chicks often lose weight. 'Good' and 'bad' days are often the same for many young but this does not seem to be related to how much food they receive.

Young are not deserted by the adults but fledge when they are ready.

There are marked differences in growth rates at different colonies and young can sometimes grow better if given additional food.

Fledging weight, peak weight and fledging date on the Isle of May had no influence on the chances of young Puffins surviving to return to the colony.

CHAPTER 11

Predators, pirates and competitors

Puffins, Puffin eggs and fish are attractive to a wide range of birds and mammals, the results of whose activities are often very obvious in the form of eviscerated corpses or broken eggs. It is a hard person indeed who can watch a pair of Great Black-backed Gulls pulling a still living Puffin to pieces without yelling abuse (or throwing a rock). Much has been made of the effects of these animals on the numbers of Puffins and in most cases people's hearts have ruled their heads and their actions, and predators are killed. There are few data on either the manner in which predators or parasites hunt or the impact on the prey population, but generally they seem to have only a limited impact on Puffin populations.

GREAT BLACK-BACKED GULL

Together with man, Great Black-backed Gulls are the only important predators of full-grown Puffins. These gulls breed in many Puffin colonies but they are, surprisingly, absent from some other large colonies, for example, those on the east coast of Scotland. Individual gulls are specialists, and the nests of those specializing on Puffins are surrounded by wings and other remains. Other individuals concentrate on other prey, such as Manx Shearwaters, rabbits, or eat garbage and waste from trawlers. The occurrence of Puffin-specialists varies greatly. On North Rona, where there are about 2,000 pairs of gulls and 12,000 Puffins, most of the gulls eat fish and only 93 dead Puffins were found in mid-summer (Evans 1975). Similarly, Pierotti (1983) found only a few Puffins killed by gulls on Great Island. However, on Dun, St Kilda, with 30–40 pairs of gulls, they are extremely specialized Puffin hunters and over 95% of the number and virtually all the biomass of their prey come from among the 40,000 pairs of Puffins (Harris 1980).

Puffins are nearly always caught in flight. A gull hunts by effortlessly circling in the updraughts above the colony, watching the Puffins coming, going and flying, in wheels in front of the colony. Seeing a likely target the gull makes a movement towards it. Usually the Puffin sees the gull and, frightened, drops rapidly towards the sea. The gull does not follow. However, if the Puffin makes no response the gull pursues it from above and behind, presumably aiming for the prey's blind spot. Even now the Puffin usually realizes the danger and escapes. But if it is too slow, it is grabbed in the strong bill and taken struggling to a flat area of rocks or grass with a pool or small stream near the nest or even the sea. The gull cannot use its feet to hold food so the Puffin has another, albeit slight, chance of escape when the gull changes its grip. Usually, however, its struggles get weaker and weaker and it is soon dead. If the gull lands on the sea there is an increased chance of the Puffin escaping or being stolen by a Great Skua. Gulls often swoop at groups of Puffins standing at the colonies but this is to panic them into flight rather than a deliberate attempt to catch one. Gulls have been reported to catch and kill full-grown Puffins on the ground, possibly as they come out of a burrow or become tangled in thick vegetation, or even on the sea – but this must be rare and I have not seen it in 15 summers spent in Puffin colonies.

Once the Puffin is killed the entrails and the breast muscles are eaten, then the skin is turned inside out like a glove by continual shaking, and the bones picked clean. The inside of the skull is cleaned out or the head may be swallowed whole to be regurgitated later in a pellet. Early in the season virtually all the meat is eaten but, later, often only the entrails and breast are eaten and the 'mince' regurgitated to the chicks.

On Dun, I found 5,500 adult Puffins killed during a four-year study – a loss of 1.5% of the birds breeding each season. The predation was most intense in June and early July when the gulls were feeding large chicks. Fewer were killed in July and August because many of the gull chicks had fledged or died, and some gulls had left the island.

The proportion of immature Puffins killed increases during the season. This partly reflects the increasing numbers of immatures present but, on Dun, 21% of the kills in July were immatures compared to only 8% of immatures among birds caught in mist nets, which suggests that the gulls were probably killing the most inexperienced birds. Most gulls hunt near their own nests where they have hunting territories. Gulls with territories in the main Puffin areas killed many fewer immatures (15–18% of corpses) than those nesting in the peripheral areas (up to 30%). Only gulls nesting in the area of low Puffin burrow density on Dun hunted over that area, and 40 out of 42 birds ringed there and later killed by gulls were found dead nearby. One of the remaining two Puffins was taken by a pair of gulls at the other end of Dun which specialized in stealing corpses from other gulls. In contrast, half of the 80 birds ringed in a high density area were recovered dead elsewhere. It seems as though gulls nesting elsewhere were intruding into the desirable area and taking Puffins (Taylor 1982).

Between 1973 and 1978, I ringed 1,129 breeding Puffins and 1,502 other, full-grown Puffins on Dun. By the end of 1979, 51 and 74 of these ringed birds had been found after being killed by gulls. Making allowances for how long each of these birds had been ringed the total annual mortality of breeding Puffins, attributable to gulls, was 1.5%. This is a minimal figure as some ringed birds must have been killed and not found. This mortality was not uniformly spread through the colony but was mainly of Puffins nesting at low density; 42 out of 332 (13%) of the full-grown birds ringed in the low density area were recovered, compared to 80 out of 2,224 (2.5%) in the high density area. Again, allowing for how long birds had been at risk, 0.9% and 4.2% of adults breeding in the dense and sparse areas respectively were killed each breeding season. Perhaps the higher mortality was because the wheels of Puffins in the sparse area were too small to protect the birds from the gulls. The normal loss of adults for a whole year is about 5%, so the mortality of birds in these low density areas approached the yearly norm in just three months. Here is an instance where a predator is almost certainly having a serious impact on its prey, although in only a limited part of the colony.

OTHER BIRDS

Herring and Lesser Black-backed Gulls regularly steal fish from Puffins but, probably, rarely kill a healthy adult. They do, however, eat eggs and young whenever they can get them and regularly stalk around colonies peering into burrows. A few burrows are short enough for them to reach the contents, but usually they have to wait until an egg rolls out of the nest chamber or a starving young mistakes them for its parent and rushes to the entrance. Most young Puffins disappearing from burrows before they are old enough to fly are taken by gulls, but many would have starved to death anyway. Normally, young Puffins are caught while exercising their wings just prior to fledging or while on their way to the sea.

Great Skuas kill Puffins but the numbers are small. On Foula, for example, only 91 adult and four juvenile Puffins were found annually in each of eight summers, although there were 8,000 individual Skuas and 70,000 pairs of Puffins (Furness 1977). On St Kilda, most Puffins eaten by Great Skuas were stolen from Great Black-backed Gulls.

The only birds of prey to take Puffins regularly are Peregrine and Gyr Falcon. Puffins have also been recorded as being eaten by Common and Rough-legged Buzzards and Sea Eagle, Snowy Owl, Short-eared Owl and Raven The most unusual predator recorded is an angler fish *Lophius piscatorius* which was found with a Puffin in its stomach (Kaftanovskii 1951). Eggs are taken by a wide range of birds including Magpie, Jackdaw, Crow, Raven and gulls.

MAMMALS

Until man introduced, deliberately or otherwise, mammals to isolated islands, Puffins were fairly safe. Arctic foxes and red foxes kill Puffins when they can get to the colonies and the former certainly excludes Puffins from some suitable areas in the northern Arctic. Otters take adults from burrows close to the sea and mink are credited with killing the last few Puffins in Sweden. Wild cats and feral cats also catch Puffins. I have twice seen grey seals make threatening dashes at Puffins sitting on the sea but this may have been in play.

Brown and black rats take and eat eggs and probably kill young, although, surprisingly, Cott (1952) found that in experiments Puffins' eggs were less acceptable to rats than those of gulls, Razorbills and Guillemot. Similarly, hedgehogs did not have a high opinion of Puffin eggs, but they are unlikely to get the chance to try them in the wild! There is circumstantial evidence that rats have caused the decline of many populations. For instance 'rats have driven them off the tops of Handa into more secure crevices in the face and slopes' (Harvie-Brown and Buckley 1884): 'but rats got ashore (to Ailsa Craig) from a wreck in 1889 and from then onwards the Puffin's doom was sealed, although the end was somewhat delayed' (Gibson 1951); 'at Ramsey the appearance of rats long ago resulted in the extermination of the Puffins, and this process is going on today at many islands recently invaded by rats' (Lockley 1953). Other islands where declines have been ascribed to rats include Puffin Island (Anglesey), Lundy and Shiant Islands. However, as is discussed later, rats may have been the last straw to the populations that were already under threat.

PARASITES AND DISEASE

A few ticks *Ixodes* are sometimes found attached to the undersides of the feet and around the eyes and mouth of young Puffins and the occasional adult. Severely infected birds, which may have several hundred ticks, are often weak and badly scratched. Dickinson (1958) found a few very sick young which had only a few ticks but with swollen heads and closed eyes, and thought this might have been caused by the toxic effects of tick saliva.

These ticks and other parasites probably transmit a range of viruses to Puffins but serious outbreaks of disease are rare. Very large numbers of dead young were found on Burhou, Channel Islands in 1913 and 1949. In the latter instances there was a plague of the common red or poultry mites *Dermanyssus gallinae* but it is not known whether they transmitted a disease or only weakened the young by sucking the blood (Dobson 1952). I have also seen fledglings dying with paralysed legs, which were extended horizontally out behind the young, rather like the disease puffinosis in Manx Shearwaters. Puffins presumably harbour various other diseases but no published accounts have come to my attention. Some adult Puffins were found dead on the Farne Islands, apparently poisoned by the toxin produced by the bacterium *Clostridium botulinum* which killed many other seabirds there at the time.

KLEPTOPARASITISM

Fish dangling from the bill of a Puffin are very tempting to other birds. The commonest thieves are Arctic and Great Skuas, Herring and Lesser Black-backed Gulls. Less common are Great Black-backed and Black-headed Gulls and Jackdaws (which are, however, sometimes very active and obvious). Kittiwake, Razorbill, Common, Arctic and Roseate Terns and Crows have been recorded but they can hardly be considered a threat to Puffins. On Skokholm two Razorbills, possibly a pair, sat on the sea until they saw a Puffin carrying fish, whereupon they chased it for up to 1.5 km, and continued to chase Puffins even after all other Razorbills had left the area (Warman *et al* 1983). These two Razorbills also attacked Puffins with fish sitting on the sea; gulls and skuas do not do this. Other species, for instance Raven and Common Gull, which glean fish dropped around the colonies, may occasionally make threatening movements towards Puffins but these are rarely successful.

Skuas

Arctic Skuas are the most specialized of kleptoparasites, chasing Puffins both in the open sea and at the breeding sites. The skua circles above the colony, often on an updraught of air, until it sees a fish-carrying Puffin which it then pursues from behind and slightly to one side. The skua's aim is to persuade the Puffin to drop a fish whilst still high in the air so that the fish can be caught before it hits the land or sea. Fish falling on the ground may be lost or eaten by a gull, crow or other gleaning species. The Puffin is often frightened into dropping its fish, in marked contrast to the tenacity with which a Puffin holds onto its fish when caught by a gull near its burrow. If the Puffin does not release the fish the skua may snatch at the fish or buffet the Puffin. The nearer the colony the Puffin can get without being seen, the greater the chance of its reaching the burrow safely (Grant 1971). A Puffin can also reduce the chances of losing its fish by coming to the colony with other Puffins (i.e. by confusing or swamping the predator). It also pays the Puffin not to carry too large a load of fish, as such birds are chased preferentially, probably because they are obvious and perhaps fly more slowly.

If pursued, a Puffin has several alternatives. First, it can try to out manoeuvre the skua; a few manage this. Second, it can press on regardless, hoping to gain the relative safety of air space close to the cliff. The skua attempts to prevent this and, especially when several co-operate, usually succeed. Third, the Puffin can abort the trip and try to return to the sea, but this usually ends in failure. Fourth, it can just give up and release the fish, thereby preventing any rougher treatment and the associated risk of injury. Even if the skua succeeds in making the Puffin drop the fish it often fails to retrieve it. At Vik, in Iceland, Puffins nest 1 km inland; about 4% of all loads brought in by Puffins were dropped – 1.7% were eaten by skuas, 1.1% fell to the ground and were eaten by gulls, and 1.2% were completely lost in the vegetation (Arnason and Grant 1978).

At Foula, Furness (1978) observed that Arctic Skuas rely mainly on their ability to outmanoeuvre the Puffin in flight and often began chases from the same height, usually but not always from behind. Less than 1% of the Puffins were chased and a fifth of those that were, lost their fish. Factors which seemed to influence the success or otherwise of chases by skuas were the speed of the Puffin's reaction, the height of the victim above the sea and local visibility (Great Skua), or the duration of the chase (Arctic Skua). A high flying Puffin can use gravity to gain speed but it cannot then land safely on the sea and would certainly drop the fish. At Hermaness, also in Shetland, only nine out of 818 fish-carrying Puffins lost their fish (Albon 1974). The success rates of both species of skua in Shetland are far lower than at inland Vik in Iceland. Nesting inland appears to have serious drawbacks for Puffins and they probably do this only when nesting habitat near good feeding ground is scarce.

Gulls

Some Herring Gulls and Lesser Black-backed Gulls specialize in stealing food. The frequency of attacks on fish-carrying Puffins varies from colony to colony, being very low in Iceland and St Kilda and high on the Isle of May and Great Island (Table 17). Gulls do not normally chase Puffins in flight and, if they do, their effectiveness is very low as Puffins can easily outpace them. Instead, the gulls stand around the colony waiting their chance to pounce on a Puffin as it lands. Sometimes they seem to try to predict where a Puffin will land and move to that spot, waiting there with legs bent and neck withdrawn as though attempting to be inconspicuous. If possible, a Puffin always lands at its burrow entrance and dives directly in; this facility is one of the main advantages of burrowing in a slope. If the Puffin is caught by a gull it usually hangs on to the fish, even if feathers are being pulled out, and strives to get down the burrow. Many succeed even though they may drop a few fish. Puffins ambushed after landing sometimes try to take off again with the fish but they rarely succeed. Puffins with fish often circle waiting for other laden Puffins. They then land together. This helps prevent the gull track an individual Puffin, confuses or swamps the gull and sometimes causes gulls to squabble, so increasing the chances of a Puffin getting to its burrow (Pierotti 1983).

Puffins thwarted by a gull standing beside their burrow may land and wait on a nearby rock (Plate 14). Presumably they are too far away for the gull to press home an attack. Mylne (1960) graphically described the scene:

> If the Puffin landed near-by, the gull would attack at once; if further away, it would often wait in a very tense attitude for a considerable time before the wary (and usually clearly terrified) Puffin would dare to approach and make a dash for its burrow. It was most interesting to watch the battle of wits which thus followed when a Puffin landed just too far away to stimulate an immediate attack from the gull, and it provided the strongest impression of birds 'thinking' I have ever witnessed. Both gull and Puffin, perhaps only ten yards apart, would stand watching each other intently, each providing a stimulus to the other but in neither case strongly enough to produce a reaction. The mental struggle for the Puffin between fleeing and feeding its

chick was usually resolved in favour of approaching the burrow, provided that the gull remained still. For the gull it appeared to be a more subtle conflict between attacking at too great a distance and waiting for its victim to move, either reaction (when considered in human terms) seeming to involve an element of calculated risk.

A single Herring Gull on Skomer, watched by Hudson (1979b), used two attack strategies – either it took off and crashed into the Puffin (61% of attacks) or it chased the Puffin around the colony after it had landed, trying to catch it by its wing or tail. The former technique was used for Puffins 4–5 m from the gull and was marginally less successful (16%) than the chasing technique (18%) which was used for Puffins landing closer. The gull's rate of food intake was highest when it attacked Puffins nesting at (for Skomer) a high burrow density but the gull's activities scared away other Puffins. The gull was, therefore, forced to make a compromise and usually spent only about an hour and a half in the area at any one time. Hudson thought that as the gull concentrated its activities on a high-density area it might adversely influence the growth of Puffin chicks there. However, Puffin chicks have been shown to grow better where the density is high, so this level of kleptoparasitism (the maximum loss to a pair was one load per day) is probably unimportant.

Up to 19% of all load-carrying landings on the Isle of May were sometimes lost to gulls but some Puffins managed to save some fish even if caught. Of 123 determined gull attacks witnessed, the Puffin escaped in 62 cases, lost all the fish in 22, most of the fish in 8, half in 16 and some in 15, so that on average about two-thirds of the fish were lost in each successful attack. Loads were lost at all times of day, the numbers lost being usually in direct relationship to the numbers of loads being brought. However, on a few days there was a suggestion that gulls bothered little when only a few Puffins were coming ashore with fish, hunted when there were moderate numbers of Puffins, and gave up when large numbers of Puffins were feeding young. It would seem advantageous for a Puffin to come ashore with many others, so that the territorial gulls become 'swamped', but this is difficult to establish. The Isle of May gulls had little impact on the growth of most Puffin chicks, the exceptions being a few pairs nesting where landings were difficult. These were persecuted remorselessly every year and their young grew extremely slowly.

Nettleship (1972) found that the 1,500 pairs of Herring Gulls had a great impact on the 100,000 pairs of Puffins on Great Island, especially so on those pairs burrowing in level ground. Chicks of such pairs received only two-thirds the number of feeds of those on the slope, the remainder was lost to gulls. Puffins could fly directly into the burrows in the slope but had to land and then run to burrows on the level, thus exposing themselves to ill treatment. Even though gull disturbance may appear serious, it still remains to be shown that it is so severe that the adults cannot compensate by bringing in more fish. Great Island Puffins could, on the face of it, not cope, but it is conceivable that food was already short, and they were stressed as a result, so that gull interference was the last straw. A decade later, Pierotti (1983) studied Great Island from the gulls' point of view and found that gulls did not depend on Puffins as a crucial food source and did not switch to Puffins as an alternative source even when their normal food was short. He concluded that parasitic gulls do not have as large a negative impact on Puffins as some studies suggest. I agree with him.

COMPETITION FOR BURROWS

In most areas Puffins nest in discrete colonies, usually with few other species. The only potential competitors are Manx Shearwaters, Razorbills and rabbits. Other birds are usually either so infrequent (Black Guillemots in Shetland) or so small (Storm Petrels in some southern colonies. Leach's Petrel in northern colonies) that competition is trivial. In Iceland the Puffin appears to win out in competition with Black Guillemots because it breeds earlier (Gudmundsson 1953). The Razorbill probably poses little threat, though occasionally there is competition, as on the cliff edge of Skomer. In most cases species are adapted to different habitats and this reduces competition.

Little is known about the interactions between rabbits and Puffins but actual physical contact is probably limited. Rabbit burrows are usually much larger and longer than those of Puffins and the only serious overlaps are in the short burrows or stops which rabbits use for breeding. Rabbits may take over Puffin burrows in the winter, but leave in the spring. A soft, rabbit's nose is no match for a Puffin's beak, but unlike Manx Shearwaters, Puffins do not dig out the rabbit stops and kill the young. Rabbits certainly help Puffins by starting burrows in short turf, a substrate which appears to defeat the birds. Unfortunately, large numbers of rabbits and Puffins often result in severe soil erosion.

Manx Shearwaters are the only serious competitors for burrows but there are only a few areas where the two species overlap. One such colony is Skomer (Ashcroft 1976). Here Puffins tend to nest in deeper burrows near to the cliff edge among short vegetation, whereas shearwaters often burrow away from the cliff edge, sometimes well inland. Manx Shearwaters appear happy to burrow both on flat ground and among tall vegetation, and to overcome the problem of getting to such burrows without being killed by gulls, by coming to land at night. On parts of Skomer where Puffins and Manx Shearwaters both occurred, there was much competition for burrows and some 15% of entrances were used by both species, Puffins breeding in one branch of the burrow, shearwaters in another. Competition with shearwaters resulted in 5–10% of Puffin eggs being broken or deserted, while shearwaters nesting in Puffin colonies similarly had a significantly lower breeding success than those nesting in similar areas without Puffins. Therefore, the main effect of competition, on both species, was a reduction in the number of young reared. In Puffins this may have affected the population, because insufficient young were being reared to replace the adults dying. The Skomer situation is, however, unusual as only in a few other places do significant numbers of shearwaters and Puffins nest side by side. In most colonies competition for sites is intra-specific rather than inter-specific, that is Puffins only compete with Puffins.

SUMMARY

At some colonies Great Black-backed Gulls eat large numbers of full-grown Puffins which they catch in flight. On St Kilda, this predation had a serious effect on the survival of Puffins nesting at low burrow density, but not on those at high density. Other birds and mammals kill few Puffins.

Arctic Skuas steal fish from Puffins at some colonies. They are most successful where Puffins nest inland. Parasitism by Herring and Lesser Black-backed Gulls is more widespread. These species specialize in attacking Puffins just as they arrive at their burrows. Although this behaviour is conspicuous, the proportion of loads lost is usually low. In Canada, Puffins burrowing in flat ground lost many more loads than those in steep slopes where they could land right at the burrow entrance. This has an adverse effect on the growth of Puffin chicks. However, in general these gulls are more a nuisance than a serious threat to Puffins.

The Manx Shearwater is the Puffin's only serious competitor for burrows, but this occurs at only a few colonies.

CHAPTER 12

Man and Puffins

Man has been a predator of Puffins ever since he first reached the isolated, seabird islands. Until recently, coastal human communities ate large numbers of eggs, young and adults of many seabirds, and also killed them for their feathers. With improvements in the standard of living and better methods of preserving food, these often arduous and dangerous activities have become redundant. However, in a few places tradition and the desire to retain old customs and skills keep the practices alive. Although I am somewhat of a traditionalist, and certainly not adverse to gnawing on a (cooked) Puffin, I was surprised to see a mural on the wall of a school at Heimay, in the Westman Islands, depicting six ways of slaughtering seabirds. These included fleyging Puffins and clubbing Gannets. Strong stuff for bird protectionists. Still, the amount of protein provided by the bird-fowlers of the Faeroes and Iceland is considerable and there is little evidence that their activities are having an adverse effect on the numbers of Puffins.

It is mainly full-grown Puffins which are killed, though some fledglings are eaten as they are considered especially tasty. Young were also taken from burrows (e.g. on the Scilly Isles and the Isle of Man) but this was labour-intensive and soon lost favour. On Røst and Vaerøy in Norway, adults were, and still are, illegally taken in the spring when they are very fat. Puffins are eaten fresh, either boiled, or as in a Faeroese traditional dish, stuffed with a rich cake mixture and roasted. They are also dried, smoked (especially in Iceland), salted or deep frozen for later use. The meat is dark and not at all fishy-tasting although, in past times, the Church allowed them to be substituted for fish the week prior to Easter. Dixon (1896), recalling his time on St Kilda, considered that dried Puffin, maybe a year old, was one of the few delicacies of the island, but recalled that Ligon in *History of Barbadoes* had complained of the taste of

147

Puffins he received from the Scilly Isles and considered them only fit fo servants. At the start of the nineteenth century, the people of St Kilda 'boned Puffins, wrapped the flesh in the skins, packed them in pots, and transporte them to London where they were eaten with vinegar (Gibson-Hill 1948). Th same happened on Puffin Island in North Wales where Puffins were 'farmed and then pickled.

EGGS

Opinions varied from community to community about the palatability o seabirds' eggs. For instance, some people prized Fulmar eggs whereas other would only eat them under duress. The same was true of Puffin eggs, thoug the difficulty in collecting them prevented large-scale use. It was always fa easier, though more dangerous, to harvest those of Guillemots. The merits o the eggs of a wide range of birds have been assessed by a series of carefull controlled experiments using an egg-tasting panel, supervised by Cott (1951- 54). The eggs were scrambled and served unlabelled and unseasoned to a serie of observers. These people were asked to score them for general palatibility o a scale ranging from 10.0 (ideal) through 9.0 (very good), 8.0 (good eg; flavour), 7.0 (barely perceptible 'off' or foreign flavour), 6.0 (definite but no unpleasant 'off' flavour), 5.0 (unpleasant), 4.0, 3.0 ('off' and becoming in creasingly unpalatable) to 2.0 (repulsive and inedible). Hen's eggs averaged ou at 8.7, the highest for any of the 212 species tasted; presumably humans ar conditioned to hen's eggs. Controls showed that there was a remarkabl consistency within and between observers.

The egg panel scores ranked the palatibility of eggs of North Atlanti seabirds as follows:

8.3 Lesser Black-backed Gull	7.0 Common Gull, Roseate Tern
8.2 Kittiwake	6.8 Arctic Tern
7.9 Herring Gull	6.6 Black-headed Gull, Sandwich Tern, Puffin
7.8 Razorbill	6.2 Little Tern
7.7 Fulmar, Great Black-backed Gull, Guillemot, Black Guillemot	6.0 Common Eider
	5.4 Gannet
7.3 Common Tern	5.1 Cormorant
7.2 Great Skua	4.4 Shag
7.1 Manx Shearwater	

From this, one should obviously restrict one's egg eating to those of chicken and the larger gulls!

Other published accounts vary as to the flavour of Puffin's eggs. Some writer tell how they were never collected by eggers because the 'white' was a livid blu colour and the eggs were generally very bad. The Flamborough fowlers Bristowe and Waterton, found them just as good as Guillemot eggs, but note that they were less 'requested' because the shells were fragile and easily broken In contrast, Naumann thought that they tasted of oil.

FAEROE ISLANDS

Bird-fowling continues on several of the main islands as an exciting and energetic sport which still supplies many tons of useful meat a year. Much has been written about the fowlers of Mykines, especially their activities during the last decades of the nineteenth century and during the early 1940s. The following accounts are based on the writings of Nørrevang (1977, 1978) and Williamson (1970). Some practices have died out but the main tradition of netting flourishes still.

The fowlers caught some of the first Puffins returning in the spring as a welcome change in the diet of salted meat and birds which they had eaten through the winter. Puffins were netted or dug out of those burrows which the fowler's dog had shown to hold birds; digging-out was time-consuming and caused considerable damage to the colonies, so was practised only on a limited scale. When the birds had laid, the fowlers systematically crawled around the colonies, pulling birds and eggs from burrows using a stick with an iron hook or bent nail at one end. This was arduous and dirty work needing the oldest clothes and tough skin! If a bird could not be reached, then a shaft was dug half way along the burrow and another attempt made from there. Subsequently, such shafts were always carefully filled in. It was believed that up to six adults might be taken from a single burrow before the egg was deserted, so that presumably there was a surplus of adults waiting a chance to get a burrow. In some places colonies were extended by using a trowel to make short holes in the turf which were readily taken over and enlarged by Puffins. Some colonies in earthy areas became very eroded by Puffins extending their burrows every year, and probably by the activities of the fowlers, and large parts of colonies sometimes fell into the sea. Fowlers trampled-in burrows during the winter to encourage the birds to dig new holes which, being short, were easier to work.

The numbers of birds killed was normally small, but eight men collected 1,360 birds from burrows on Mykines on one day in 1942. This practice was said to have had little effect on the population, but in the nineteenth century it was prohibited on Nólsoy because of the damage caused. On Mykines burrow-robbing was done in isolated and relatively inaccessible colonies where no netting was undertaken. Each colony was exploited every third year.

The vast majority of Puffins are killed in July using the famous *fleygastong* – shortened to *fleyg* in English and *stong* in Faeroese. This is a large triangular net fastened to a pair of wooden supports lashed to a 3–4 m-long pole (Plate 19). The pole is held with one hand near the bottom of the pole and the other much higher up. The net is laid flat on the ground near a place where Puffins regularly alight or where they will fly close to the cliff to look at decoys (Plate 21). The pole is levered up as quickly as possible to make the net overtake any bird which hesitates. Traditional, good fleyging sites are limited and jealously guarded and sometimes improved by stone walls behind which the fowler lurks. A fleyging place is never changed, because this upsets the Puffins and some have been in use for centuries. New ones are, however, established from time to time to replace those destroyed by time and weather. Most of the fleyged birds are immatures because it is these which fly along the cliffs, and, no self-respecting hunter would kill a bird carrying fish. Weather greatly influences the catch. On warm and calm days Puffins do not fly near the cliffs, whereas on very wet days few immatures visit the colonies. Large numbers of birds sometimes fly in with drizzle. Good catches come with a moderate wind blowing along the cliffs; then a single man can catch 200–300 birds a day. The highest recorded individual catches are 1,201 on Vidoy (a bird a minute), and over 900 on a day when nearly 10,000 Puffins were fleyged on Mykines.

The birds are carried home tucked into waist bands, or on the back using a headband (Plate 22), or on ponies. Plucking, within three days of death, is usually done by the women, each of whom can manage 200–300 a day if the children remove the heads, wings and feet. Each woman is reputed to swallow a pound of feathers a year – no Safety at Work Laws operate there. In earlier times the birds were split, salted, and packed in large barrels. Now, many Puffins are frozen and sold in supermarkets.

The catch varies considerably. On Mykines 80,000 were caught in 1874 and the annual kill on that island fluctuated between 18,000 and 67,000 from 1890 to 1896. By 1900, 75,000–100,000 were killed annually on Vidoy, and maybe 100,000–200,000 on the other islands, suggesting a Faeroese total of around a third of a million. The annual total was put at 400,000–500,000 in the 1940s including an average harvest of 30,000 on Mykines. The maximum catch on Nólsoy was 32,000 in 1908, but the average catch was only 20,000; since then the Puffin population has declined due to loss of habitat, and the numbers killed have been halved. Vidoy claims the island record with 120,000 in a season. The population there is now in the region of 30,000 pairs, yet 12,000 birds were taken at the main colony, Seydtorva, in 1979, compared to a recent maximum of 18,000 in 1959. There are no good estimates of the present Faeroes kill but it probably does not exceed 50,000. Formerly Puffins were shot at the colonies but this was made illegal in 1942. Now they can only be shot from 1st September to 15th March.

The record catches were made when the Puffin population appeared to be stable. Such catches are often boastfully inflated but on the Faeroes tithes had to be paid to the crown, church and parson, so the numbers may well be under-estimates! Still, the fact that between a quarter and half-million Puffins, mostly non-breeders, could be removed without serious effect shows how enormous the population was. To judge from the fragmentary data on the dynamics of British populations, the populations would have had to be at least two million pairs to support this loss on an annual basis.

ICELAND

Large numbers of Puffins have been killed since time immemorial (details from A. Petersen). On the Westman and Breidafjordur Islands between 1850 and 1860 many birds were caught by nets placed over burrows. This seriously depleted the breeding population and was banned from around 1870. Birds were also hooked out of burrows and this method continued until the Faeroese fleyg was introduced around 1875. Hunting is now restricted to fleyging, and shooting at sea from 1st September to 19th May. Fleyging is allowed at any time during the summer but is mainly practised in July and August when most Puffins are at colonies. Up to 200,000–400,000 Puffins were killed annually 1850–1920, and Lockley (1953) guessed that 250,000 were killed in Iceland in 1950. The present catch is estimated at 150,000–200,000 (Petersen 1982).

Pettingill (1959) described the fowling technique on Ellidaey in the Westman Islands. He saw three catchers net 1,300 birds in a day; this would be close to a maximum catch as 400–600 was considered 'common' around 1850, and 200–300 'good' at the turn of this century.

> The fowler sits half hidden in a trench at net-length back from the cliff edge near an open area where non-breeders like to stand and to which they are seduced by about a dozen dead Puffins which are stood there as decoys. The net is a bag of coarse netting suspended between the prongs of a fork 1 m in length at the end of a 4 m long pole. This is usually kept on the ground near the decoys. Puffins flying along the cliff hesitate, presumably deciding whether or not to land on seeing the decoys standing on this desirable open area. Such hesitation is often fatal as the net is quickly lifted up to engulf the fated bird. Strong winds are the best conditions for fleyging as birds then all come in a predictable direction and land in the updraughts.

In the Westman Islands, 843 out of 988 birds ringed as young and later killed by bird-fowlers were four years old or less. Breeding adults are less likely to be caught, as they come and go directly to the burrows, and Westman Islands catchers avoid netting fish-bearers (Petersen 1976a).

The regulations governing fowling are very strict. Some excerpts of the '1966 Act concerning bird-hunting and bird protection in Iceland' are given below:

> Only the landowner has the right to hunt birds within the boundaries of his property, and only he has the authority to dispose of this right, unless other legal provisions stipulate to the contrary.
>
> The bird-hunting rights, in part or in full, on any property may not be disposed of finally. Disposal of them may, however, be made for a limited period, which may in no case exceed ten years at one time.
>
> From 1st September to 19th May: it is lawful to hunt Razorbill, Common Guillemot, Brünnich's Guillemot, Black Guillemot, Puffin (otherwise they are protected).
>
> In restricted areas where the hunting of Gannet, Cormorant, Shag, Fulmar, Great Skua, Glaucous Gull, Kittiwake, Razorbill, Common Guillemot, Brünnich's Guillemot, and Puffin, or the taking of their eggs or young, has been or is considered to be a contributory source of the means of livelihood of the local population, the future enjoyment of such privileges shall not be impaired by the protective measures of this Act. It shall, however, be unlawful to shoot the species during the period in which they are protected according to this Act, and birds on bird-cliffs may never be shot.
>
> If birds are caught in nets that have been laid for other purposes (to catch fish or seals), they must be freed from the nets and released if they are alive when the nets are visited. But birds that are found dead in such nets may neither be kept nor used in any way.

Nets may not be used for bird-hunting on land. It shall, however, be permitted to catch Puffins by net in places where their burrowing activity interferes with Eider-duck breeding. This method of catching Puffins may only be employed if a watch is kept on the nets and the birds are taken from them immediately they are caught, or if the nets are visited for this purpose at least twice daily. It is permitted to use handnets (hafar) for the hunting of Puffins and other cliff-nesting seabirds.

It shall be unlawful for ships and boats to sound steam whistles or sirens unnecessarily in the vicinity of bird-cliffs.

Icelandic seabirds are well looked after as well as eaten.

NORWAY

Until recently bird-fowling was an important activity in many places in northern Norway. It was never practised in the southern colonies where there are, anyway, relatively few birds, but birds were shot at sea during the autumn and winter. The following account is mainly taken from Kolsrud (1976) augmented by observations supplied by H. Bratrein and R. Barrett. Originally the fowling was on a small scale for food, but the development of feather-filled mattresses and dynas (duvets) in the sixteenth century brought about a rapid change. Eiderdown from nests was the preferred filling for beds but this had to be laboriously picked clean and it took two to four man-weeks of work to make one down cover. The feathers of Puffins and, to a much lesser extent, other seabirds, were easily come by and because the birds were caught alive and then killed, the feathers needed no cleaning. All the feathers were used except those of the wing and tail. Birds were plucked as soon as possible after death. It took 3–4 minutes per bird, 50 birds gave 1 kg of feathers and it needed 300 birds to fill a duvet, slightly more for a mattress.

Whereas Razorbills and Guillemots were mainly caught at sea, using nets strung across an open, floating wooden frame on which the birds landed and became entangled, Puffins were caught at the colonies where they were dragged from burrows by hand or with a stick with an iron point or a straightened-out halibut hook. This practice occurred between the sixteenth and the present century at colonies where there were reasonably short burrows in earth, but it was impracticable where birds nested among boulders. In about 1700 a new method was introduced, that of spreading old fishing nets over the colony to trap birds already underground. The technique varied somewhat; for instance at Lovunden the nets were set over the colony one day and taken in the next and catches of up to 150–200 per day were made throughout June. At Røst and Vaeroy the nets were spread over grassy colonies to catch the fat, pre-breeding adults whereas on Sør-Fugløy nets were set over rocky screes. In some areas nets were set on poles rather in the manner of modern mist nets. Elsewhere, up to 500 birds a day were caught in nets held high between two men walking uphill towards groups of birds standing at the colony. Long bamboo poles were used on Sør-Fugløy to knock, down birds flying around the colony but the fleyg never found favour in Norway.

Perhaps the most specialized technique was the use on Røst and Vaeroy of dogs to catch fledglings as they left the colony at night. The dogs were small and agile with a very flexible neck, ear openings which could be closed to prevent earth entering, and five fully developed toes on each foot to give a secure grip on the boulders. They hunted silently and brought the young back unharmed. A good dog could catch 120–130 young per night for the three weeks when the young were fledging. Some farmers had up to 12 such dogs which were a problem to feed when the seabirds were not ashore. Still, they had to be thin to enter burrows!

Some communities got a fair proportion of their income and much of their food from Puffins, and during the Second World War these birds saved many people from starvation. On Røst during the war each man and his dogs collected 1,000–1,200 young per season – enough meat for his family for three months. At Lovunden the catch was 15,000–20,000 Puffins per man per year, reaching 30,000 during the war. Over 2500 kg of feathers were shipped from Sør-Fugløy to Bergen over a 16-year period and Bratrein reckoned that this represented 125,000 birds or 20% of the estimated chick production each year. In addition about 3,000 eggs were taken annually.

Although the taking of seabirds at or near colonies is now prohibited, many are known to be killed on some of the more remote islands. These numbers are usually small but many breeding birds are killed on some of the islands in the Røst Archipelago each spring – surely a wasteful procedure. In most of the country Puffins can legally be shot between 21st August and 28th February, but Puffins have been legally protected in Rogaland since 1971.

Large numbers of birds are sometimes drowned accidently on baited long-lines set for fish. One boat caught 294 seabirds, including 107 Guillemots and 89 Puffins during 75 days fishing between mid-March and mid-June 1969. Assuming this sample was representative of the whole fleet, Brun (1979) estimated that 18,000 Puffins were killed that seaon in that way.

RUSSIA

Birds were occasionally caught on Little Heno Island, Murmansk, using large-mesh fish nets spread over the burrows, and burrows were dug up to get eggs on the Ainov Island (Pearson 1904). Many seabirds were exploited in Russia but Kaftanovskii (1951) concluded that there was nothing to recommend the development of any commercial interest in Puffins and that they would soon be exterminated if large-scale killing was allowed.

NORTH AMERICA

Many seabirds suffered last century from overexploitation by men. Whereas the old-established European settlements which depended on birds rarely over-exploited their resources, these newly formed communities had no traditional harvesting methods and often killed too many birds. For instance, in the 1850s, parties visited Matinicus Seal Island and spread herring nets over the rocks in the evenings to catch the birds as they came out in the morning. By 1886 the colony was reduced to 25–30 pairs and their final extermination was probably effected the following year by milliner's agents 'who carried out a most destructive season's work' (Palmer 1949). Similarly, hunters reduced the Puffin populations on the islands along the St Lawrence north shore and off the Labrador coast, as well as exterminating the Great Auk there. Birds were shot and dragged out of burrows by a fish-hook lashed to a stick, and the colony on Perroquet Island, Bradore Bay, Quebec, was so systematically dug up by egg collectors that the suitable nesting habitat was greatly reduced.

Birds are still shot at sea in Newfoundland and Labrador, but the extent of this mortality is not known. The few data on hunting that exist suggest that numbers shot each year (especially of Guillemots) may be high.

GREENLAND

Greenlanders shoot virtually any seabird which comes within range. Worse, they consider Puffin eggs such great delicacies that until recently (or so it is said), they were collected wholesale by digging out the burrow above the sitting birds. The turf over the burrows was not replaced so colonies were quickly destroyed. Complete protection was introduced in 1960; this may have helped some colonies but others are still 'egged'.

BRITAIN

The best known, and last community in Britain to depend on seabirds was that on St Kilda. Although by the time the island was evacuated in 1930 birds were far less important, for many centuries the inhabitants obtained much if not most of their protein from birds. The most utilized species, in decreasing order of importance, were Fulmar, Puffin, Gannet and Guillemot. Some 90,000 Puffins were thought to have been killed in 1876 (Sands 1878). The majority of birds were taken for feathers to help pay the rent of the island. Some Puffins were eaten fresh, some were preserved, some were dug into the ground for manure, but most were thrown away. After 1902, Puffins were only killed for food.

Adult Puffins were caught with nooses. The usual method was to use a pole about 4–5 m long to which was attached a slightly curved hazel twig ending in a horse-hair noose stiffened with a Gannet quill. The noose was slid along the ground using the flexible twig to lift it over bumps, and then quickly flicked over the head of a Puffin (Plate 19). Once the noose was over the head of the bird it was immediately jerked away before it could panic and frighten off its companions. The St Kilda record was 620 birds caught in a single day (Kearton 1906). Another method, often used by children working the safe inland boulder colonies, was to lay a short length of rope with up to 40 horse-hair snares over a boulder or along a ledge. Puffins were usually caught by the feet, sometimes by the head. The nooses had to be reset when three or four birds were caught but even so a skilled operator with four or five sets could kill up to 280 birds in a day; the speed record was 127 in three hours (Kearton 1906). Early this century the younger people took to shooting Puffins but this was considered unsporting, or perhaps wasteful, by the older inhabitants. Some eggs were also taken for food, and dogs were used to indicate which burrows were occupied.

Less refined methods were used elsewhere. Up to 500 birds were caught in a three-day period on Ailsa Craig by placing nets over the colonies at night (Gray and Anderson 1869). This was extremely wasteful as it killed breeding adults leaving young to die in the burrows. At the same colony, adults were knocked out of the air with a pole – rather clumsy compared to the fleyg, but David Bodan was credited with killing 960 in 1826, and this was bettered by 240 by Andrew Girvan in 1900 (Gray 1871, Gibson 1951). Puffins were also killed on Foula, Berneray and Mingulay, for food and for bait for lobster creels. In Wales nets were set on short stakes among or below the burrows. Every Whit Monday, men from Tenby used to slaughter Puffins on Caldey, but it is not clear whether this was for food or fun (Mathew 1894). There was no British tradition of shooting Puffins at sea for food, although Breton fishermen were still doing it at Skomer in the 1960s, but Puffins were shot for 'sport' on the south coast of England last century.

In most maritime areas a few Puffins are accidently caught in fishing nets, especially drift nets set for salmon. Most fishermen dislike killing these birds, and birds are also troublesome to remove from nets, so nets are often set where there are few birds.

SUMMARY

Puffins were once an important source of food for many island communities which developed specialized techniques for killing them.

Large numbers are still killed in the Faeroe Islands and Iceland but Puffins are now legally protected during the breeding season in all other areas, although they can sometimes be shot in winter.

Puffins are sometimes accidently drowned on baited fishing lines or in nets but such losses are usually small.

CHAPTER 13

Pollution

With increasing industrialization man is altering the environment at an unprecedented rate. The resulting changes have an important influence on the lives of all animals, including seabirds which have evolved in relatively stable, or at least slowly changing, conditions. Any change is likely to be for the worse.

Three major types of pollution affect seabirds: oil, toxic chemicals and man-made artefacts. Oil pollution is obvious and sometimes spectacular in that large numbers of birds are seen to be affected; pollution by chemicals is insidious in that the effects are often hidden but may well seriously affect populations; and artefacts usually have little effect on populations. All of these cause great suffering but there is much debate as to the influence of oil and chemicals on seabird populations. Bourne (1976b) reviewed the information then available on the incidence and effects of pollution on seabirds. Here, I mainly restrict my attention to pollution and Puffins.

OIL

Oil is a very obvious and disturbing cause of seabird mortality, the more so because almost invariably it is man who has introduced it, either deliberately or by accident, onto the surface of the sea. Oil kills birds by destroying the waterproofing of the plumage which results in increased heat loss and waterlogging. Oil also poisons birds if they preen it off their feathers and swallow it. Oiling is not a recent phenomenon; for instance, large numbers of auks, including Puffins, were killed in east Scotland in June 1915 (Baxter and Rintoul 1916).

Oiling falls into three distinct categories. First, major spectacular incidents which result from the wreck of a tanker or a malfunctioning of an oil well. Such disasters attract much publicity and the names of some, such as the *Torrey Canyon* and *Amoco Cadiz*, have become associated in the public mind with the deaths of large numbers of seabirds. Second, oil is lost from tankers and from other ships when they are bunkering or unloading, due to ruptured pipes or human error. It can come from tankers deliberately pumping dirty ballast water or tank washings into the sea. These incidents attract far less attention and, for example, in January 1979 about 3,000 birds were killed in Cornwall without a national outcry. Third, there is background pollution which comes partly from the second type of incident, partly from even smaller spillages, or from spillages in areas where there are no birds and which go largely undetected. Several decades ago these small incidents and the present background level would have given rise to great public concern. They are now, regrettably, an accepted part of life and public outrage is confined to some unusually large spill or when holiday beaches are threatened. Pollution by fuel oil which can come from any ship is more of a problem around Britain than crude oil which comes solely from tankers.

The numbers of birds killed by oil is difficult to assess. It is usually possible to have sufficient people mobilized after a major incident in the more populated parts of the North Atlantic coast to count corpses or collect oiled, live birds. Many birds are overlooked so such counts are minimal. A sample of 410 dead, oiled auks was marked and thrown into the Irish Sea, only 82 (20%) were later found ashore even though searches were made. In addition, one was later recovered from the seabed showing that some dead seabirds sink (Hope Jones *et al* 1970).

MAJOR OIL DISASTERS

Few of the major oil disasters have killed large numbers of Puffins. The supertanker *Torrey Canyon* which ran aground off Cornwall in March 1967 spilled a huge quantity of oil which polluted the Cornish and Breton coasts and oiled many thousands of auks, but relatively few dead Puffins were found. Even so, the numbers of Puffins on the Sept-Iles (Brittany) declined from 2,500 to 400 pairs and about five-sixths of the French auk populations was eliminated. Breton colonies suffered again, in March 1978, when the *Amoco Cadiz* was wrecked releasing 220,000 tons of crude oil which killed at least 4,572 birds including 1,391 Puffins (Hope Jones *et al* 1979). This resulted in a further 44% reduction in the Sept-Iles Puffin population (Pénicaud 1979). Many of the Puffins could not fly, having moulted their primaries, and they were possibly already weakened by adverse conditions further south in the Bay of Biscay (Mead 1978). They just could not cope with the oil.

Such large numbers of oiled Puffins are exceptional and Puffins usually escape oiling. For instance, there were only 187 oiled Puffins in a major incident in eastern Scotland and north-east England, in January and February

1970, compared to 955 Little Auks, 1,599 Razorbills and 5,203 Guillemots (Greenwood *et al* 1971). Between 1976 and 1979 the 173 Puffins collected in 15 large oiling incidents represented only 1.5% of the oiled auks counted (Table 18). The story is the same elsewhere. There were 52 Puffins among 1,616 oiled birds in northern Norway in 1979 and four among 668 auks killed by two major spills off eastern Canada in 1970 (Barrett 1979, Brown *et al* 1973). Puffins winter well away from land and it is conceivable that even if they do get oiled they never float ashore. However, the available evidence suggests that Puffins rarely congregate away from the colonies so any oil spill in the open sea is unlikely to kill more than a few individuals.

OTHER MORTALITY

The effect of the now accepted 'normal level' of oil pollution is harder to assess but Puffins seem to suffer far less than the other auks. Between 1976 and 1979 the five-times-a-winter Beached Birds Surveys of the east coast of Britain found only 133 dead Puffins compared to 4,588 other auks (RSPB-Seabird Group). Further, only 45% of the Puffins were oiled compared to 67% of the other auks. Some birds of both groups may well have been oiled after dying but this should not invalidate the comparison. Similarly, Hope Jones (1980) found only 39 Puffins (one oiled) compared to 403 Guillemots (190 oiled) and 108 Razorbills (56 oiled) among 2,513 corpses collected on Orkney beaches in two years. In most winters, extremely few dead Puffins are recorded e.g., in 1975 only five during a survey covering 4,095 km of European beach (Lloyd 1976). There are, however, exceptional years such as 1978, when 227 Puffins were found dead along 4,475 km of similar beach.

The only decline in Puffin numbers which can be attributed with any certainty to oil is the recent decline of the Breton colonies, and these populations were declining long before a major spillage occurred nearby. Otherwise, the evidence is circumstantial in that birds are absent or in reduced numbers today in some areas where there have been large kills and chronic oiling in the past. Probably, oiling is unimportant in limiting Puffin populations. However, distinction must be made between the effects on the populations and on the individual birds. Oiling certainly causes great suffering to individual birds and misguided attempts to clean and rehabilitate them results in further suffering. Oil pollution is undoubtedly bad and should be resisted and not accepted as a necessary evil.

CHEMICALS

Whereas the effects of oil pollution have been noticed for a century or more, the first signs that chemical pollution might pose a serious threat to seabirds were not noticed until the 1960s. This was partly because large scale chemical pollution is a fairly recent phenomenon and partly because it is difficult to prove that a chemical has caused death or illness in a bird unless the dose is massive.

Usually, birds die as a result of food shortage, adverse weather or predation, but many of these birds might have coped with such threats if they had been uncontaminated. Chemical induced damage to populations may be insidious and manifest itself only when birds become sterile, or their eggs malformed (with a thin shell or even none at all) and fail to hatch. Alternatively, eggs may become broken if the normal incubation behaviour is disturbed. However, all these changes are extremely difficult to monitor.

A vast range of pollutants is now being added to the environment. Many of these chemicals or their derivatives end up in the sea, either via rain or by run-off into rivers. Those which do not readily break down find their way into planktonic animals and, as these are eaten, into fish or other organisms which are food for seabirds. Increasing numbers of chemicals are being detected in seabirds and their eggs. The levels tend to be very low and are usually expressed as parts per million (ppm). Here, concentrations are expressed as ppm wet weight unless otherwise stated. The best known contaminants are the chlorinated hydrocarbons which include DDT (dichloro-diphenyl-trichloro-ethane) and its breakdown product DDE, chlorinated cyclodienes such as aldrin and dieldrin, and PCBs (polychlorinated biphenyls). All these are fat soluble and so are passed up food chains and are frequently concentrated by predators. In seabirds they accumulate in the large deposits of subcutaneous and mesenteric fat, and there apparently do no harm. However, during food shortage, moult, migration, or at other times of stress this fat is mobilized. Chemicals are then liberated and circulate in the blood until they are reabsorbed into the decreasing quantities of fat. Thus when the last of the fat is used, large amounts are liberated into the blood stream. By this time the bird is probably in fairly dire straits and these chemicals may well be the last straw and result in death.

Heavy metals, although often very toxic, occur naturally in the sea so seabirds presumably have some tolerance to them; indeed, traces of many are essential to life. They are insoluble in fat and have low solubility in water, and so are perhaps less easily passed up food chains. Little is known of the effects of these metals but the levels of cadmium in Puffin, Fulmar and Manx Shearwater are among the highest recorded from any wild vertebrate.

Cadmium is concentrated by these pelagic birds to a level which would seriously harm other species. Even though the cadmium could damage their kidneys the birds seem to have evolved a way of coping with it, as it does them no apparent harm. The cadmium may well originate from natural sources (Bull *et al* 1977).

Most information on the occurrence of pollutants comes from the analyses of eggs and birds found dead, and both sources have their short-comings. First, the relationships between the levels in a female and her eggs are far from clear, so that it is difficult to compare the results and heavy metals in particular are not passed from the female to the egg. Second, results from dead birds are difficult to interpret. If the bird died of starvation the bulk of the pollutants will be in the liver, if it died of an accident they may be scattered through the fat, muscle, brain and other tissues. As an example, Guillemots found dead, and 40% underweight, had 23, 19 and 12% of the total body loads of PCB, DDE and dieldrin respectively in the liver (Parslow and Jefferies 1973). In shot birds the three figures were all 1%. Thus, it is difficult to compare analyses of dead and healthy birds. Recently, attention has focussed on healthy birds as their analysis provides a much more useful base line against which to measure change. Ideally the whole body would be analysed, but this is technically difficult and very expensive. A detailed tissue analysis, including heavy metals, of a single corpse would cost thousands of pounds. Usually, just the liver, fat and muscle, and sometimes brain and kidney, are examined since these provide a good guide to pollution levels in the bird generally.

POLLUTANTS AND PUFFINS

Several points have emerged from the analyses of Puffins (Table 19). First, the levels of PCB and DDE are highest in the livers of birds found dead, presumably because of concentration there as fat stores are used up as the birds slowly die. Second, Puffins contain only low residues of PCBs and organochlorine residues in most tissues, except for some PCBs in the fat. Third, Puffins living in west Britain, have more cadmium in their livers and kidneys than similar birds from the North Sea. This difference fits extremely well with the different migration patterns – North Sea birds remain in the North Sea, those from the west coast disperse widely over the Atlantic where cadmium levels are relatively high. The wide variation in the levels of other pollutants in these western birds might also be due to their very dispersed wintering areas. Fourth, birds accumulate cadmium during their lives; none was detected in eggs from the Isle of May and only 5 out of 19 eggs from St Kilda had even a trace.

Amount of cadmium in the livers of Puffins found dead and killed in Britain

	Age	Number	Mean amount in liver ppm dry weight ± SE
Found dead			
North Sea coast	Juvenile	2	0.2 ± 0.04
	1st winter	6	3.1 ± 1.4
	Older	17	14.5 ± 4.3
Atlantic coasts	1st winter	2	1.4 ± 1.0
	2nd year	4	32.4 ± 6.9
	Older	7	16.8 ± 7.6
Killed			
Isle of May	Juvenile	3	ca. 0.5
	Adult	10	1.0 ± 0.3
North-west Scotland	Adult	10	19.9 ± 2.8

Eggs from several colonies have been analysed (Table 20) but comparisons between years, or even colonies, are difficult because there is great individual variation. However, levels are low and there is no suggestion that these pollutants had caused any thinning of the egg shell, as has been shown in some water and predatory birds.

Chemicals pass from the female to the egg but there is no significant relationship between the levels of PCB in a female Puffin and her egg. The constituents of the egg come both from food eaten by the female at the time and from her fat, so that some fat soluble substances become incorporated in the ·yolk. The amount of PCB going into the egg will depend on how much PCB is in the female and whether she is forced to draw on her fat reserves. Eggs are useful indicators of the level of chemicals in the bird which laid them, but full understanding of the effects of chemicals regrettably necessitates killing the birds.

Possible effects

Puffins have such low levels of pollutants that it is tempting to think that they can have little effect, but many chemicals are so highly toxic that they can be lethal at extremely low levels. There is the added problem of demonstrating that the pollutants actually cause death when large numbers of birds are found dead in suspicious circumstances. In 1969, 10,000–20,000 Guillemots were found dead or dying in the north Irish Sea. There was no obvious cause of death but the birds were extremely underweight and had concentrations of up to 880 ppm of PCB, 25 ppm of DDE, and 0.8 ppm of dieldrin in their livers (Holdgate 1971). The average Guillemot found dead had 4,660 μg of PCB residues in its body, twice as much as Guillemots shot slightly further north a few weeks later (Parslow and Jefferies 1973). This would seem reasonable evidence of PCB having adversely affected the survival of these birds, but these two samples of birds might have belonged to different colonies (Bourne 1976b). These Guillemots were probably already suffering from food shortage, bad weather and the fact that many were in moult, and so flightless. Pollutants were probably, again, the last straw.

A further wreck occurred in the same area in early 1974. These birds, also, had relatively high levels of PCB and dieldrin. Although most birds were thin, post-mortem examinations gave no clear pattern of the causes of death. The report on this wreck concluded 'whatever the effect of these man-made compounds may be, their presence is surely undesirable' (Lloyd *et al* 1974).

PCB AND PUFFINS

The documentation of disasters, the routine examination of bodies of birds found dead or deliberately killed, the detailed monitoring of the numbers of birds at colonies, and studies of breeding biology *may* produce some suggestive evidence of the adverse effects of chemicals. It will, however, need many years of work to collect data and even then it may be difficult to determine the true chemical culprit from among many possibilities. More direct evidence is required and that can only come from carefully designed studies. Most monitoring of the effects of chemicals on wild birds has involved taking individual animals into captivity and feeding them contaminated food. Such experiments are essential to test the toxicity of pollutants, but the animals are subject to stresses so different from those they encounter in the wild that it is far from certain that the findings on the sub-lethal effects of chemicals can safely be applied to wild populations. Field studies are desperately needed.

There are two possible approaches. First, one can compare the biology, breeding output and behaviour of a species in two colonies, one where the adults were 'dirty' (that is they have high levels of pollutants), the other where the birds were 'clean'. Almost of necessity this means that the two colonies will be widely separated and therefore any differences caused by pollutants are likely to be masked by the normal variation in almost every aspect of the birds' lives. The second approach is to find a 'clean' population of birds and to make a few individuals 'dirty' by introducing minute quantities of chemicals, under all the proper licences and constraints which quite properly govern such work. These birds can then be compared with their normal neighbours. This approach has been adopted for Puffins and PCB (Harris and Osborn 1981).

Small plastic implants containing PCB, or sucrose as a control, were slipped under the skin of Puffins so that PCB was gradually introduced into the body, just as it would be if the bird was eating contaminated fish. The process of implanting had no detectable adverse effect on the birds and all were subsequently seen at the colonies. Samples of these birds were later killed and chemical analyses showed that the PCB had gone into the body and had raised the level of the fat tenfold. Many of these dosed, and apparently healthy Puffins had more PCB in their bodies than the Guillemots which had been killed in the

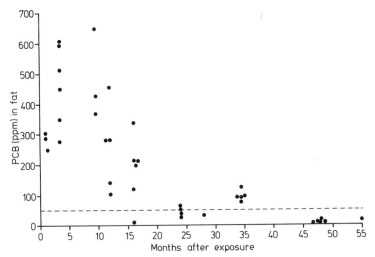

40   *The levels of PCB (ppm wet weight) in the fat of Puffins at various intervals after being exposed to the chemical. The dotted line is the maximum level recorded in control birds from the same area. No deleterious effects of the chemical were noted.*

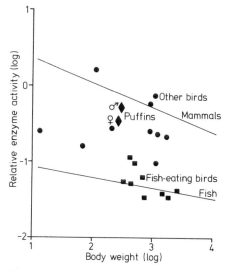

41 The relative hepatic enzyme activity found in the Puffin (diamond), seabirds (squares) and other birds (circles). Puffins and most other birds had levels similar to mammals (upper regression line) whereas other fish-eating birds had levels similar to those in fish (lower regression line). (Redrawn after Walker and Knight 1981.)

1969 Irish Sea wreck. These birds and a series of normal adults were then followed in detail to find out how well these birds bred and how well their young grew.

The PCB did not interfere with the Puffin's ability to obtain a burrow, nor with its fertility or ability to rear a nestling which then grew and fledged normally. There was no difference in the birds' behaviour. Neither did it affect the survival of the birds. Quite obviously these high levels of PCB had no effect on these particular Puffins.

Because PCB is 'tied-up' in the fat and birds are continually acquiring more, albeit a minute quantity, through their food, it is sometimes thought that the birds must gradually accumulate an increasing load. However, the subsequent analyses of these dosed birds showed that this was not so, as amounts in the body declined quite sharply after the first few months; however even after 16 months the levels in the fat were four times the normal 'background level' (Fig. 40). This monitoring of the rate of excretion continues as it is very important to learn how birds cope with toxic chemicals.

Fat-soluble substances, which include pollutants such as PCB and dieldrin, are only slowly excreted by vertebrates other than fish. Within the body they are converted, sometimes very slowly, into water-soluble products which are readily excreted in bile and urine (Chipman and Walker 1979). The enzyme microsomal mono-oxygenase, which is found in the liver, has an important role in this breakdown of dieldrin and PCB into water-soluble products. If animals take in these compounds faster than this enzyme can break them down, then they will accumulate in fatty tissues.

Fish-eating birds have a much lower hepatic mono-oxygenase activity than other birds which, in turn, have a lower level than mammals (Fig. 41). Fish have the lowest level of all, presumably because they eliminate unwanted fat-soluble compounds into the constant stream of water which passes across the gills. Seabirds may not have evolved an efficient enzyme system for detoxification simply because there was no need. Puffins are exceptional in having a much higher level of microsomal mono-oxygenase than any other seabird of the same body weight (Walker 1980), and appear to be able to cope with these fat-soluble pollutants better than most seabirds. A fact which emphasizes the need to know a great deal about any bird before we can predict how it will cope with a changing environment.

ELASTIC AND OTHER ARTEFACTS

The seas of the world are now littered with astronomical numbers of a variety of man-made articles, litter and garbage. Small floating objects are attractive to seabirds, which sometimes swallow them.

A juvenile Puffin found in Yorkshire in 1960 had died of acute gastritis caused by the remains of rubber bands in its stomach (Bennett 1960). Between 1969 and 1972 elastic threads of various types were found in the stomachs of many Puffins in the North Sea; for example, in seven out of 69 found dead in east Scotland in March 1969, and in two out of nine shot off Hordaland, Norway, in 1970 (Parslow and Jefferies 1972, Berland 1971). Now, about one in ten Puffins have elastic in their stomachs. The pieces are normally short but sometimes they become entangled into knots some 10 mm in diameter.

Some of this elastic is of the sort used in clothing and presumably it gets into the sea as a result of the deliberate dumping of waste off-cuts, or with the rotting of lost clothing. The elastic threads have a density similar to that of sea water and sink slowly with an action reminiscent of a swimming pipefish. Perhaps Puffins mistake black elastic for fish, red elastic for marine worms. They also bring ashore short pieces of pale-blue braided nylon as nest lining but do not appear to swallow these. Other artefacts found in Puffin gizzards include small pieces of nylon thread (sometimes in tight, tangled knots), plastic beads and small (4 mm × 2 mm) black plastic cylinders. Many seabirds whose food contains hard material, e.g. chitinous squid beaks and large fish bones, regurgitate the undigestible remains as pellets. Puffins do not do this so possibly these artefacts remain in the gizzard.

Seals, Puffins and seabirds which dive for their food often get entangled in fishing nets, especially the almost invisible, floating drift nets set for salmon. They also get snared in the off-cuts of fishing netting which are now commonplace in inshore waters. Although these nets cause great suffering to the individual animals concerned, they probably have only a trivial effect on Puffin populations.

SUMMARY

Relatively few Puffins are washed ashore dead and only a small proportion of them are oiled.

There is little evidence that oiling has caused more than local declines in Puffin numbers.

Puffins now have accumulations of some toxic chemicals in their bodies. The levels of cadmium are quite high but this is probably natural.

At the levels detected, PCB has no observable detrimental effect on the survival or breeding of Puffins.

Puffins seem to be able to cope with fat-soluble pollutants better than most species of seabirds.

Puffins sometimes swallow elastic, perhaps in mistake for fish.

These pollutants are very worrying, but the suggestion that they might have caused a decline in the numbers of Puffins must be considered unfounded.

CHAPTER 14

Migration, survival and winter at sea

Ringing or banding is an extremely valuable tool in the study of migration. Even if we have no particular interest in a species we are still slightly awed by news of some extremely distant or rapid recovery, or at the ages attained by ringed seabirds. Although Puffins produce such recoveries (e.g. young ringed in Britain and later reported killed off Newfoundland, or washed ashore in Sicily) most recoveries are much more mundane although still interesting. This chapter pieces together the scattered available information on where Puffins go in the winter. It also considers the survival of ringed adult and young Puffins as this is at least as important an aspect of ringing as the superficially more interesting distant recoveries. Much of this information refers to British Puffins, mainly because many more Puffins have been ringed here than elsewhere. However, I have been given access to foreign recoveries by the various ringing schemes in other countries.

Many tens of thousands of Puffins have been ringed after being caught in burrows, by fleyging with a large landing net, by slipping a small crook around the leg, in barrel-traps with swivel lids which deposit the birds at the bottom when they walk on the lid and with mist nets, but very few have been heard of again, and only 792 out of 106,000 Puffins ringed in Britain and Ireland have been recovered. This recovery rate (0.7%) is far lower than those of Razorbill (3.0%), Guillemot (2.7%) and Black Guillemot (1.4%) and lower even than the trans-equatorial migratory Manx Shearwater (1.4%) and Arctic Tern (1.2%). The paucity of recoveries is almost certainly because Puffins spend

166

most of their life in areas where there is nobody to find the rings when they die, and some may die in burrows. Even within one country there are great variations in the recovery rate. In Britain, Puffins ringed on the east coast have a higher chance of being recovered than those ringed in the west; e.g., 59 (0.5%) out of 12,541 full-grown Puffins ringed on the Isle of May have been reported, compared to only six (0.2%) of 3,756 ringed on St Kilda. The former birds rarely leave the North Sea, where one might expect that there was a reasonable chance that a bird dying would be washed ashore and found, the latter move to less densely populated areas (below).

METHOD OF RECOVERIES

Most recoveries come from birds dying or becoming moribund which are then washed ashore. The cause of death is rarely known. About 28% of ringed Puffins washed ashore in Britain are reported as being oiled, but it is impossible to know whether the oil caused the deaths, or the birds became oiled after death. In a few specific areas recoveries come from birds shot for food or sport (e.g., 26 out of all 52 recoveries in Scandinavia) or drowned in fishing nets. Young Puffins become caught in nets set for salmon in European waters, and all 16 reported from such nets set off Co. Donegal and Co. Mayo, Ireland, were less than two years old.

Puffins are numerous on these fishing grounds, arriving in April and May and remaining until mid September, and up to 20–30 birds are sometimes caught in one set of nets fished overnight. The fishing, and thus the recoveries, are concentrated between the end of May and mid July. Nine recoveries were between 1975 and 1978, and five were in 1977, when the fishing was most intense and happened at night. Birds are certainly there at other times. None were reported in 1979, when most fishing was by day, which suggests that Puffins can usually see the nets. Maybe these inexperienced birds become caught at dawn and dusk as there is no direct evidence that Puffins feed at night. Sad as these deaths are, fishing has shown us this important summering ground for immature Puffins. Similarly, shooting has shown that many juveniles winter off southern Norway; in recent years there have been fewer recoveries from this area, either because there is less shooting or because, now that shooting is illegal, few rings are returned. The pattern of recoveries in the west Atlantic is somewhat different, for although 28 out of 33 recoveries of birds shot were less than 18 months old, 31 out of 35 recoveries from nets were of older birds. The reason for this difference is not clear.

Although the modern rings of stainless steel, monel or incoloy last much longer than the earlier aluminium ones, they tend to be smaller and darker and far less obvious. They are also hard to remove, so that squeamish finders fail to remove them and forget the number before they can write it down. The recovery rate of birds ringed as full-grown (but not that of chicks) is greatly increased if the bird also has a colour ring, as shown by recoveries from St Kilda and the Isle of May:

	No. colour ringed	% recovered	No. with plain, numbered rings	% recovered
Ringed as full-grown				
St Kilda	1540	0.3	2024	0.1
Isle of May	2751	0.8	4287	0.3
Ringed as young				
St Kilda	3129	0.4	1689	0.3
Isle of May	1630	0.7	270	0.7

Old birds that die are mostly washed ashore and a colour-ring draws attention to a corpse on a tideline, so increasing the chance of the bird being examined. Young birds predominate among those shot or caught in nets and the chances that a ring will be seen are high in such cases even if a colour-ring is not present, so colour-ringing does not increase the recovery rate.

MONTH OF RECOVERY

There is a marked peak in the numbers of recoveries of older British ringed Puffins in the early part of the year (Fig. 42) which is partly due to 'wrecks' at that time of year, e.g. in north-east Britain 1969, Bay of Biscay in 1978 and 1979, and the *Amoco Cadiz* oiling incident in Brittany in 1978. However, some mortality occurs in most years at a time when many adults are either flightless or

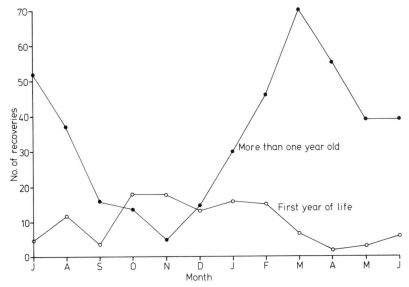

42   *Monthly distribution of recovery dates of Puffins ringed in Europe and later found dead or presumed dead. Birds older than one year had a large peak of recoveries in the spring when many are flightless or migrating.*

passing close to land during their northward migration. Juveniles, which moult later in the year and over a much wider time span than adults, and do not return to the colonies in their first summer, do not have a similar mortality.

SURVIVAL RATES

As is usual in birds, there is heavy mortality of young in their first year of life. Among young Puffins ringed in Britain before 1975, 36 were recovered in the calendar year of ringing (i.e. were less than six months old), 41 in the next full calendar year, 32 in the next and 15 in the third.

It is difficult to calculate accurate survival rates from past recoveries because the large numbers needed are only now accumulating, following the great increase in ringing of Puffins in the 1970s. However, an examination of the age distribution of Farne Island ringed birds killed in a 'wreck' in spring 1969, suggested an annual mortality of 4.5% (Mead 1974). More satisfactory estimates of the survival rates of seabirds come from detailed studies of individually marked birds where the ringer produces the recovery data rather than the general public. The limited scope of these population data is more than offset by their accuracy. Annual survival rates of adults have been measured on Skomer and the Isle of May (Ashcroft 1979, Harris 1983).

% of Puffins surviving from one season to the next

		Skomer	*Isle of May*
Breeding birds	1972–73	91.8	
	1973–74	95.4	94.3
	1974–75	94.9	
	1975–76	94.7	
	1976–77		
	1977–78		96.2
	1978–79		97.8
	1979–80		97.1
	Mean	94.2	96.3
		Skomer	*Isle of May*
Breeding not proved	1972–73	88.0	
	1973–74	88.5	94.8
	1974–75	88.5	98.4
	1975–76	92.7	94.7
	1976–77	86.8	97.9
	1977–78	88.2	94.7
	1978–79		91.1
	1979–80		94.8
	1980–81		93.5
	Mean	88.8	95.0

The seemingly higher survival of breeding adults almost certainly arises from their very high fidelity to their nesting area, where they are easily found, rather than from any real difference in the mortality rates between the two classes. Such estimates of survival rates are minimal figures as some of the missing birds are not dead but are lurking in an out-of-the-way part of the colony, or they may not have visited the nesting areas that year. Indeed, it would appear that each year up to 5% of Puffins fail to turn up at the colonies and sometimes birds miss two seasons. These errors are not important in long-term studies, as most of the missing birds will be found later. Puffins sometimes suffer severe overwinter mortality. The survival of Isle of May Puffins between 1982 and 1983 was probably only 75–80%, i.e. four to five times the usual mortality (Harris and Wanless 1984). The frequency of such events obviously affects the overall survival estimate, but they appear to be rare. The overall annual survival rate of Puffins is probably 95–96%.

Neither the sex nor the fact that a breeding adult does or does not breed one year influences its chances of survival. This suggests that breeding does not impose any lasting strain on the birds. The place where the Puffin nests in a colony does, however, sometimes influence its chances of survival. For instance, 4.2% of adults breeding at low density on St Kilda were killed each May–July by Great Black-backed Gulls. This was about four times the figure for adults nesting at high density nearby.

The average annual survival rate of adult Puffins is among the highest recorded for birds. The mean expectation of further life for a Puffin once it reaches breeding age is about 20 years, giving a total age of 25 years. Any small change in the mean survival rate has a great effect on the expectation of further life; e.g. an annual survival rate of 97% means that the further expectation of life is 33 years, 96% gives 25 years, but 94% only 16 years.

The survival rate also has great implications if we try to model the population dynamics of a species, so care must be taken to get it right. The calculation of average life expectancy assumes that survival is not related to age (that is birds do not suffer from the effects of senility). Only time will tell if this assumption is valid. However, ringed Puffins have survived up to 29 years in the wild and the introduction of better-wearing rings is sure to show some very old birds in due time.

The survivals of three- and four-year-old Puffins on Skomer between 1977 and 1978 were estimated at 58% and 63%, whereas the survival of older birds was 88% (Hudson 1979). On the Isle of May there was no suggestion of such an age-related difference in survival. Indeed it seems unreasonable to suppose that four-year-old birds would survive much less well than birds a year or two older, and some of the missing birds may have moved to other colonies.

The estimates of the survival of chicks from fledging to breeding age are almost certainly too low, it being difficult to determine how many move to other colonies. Rothery (in Harris 1983) modelled the retraps of young Puffins on the Isle of May and found that 60% survived to return in their third year and about 30% survived to breeding age. My colour-ringing suggested that 23% of the birds which did survive were living elsewhere, i.e. a total of 39% survived to breed. This is an extremely high survival rate, but then the Isle of May is an extremely good place to be a Puffin. On Skomer, 10–16% of ringed young returned to the colonies when old enough to breed (Ashcroft 1979) but no account was taken of possible emigration so the true survival was doubtless higher.

INTER-COLONY MOVEMENTS

Most seabirds return to breed in the colonies where they were born. Obviously, a few must go elsewhere or new colonies could not be formed, but until recently it was thought that there were few such adventurous birds. Indeed, mortality rates both of young and old birds, calculated from their recapture or frequency of sighting, usually assume that all marked birds missing from a study colony are dead. The amount of emigration is always under-estimated because it is easy to find the majority which returns to the study colony, but very hard to find the few which move to distant colonies. Recent studies on Herring Gulls have shown that many of the young, though still a minority, breed away from their natal colony (Monaghan and Coulson 1977). Similarly, the Manx Shearwater was once thought to be an extremely conservative species but it is now known that about half the females emigrate from the colony where they were reared (Brooke 1978).

There is little comparable information on auks because of the difficulties in retrapping enough birds, but casual colony-visiting is widespread in Puffins. I attempted to find out whether Puffins from the declining colonies on the west of Britain were moving to the east coast where the colonies were expanding. Between 1973 and 1978 about 20,000 Puffins were colour-ringed to indicate where they were ringed, the year of birth if ringed as nestlings, and breeding state. This meant that about one in every 150–300 Puffins in Scotland had a ring. Many more Puffins were ringed with normal, numbered rings. As expected, most of the Puffins were later seen where they were ringed. However, there were some long distance retraps or sightings at other colonies. These and those documented by normal ringing are shown in Fig. 43. The movements from Britain and the Faeroes to Iceland are particularly interesting because it is often thought that Puffins in these areas belong to different races. None of these movements refer to breeding birds so the records could indicate casual visiting rather than emigration. A chick from the Farne Islands has been found breeding on Kjør in south western Norway, but Puffins in these two areas belong to the same subspecies. These long-distance movements are exceptional. As far as population dynamics are concerned, the numerous short-distance movements are more important.

I followed the movements of birds between the colonies scattered along 250 km of coastline in Britain between Northumberland and Aberdeenshire (Harris 1983). Of 9,353 Puffins ringed on the Farne Islands, 114 were caught (and many more seen) about 100 km away on the Isle of May, two at nearby

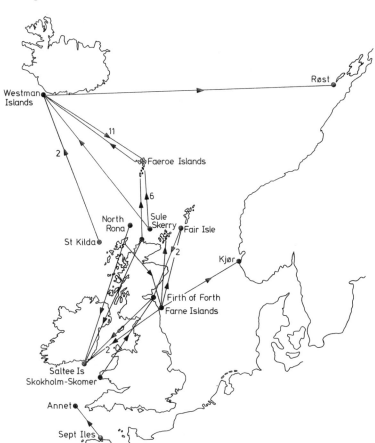

43   *Long distance inter-colony movements of Puffins. Arrows indicate the direction of movements, numbers refer to the number of recoveries (if there were more than one).*

Craigleith and one at Inchkeith; all but 12 had been ringed as chicks. These movements were anticipated as the large Farne Islands colony was overcrowded and the other colonies were small and increasing rapidly, so that immigration was certain to occur. Some Farne Island young appeared to be choosing to move to less crowded areas. Unexpectedly, there were reverse movements as 18 of the 11,137 Puffins ringed on the Isle of May were found at the Farne Islands and five on Craigleith. Nine of the 23 were breeding when found, compared to only 30 young bred on the Isle of May found breeding on the Isle of May itself during the same period. This suggests that 23% (9/39) of the young may have changed colonies.

Similar movements have been recorded elsewhere. There is, for example, a regular three-way traffic of Puffins between Skokholm and Skomer (5 km apart) and Great Saltee (105 km from the other two) in the southern Irish Sea. Inter-colony movements have also occurred within Norway, Iceland and the Faeroe Islands. In the west Atlantic at least 36 birds from 438 young ringed on Eastern Egg Rock were seen on Matinicus Rock (42 km away) in one season, and a single two-year-old visited Machias Seal Island 187 km away (Kress 1982). A few colonies have participated in far more intercolony movements than would have been expected. In Britain, the most striking are Faraid Head and the Pentland Skerries; in Ireland, Great Saltee also has had a good selection. There are relatively few Puffins on the Pentland Skerries, yet during a single visit in June, Sarah Wanless saw two Farne Islands and a single Isle of May young among 160 looked at closely. All these colonies are at places where migrating Puffins are forced to come close to land. Maybe they come ashore for a rest.

Even if a ringed young is caught subsequently at its natal colony it cannot be assumed to be resident there, for some change colonies later in life. One chick from the Farne Islands was caught as an immature on the Isle of May and is now resident again on the Farnes. Although Puffins ringed as young on the Westman Islands visit other colonies, where they are caught by fowlers, all birds later found in burrows were at their natal colonies (Petersen 1976a). Some idea of the extent of these movements comes from the sightings of 310 full-grown Puffins individually colour-ringed on the Farne Islands in 1969 by N. Brown. Of the 258 found later, 231 (75% of the original number) were seen only on the Farne Islands, 14 (4.5%) were seen both on the Farne Islands and later on the Isle of May (12), Coquet Island (1) and Fair Isle (1) and ten others were seen only on the Isle of May, two on Coquet and one at Auskerry, Orkney. Fifteen of those on the Isle of May, were either breeding or were seen regularly for several years. Both sexes move, for the birds caught on the Isle of May included nine males and 13 females. There is no record anywhere of a breeding adult changing its colony. However, single breeding birds from the Isle of May and Craigleith were seen on Coquet and the Isle of May, respectively, later in the year that they were ringed; despite intensive searching they have not been seen again so were presumably just visiting.

In conclusion, there are few long-distance inter-colony movements but there is a regular interchange of young birds between adjacent or nearby colonies. Some immatures and a few adults land at colonies away from their own. Certain colonies seem to have a fascination for passing Puffins or it just may be that they are placed where large numbers of Puffins pass on migration. This casual colony visiting is well known with storm petrels and even some passerines. Probably, such wanderings are common among colonial birds.

MIGRATION PATTERNS OF PUFFINS IN BRITAIN

Puffins reared in north-east Britain do not move very far. All recoveries of first-year birds are in the North Sea, with a notable concentration in southern

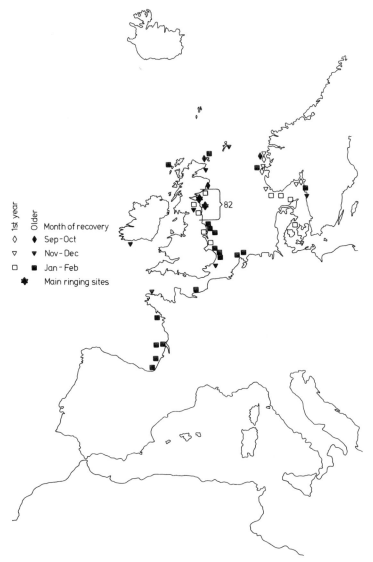

44 *Winter recoveries of Puffins ringed on the Farne Islands and in the Firth of Forth (stars). The totals near the colonies refer to the number of local recoveries within the bracketed area.*

Scandinavia which is probably due to past hunting pressure. Most older birds are reported within 200 km of the colonies (Fig. 44) but a few recoveries have come from slightly further afield including western Scotland (two in winter, two in summer), southern Ireland (one in winter), the Channel Islands (one in winter), northern France (one in winter and a 22-month-old bird in summer)

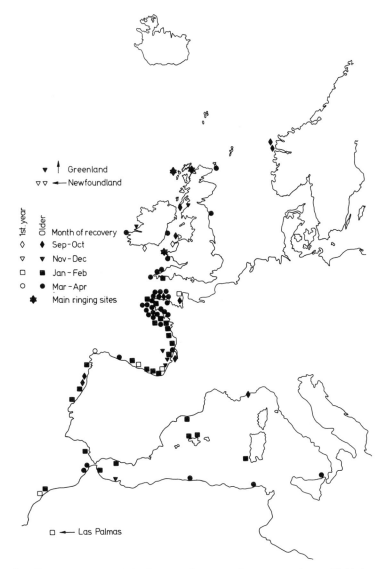

45   *Winter recoveries of Puffins ringed in west Britain, mostly on Skokholm and Skomer, St Kilda, and the Shiant Islands (marked by stars).*

and the Bay of Biscay (five in winter). The first of the recoveries outside the North Sea was not until December 1975 (by which time there had already been 106 recoveries) so perhaps the recent rapid increase in the numbers of Puffins breeding on the British east coast is causing birds to move further afield in winter.

Puffins from Wales, Ireland and the Outer Hebrides move much further (Fig. 45). First-year birds have been recovered south to Morocco (one bird) and the Canary Islands (one) and west to Canada (two). The last two were among the first recoveries of ringed Puffins, and were remarkable in that they were ringed on St Kilda in the same week and killed off Newfoundland only a day apart. This started speculation that many Puffins might winter there, but it was 36 years until the next British Puffin was recorded so far west. The far more numerous recoveries in later winters include 11 in the Mediterranean, as far east as Sicily, and three on the north-west African coast south to the Morocco/Spanish Sahara border. The recovery in north Italy was a St Kildan Puffin, and assuming that it came via the Straits of Gibraltar, this is a movement of 4,100 km, which is further than the trans-Atlantic movements. Most western birds leave British and north European waters in the winter; the Welsh adults shot off Norway in September and October, and caught in a salmon net off Greenland in December, are quite exceptional. The large numbers of recoveries in north-west France in March and April, which include moulting and migrating birds, contrast with just two autumn recoveries there and must mean that birds moving south in the autumn keep well away from land. The summer recoveries are all quite close to the colonies except for two in the Mediterranean, one of which was 14 months old and so may well have spent its first summer there, the other was an adult which was found dead in early May, which could have died sometime earlier.

The pattern of recoveries of birds ringed in Sutherland, Caithness, Orkney (mainly Sule Skerry) and Shetland (Fair Isle) is intermediate. Some first-winter Puffins go into the North Sea, others to Greenland and Newfoundland or as far south as the Canary Islands. Older birds go mainly south in winter, to the Bay of Biscay and Mediterranean. It is not clear whether Puffins go to and from there via the North Sea or the Atlantic, but the lack of recoveries in the Irish Sea of birds ringed in Scotland shows that there is little migration through that area.

Until 1971, only 13 British-ringed Puffins had been recovered in France and north Spain. Yet there were nine recoveries in 1977, 14 in 1978 (plus another 11 killed in the *Amoco Cadiz* oil incident) and 19 in 1979. This increase was far too marked to have been due to more Puffins having been ringed in recent years, but the reason for it is unknown. Since then numbers have declined again, with eight recoveries in 1980 and three in 1981.

OTHER POPULATIONS

Even less is known of the movements of birds from other areas. Fewer have been ringed and the rates of recovery are even lower. Two birds from Burhou, Channel Islands, have been recovered on the English south coast, a third in the north Irish Sea. Six other recoveries are all in northern France; probably the Breton and Channel Islands birds disperse in a similar way to those from western Britain.

Some Norwegian birds move south and there is a clump of recoveries shot or caught in fishing nets in south-west Norway. Some enter the North Sea, as is shown by five adults recovered in east Britain south to Norfolk, and one in Germany. However, others go westwards as there are winter recoveries in Greenland (3), Newfoundland (1), north Iceland (2) and the Faeroe Islands (3). All but one of these birds are from northern colonies and all but two are in the first winter of life. The exceptions are a first-winter bird from Runde shot in the Faeroes, and second-winter birds from Iceland and the Faeroes. Single birds from Russia have been found in Finnmark and Sør-Trøndelag in Norway (Norderhaug *et al* 1977). Twenty-seven young ringed in the Westman Islands, Iceland, and one from Kangek, Greenland (out of only 121 ringed), have been recovered in Newfoundland, all in their first winter (Petersen 1982, Salomonsen 1979). A full-grown Puffin from Mykines was reported from southern Greenland in July seven years later. One wonders if it had changed colonies or was a Greenland bird visiting the Faeroes when ringed. Two other Icelandic birds have been reported in the winter – a first-year in the Bay of Biscay and a six-year-old in the Azores. Puffins are not seen in any numbers near land in south and west Iceland in the winter; a few are seen in the northern fjords but these are thought to be Norwegian birds, as indicated by the two recoveries mentioned earlier (Petersen 1982).

Puffins breeding in Iceland and Norway appear not to move very far south in the eastern Atlantic and do not enter the Mediterranean (all the Puffin skins from the Mediterranean are referable to the small southern race *F.a. grabae*). They probably do not regularly enter the North Sea as the vast majority of birds found dead in the winter on beaches around Britain probably come from the British breeding populations.

The ringing of Puffins in the west Atlantic, almost entirely on islands in Witless Bay, Newfoundland, has produced few results except that many birds get killed, mainly in fishing gear, during the summer within 100 km of the colonies. There are just seven recoveries between October and April but the only long distance movement is a bird which travelled 800 km from New Brunswick to Newfoundland within three months of fledging.

FIRST-YEAR BIRDS

The young of many bird species in their first winter migrate further than adult birds, but it is difficult to be sure whether this is true of Puffins. The three most southern recoveries in the east Atlantic, Canary Islands (2) and Morocco, and all 34 European and Iceland young which have been recovered in Newfoundland, were all in the first winter. Also, the mean distance between ringing and recovery places for 79 young recovered in their first winter was 1,651 km (S.E. 127), compared with 1,032 km (S.E. 111) for 111 birds at least 18 months old. (I excluded birds in their second winter in case they moved intermediate distances and I assumed that birds entering the Mediterranean moved through the Straits of Gibraltar.) This difference is highly significant and indicates that young do move further, but why they appear not to enter the Mediterranean remains a mystery. Maybe more recoveries will show that they do.

THE OPEN SEA

Most Puffins probably winter in the open sea, far from land. Long before ringing started it was known that numbers of Puffins occurred in the Mediterranean, with a few birds as far east as Malta and (extremely rarely) the Adriatic, and off North Africa and Iberia. Sightings were so frequent that breeding was suspected on the Berlenga Islands, Portugal, and possibly on islands in the Mediterranean. Some immature and non-breeding birds over-summer in these areas but there is no evidence that Puffins have ever bred south of Brittany. Most birds leave the Mediterranean in March and birds seen passing through the Straits of Gibraltar in April and May are probably not going to breed that year. Although numbers sometimes come within telescope range of Cape Finisterre, Spain, most pass by unseen, further out to sea. It was previously thought that Puffins migrated across the western edge of the Bay of Biscay but the recent increase in recoveries of birds washed ashore and sightings of Puffins just off Biarritz, where deep water comes close to the coast, suggest that some birds enter the Bay. Possibly, birds winter there. Large numbers have been seen moving north off western Ireland in late March and early April; probably these are birds going to north Scotland and the Faeroes. The far fewer autumn records of migrating birds points to the southward migration being even further out to sea.

In the autumn, Puffins are common in the Labrador Sea and off south-east Labrador. These birds probably came from the large Newfoundland colonies but might include migrants from more northern and eastern colonies (Brown *et al* 1975). Puffins also occur in numbers on the Grand Banks off Newfoundland, extending eastwards to 45°N, 45°W in December–March (Rankin and Duffey 1948), where they are joined by large numbers of Brünnich's Guillemots, including many from Greenland.

These few concentrations contain only a small proportion of the millions of Atlantic Puffins. Where then do the remainder spend the winter? The answer must be that we do not know. Other major wintering grounds would surely have been found by now with the increasing number of fishing and research vessels working in all the more productive areas of the Atlantic. The birds are probably dispersed over the whole ocean. Although no attempt has yet been made to collect and collate all the scattered sightings made at sea, it is obvious that they are pitifully few. It is even difficult to determine the southern edge of the winter range. Most distribution maps draw it as a line across the Atlantic from just south of the Canary Islands at 25°N, to New York at 38°N. These very southerly records are, however, exceptional as the Puffin is rare in the Canary Islands, Madeira and New York State, although more frequent slightly further north at the Azores. The northern limit is the southern edge of the arctic pack ice. Even taking the southern limit as the Azores, and a 'guesstimate' of 15 million Puffins, the density of birds would only be in the region of one every $1-2 km^2$ of ocean. Certainly, Puffins are seen in the central Atlantic more often than Razorbills or Guillemots but the frequency of sightings is extremely low. Five of the only six oceanic records of Puffins made during 101 crossings of the Atlantic where Puffins might be expected to occur were in the winter, the sixth 200 km north-west of Ireland was in July (Aikman 1958, Rankin and Duffey 1948). One of the winter records was a bird washed on deck aboard a boat and stranded! Similarly in the North Sea, with an estimated 150,000 Puffins resident in maybe a half to two-thirds of a million square kilometres of sea, few are seen in winter; for example, P. Hope Jones saw only three birds in 152 hours of systematic observations from fixed oil and gas platforms between September and April. It seems that the Puffin's life at sea is likely to remain a mystery for many years to come.

SUMMARY

Very few ringed Puffins are ever reported. Those which are, are mostly found washed up on beaches but some young birds get caught in fishing nets or shot. There is a peak of recoveries in the late winter and spring when Puffins are flightless.

The adult survival rate is about 95% per annum and the adult Puffin has an average total life expectancy of 25 years.

Most Puffins remain faithful to their natal colony but some young birds move to nearby colonies; and some immatures and a few adults sometimes visit other colonies.

Puffins from north-east Britain are mostly resident in the North Sea, whereas those from the west move much further, to Newfoundland, Greenland, the Mediterranean, and south to the Canary Islands. Puffins from north Scotland have an intermediate migration pattern. Little is known of the migration of other populations. Some Norwegian Puffins go into the North Sea, others, and some from Iceland and Greenland, move to Newfoundland. These northern Puffins do not move very far south in winter.

Most Puffins winter in the open sea far from land.

CHAPTER 15

Factors influencing numbers of Puffins

Although the numbers of most animals fluctuate between quite wide limits, the variation is much less than might be expected, given the possible reproductive output. The changes in numbers are most rapid (and probably greatest) in species with short life cycles, rapid maturation and high breeding output, and slowest in species with delayed maturity and low reproductive output. The numbers of cormorants, boobies and pelicans, collectively known as 'guano birds', which live in the waters of the Humboldt Current off Peru and Chile, increased from 6 to 20 millon and then declined again, all within a period of 12 years (Jordan and Fuentes 1966). Such an increase is possible because, when conditions are good, these birds lay large clutches, fledge many young, breed when a year old, and probably breed more than once a year. The collapse comes when their food supply fails. In contrast, the great albatrosses do not breed until they are eight to ten years old, they lay a single egg a year and take so long to rear a chick that a pair can breed succesfully only every second year. We know nothing of the pattern of changes in the numbers of these albatrosses but it is hard to envisage changes as dramatic as those seen in the guano birds. Seabirds of the albatross type can certainly increase their numbers greatly but it is usually a slow process.

The general picture of the fortunes of Puffins is of great decreases in the numbers at most southern colonies during the last hundred years with, at least in Britain, a recent partial recovery. The numbers of Guillemots at many British colonies have also increased considerably during the last decade after showing declines during the previous 30 years. It is probably not a coincidence that

British Guillemots and Puffins are together experiencing better times, because they eat similar species (although different sizes) of fish.

POPULATION DYNAMICS

The work of Ashcroft on Skomer and myself on the Isle of May has produced enough quantitative information on the breeding and survival of Puffins for us to construct very simple life-tables.

		Isle of May	*Skomer*
(a)	Nesting success—young fledged/burrow	0.83	0.64
(b)	Proportion of adults breeding	0.70	0.80
(c)	Production of young/pair (a × b)	0.58	0.51
(d)	Adult mortality %	4.0	5.0
(e)	% of fledged young needed to replace the adults dying (2d/c)	14	19.5
(f)	Minimum % of young known to survive to breeding age	39	15

Thus, each year, a thousand pairs on the Isle of May will fledge 580 young and 226 will survive to breeding age. Of these, just 80 will be needed to replace the 4% annual loss of adults if the population is to remain stable. The surplus of 146 birds or 73 pairs means that the population should have increased by 73/1,000 or 7% per annum. (If the adult mortality is 5%, the rate of increase would be 6.3%.) In fact the increase has been about 22% per annum during the last decade. This would need every pair successfully to rear a chick or for young to survive even better than adults. Such is obviously not likely. Even if no adults die the population could increase by only 11% per annum. The increase has been partly due to immigration, and ringing has shown that it comes from the Farne Islands, just 100 km away. Ringing has also indicated that the Puffin population in east Scotland and north-east England is a fairly closed unit. In 1969 there were *c.*10,000 pairs, in 1974 *c.*17,000 pairs, and in 1979 *c.*24,000 pairs – an annual increase of 9%. Given the undoubted inaccuracies of some of the figures, this is a fair agreement with our calculated 7% and is probably as fast as any Puffin population can increase. The claim that auks need more than 50 years to double their population even under optimal conditions (Ohlendorf *et al* 1978) is obviously unrealistically pessimistic. The Skomer results are less clear. There was a deficit of 2.3 birds per 100 pairs each year, i.e. the population should have declined by 1% per annum. Such a slow decline would not have been detected; and the population appeared to be more-or-less stable.

The rate of decline of a population will depend on many things. If adult mortality is much higher than normal the decline will be rapid; if no young are produced for many years but the adults survive well the population will decline only slowly. The largest recorded seabird mortality was the death of 10 million guano birds in 1965 when a change of ocean currents (El Niño) resulted in the virtual disappearance of the anchovies which was their staple food. Then mile

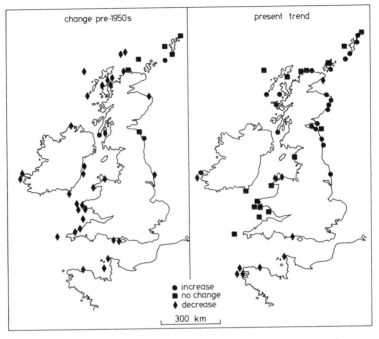

46   *Changes in the numbers of Puffins at some British, Irish and French colonies up to 1950 and at present. Some symbols are slightly offset for clarity.*

upon mile of beaches was knee-deep in dead birds. The only estimate of the rate of decline of a Puffin population comes from Skomer, where between 1920–60, numbers declined by 3.5% per annum (Birkhead and Ashcroft 1975). The colony on neighbouring Grassholm lost Puffins at a far faster rate as the numbers declined by a factor of 1,000 in 30 years – a loss of 20% per annum – but some of these birds may have gone elsewhere. We shall never know if the losses from Grassholm were gradual or dramatic, i.e. were caused by failure of breeding or death of adults. It is doubtful whether the death of all of these adults in a single disaster would have been noticed. Even today the well-organized surveys of dead birds washed up on the beaches of Europe find few of the hundred thousand or so British Puffins which must die each year.

TIMETABLE OF CHANGES

Only the most approximate timetable can be compiled to show when these declines in southern Puffin populations started or took place. Some colonies became extinct last century and others started declining in the 1890s. But the most dramatic changes occurred in the first half of the present century, as on Ailsa Craig 1910–34, Grassholm 1893–1928, St Tudwals 1922–51, St Kilda 1947–57, Rouzic 1912–60. The more southern colonies probably declined first and, with a few exceptions, lost the most birds. However, some Faeroese and Norwegian colonies also became noticeably smaller at this time. Recently, some declines have halted at least temporarily and there have been some notable increases, colonizations and re-settlements of previously empty areas. Again it is not possible to compile a timetable for the reversal of fortunes and most of our reasoning on the factors influencing the numbers of Puffins is based on the decline phase of the population fluctuations.

CAUSES OF THE DECLINES

There is no shortage of possibilities and many have been implicated in specific instances.

Man

It seems unlikely that man was directly responsible for many declines. Undoubtedly, he over-exploited colonies in the United States, Britain, Faeroes, Iceland, Greenland, and eliminated a few by digging out burrows or killing breeding adults, but several populations recovered when protection was given. The great decrease in numbers on St Kilda occurred at least ten years after the islanders stopped killing seabirds for food. Brun (1979) thought that birds shot and caught in fishing gear were the most serious factors influencing the numbers of auks in Norway, but the totals killed appear too small for this to be likely.

Pollution

It is difficult to be sure about the effects of oil pollution. Although major oiling incidents have had a serious effect on the Breton colonies, the few Puffins found oiled suggest that oiling is not a major cause of mortality. Similarly, the levels of toxic chemicals and heavy metals in adults and their eggs seem too low to depress either breeding or adult survival. Certainly, experimental work has shown that the current level of PCB is not important and is unlikely to influence populations. Many population declines took place before either oil or chemical pollution became widespread, which also suggests that these factors are not important.

Rats

Man has introduced rats to many islands and these pests are now common in several Puffin colonies. In many cases the introductions have occurred within the last 50–100 years and rats have been suggested as the probable or possible cause of the demise of Puffins on some of the Faeroe Islands and on Lundy, St Tudwals, Puffin Island (Anglesey), Ailsa Craig, Handa, Shiant Islands and others. Rats certainly eat numbers of eggs, and presumably small young, but the only evidence that they seriously affect the population is that some colonies on Vagar in the Faeroes increased after the rats were poisoned. Unfortunately, there is nothing to show that colonies without rats did not also increase at the same time. I found that only 40% of the Puffin eggs laid on the Shiant Islands produced fledged young, compared to 70–90% elsewhere in Britain. This was based on a single season and again there was no control; checking burrows might easily have scared the birds from the burrows, leaving the way open for the rats to get the unprotected eggs.

Rats are said to drive Puffins from earth burrows so that the birds seek refuge in rocks, or cliffs, as on the Great Stack of Handa. However, when a colony declines for any other cause, the surviving birds are usually found in boulder screes or cracks in cliffs, and colonizations of new areas often start in cliff sites. This suggests that rocks or cliffs are the preferred habitat when Puffins are at low density, rather than the outcome of predation by rats. It is hard to find a good word for the rat but in fairness we should note that several colonies (e.g. Great Saltee, Shiant Islands) where there are numbers of rats are no longer declining.

Gulls and skuas

Many seabirds have increased in numbers in the North Atlantic this century and some of these could well have an effect on the Puffin. Puffins are eaten by Great Black-backed Gulls and Great Skuas, but the total losses to predators are trivial in overall population terms and these particular predators are uncommon or virtually unknown at many Puffin colonies or feeding areas. The increases of Herring and Lesser Black-backed Gulls could have resulted in more Puffins having their fish stolen, but the most severe piracy recorded, on the Isle of May, was still insufficient to cause any serious effect on the breeding. Presumably Puffins on the Isle of May compensated by bringing more loads, which suggests that they had a good food supply nearby. Puffins sometimes compete with Manx Shearwaters for burrows, and with Razorbills and Black Guillemots for holes in boulder scree, while Fulmars and gulls sometimes build their nests in the entrances to Puffin burrows, but these are purely local and small scale problems. We are completely ignorant as to how these various seabirds share the food resources of the sea but there is no evidence at present that they seriously compete. Anyway, the Puffin has its own particular food preferences and expertise and should be able to hold its own in most situations.

Rabbits and sheep

Mammals have few or no adverse effects on Puffin populations although adults are sometimes killed by foxes, mink and cats.

Rabbits and Puffins occur together in many places, and rabbits start burrows in places where Puffins have difficulty in getting through the turf. These short burrows are then taken over by Puffins. The introduction of sheep onto a densely-burrowed Puffin colony causes widespread collapse of burrows but colonies which have been grazed for many years are remarkably stable (compare Plates 2 and 3). The beneficial results of grazing can be seen where grazed and ungrazed colonies occur side by side. In the former, the burrows are deep and long, and each nest-chamber has a solid roof of closely matted grass roots. In non-grazed areas burrows are short, shallow and easily collapsed as the dominant plants tend to be succulents, such as sorrel, which make for fragile roofs.

CHANGES IN THE MARINE ENVIRONMENT

The declines in numbers were widespread and various possible causes have been suggested above. In many cases they provide credible explanations but in other instances there is no obvious cause for a decline. All of which suggests that we should be looking for a common factor acting throughout the area where declines have occurred, while admitting that rats, oil, gulls, etc, might modify and almost certainly would worsen the impact in specific colonies. The declines spanned perhaps 50 years, which further suggests that the cause was subtle and acted slowly over a long period, rather than that it brought about spectacular disasters.

The most probable factor influencing the numbers of Puffins and other seabirds is food. In several of the winter 'wrecks' the full-grown birds were emaciated even though the weather had not been exceptionally harsh. There are several records of large numbers of Puffin chicks dying of starvation in Britain and very few young have been reared on the Lofoten Islands in recent years. Even when young are reared, as on St Kilda, chicks are sometimes underweight, and in many places, such as Skomer, Great Island and St Kilda, they benefit from supplementary food.

Even if we assume that food shortages were responsible for decline in Puffin numbers, we are still left with the question, what has caused the changes in the food supply? The distribution and abundance of fish are controlled by oceanographic conditions, probably modified by man's fishing activities, but the relationships are extremely complex and far from understood. However, the temperature of the sea certainly has a major effect on where various marine animals are found. Is there any recent change in the marine environment which could account for the reversal of the Puffin's fortune? Many pelagic organisms in the north-east Atlantic and the North Sea underwent a marked change of distribution in the mid 1960s probably due to a climatic shift (Coombs 1975, Dickson and Lee 1972). This affected fish stocks, e.g., a decline in the water temperature between March and May in the 1960s also resulted in improved survival of young North Sea cod (Dickson *et al* 1975). Any change in sea temperature is likely to influence the food of Puffins.

There appears to have been a slight but general warming up of the water in the North Atlantic during the early part of this century. This had several obvious ecological effects, such as the colonization of west Greenland seas by cod, and the retreat northwards of the beluga or white whale and capelin (Beverton and Lee 1965). To judge from sea surface temperatures off Plymouth, British seas were warming up this century until the 1940s, then temperatures stabilized in the 1950s and have cooled slowly since. The present decline in water temperature is predicted to continue until 1990.

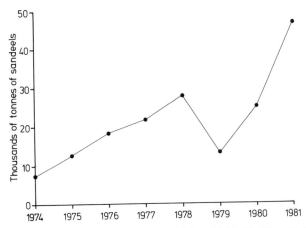

47   *Annual landings of sandeels in the Shetland fishery 1974–81. (From Bailey 1983)*

The Puffin and Guillemot are cold water species which have the southern edges of their ranges in Britain, Ireland and France, although some few and declining numbers of Guillemots also nest on islands west of Iberia. Such populations are likely to be susceptible to small changes in their environment. It will be interesting to see whether the North Atlantic continues to become colder and if the populations of Puffins and Guillemots continue to increase. However, 'It is deceptively easy to deduce casual connection between two sets of fluctuating data, especially when their reliability and true relationship, if any, are unknown. Attempts to trace the biological effects of climatic trends are peculiarly susceptible to this pitfall' (Beverton and Lee 1965). At the very least we need better monitoring of seabird numbers, their food requirements and an understanding of their population dynamics, before we can hope to link population trends with changes in sea temperature or anything else, except at a circumstantial level. It will be extremely difficult to separate truly natural changes in the environment, about which we can do nothing, from those like pollution, over which we have some slight control, if the numbers of any seabirds seriously decline.

INDUSTRIAL FISHING

There is one serious threat to the Puffin and other seabirds which eat sandeels, capelin and other small fish. This is the continuing rapid expansion of 'industrial' fishing of these fish for processing into fish meal. An average of 1.5 million tonnes of small fish was taken per annum by industrial fishing fleets working in the North Sea 1975–80 (Bailey 1983). The main species 'preyed' on by fishing boats were formerly herring and mackerel but are now Norway pout, sandeels, and sprats. All these are important foods of seabirds. At present sandeels form the largest proportion of the fish caught by these boats. In

Shetland, the catch is increasing at a spectacular rate (Fig. 47). Often it is the capacity of the factories to process the fish which limits the catch, and it is planned to double the capacity of some factories between 1982 and 1983. It is not difficult to see that this rate of increase cannot be sustained without some adverse effect. Will it be the fish stocks, seabirds or the fishing industry which suffers? Possibly it will be all three.

Over-exploitation of herring and capelin are thought to be responsible for the extremely poor breeding success of Puffins in Norway and Newfoundland respectively (Lid 1980, Brown and Nettleship 1983). Man's record of management of stocks of fish is so bad that it is not being over-pessimistic to assume that he will seriously deplete, or possibly even destroy, these fish stocks. This would have a most serious effect on the numbers of the larger commercial 'food' fish, and on whales and seabirds. Adult Puffins can presumably change their diet but all the evidence points to their doing best when they have access to oil rich fish. Thus, although British Puffins might change from the preferred sandeels, sprats and herring (all subject to heavy fishing) to the numerous other small fish such as haddock and whiting, they would have difficulty in rearing young successfully. It is difficult to see what Canadian Puffins could feed to their young if they should lose their capelin.

CONCLUSION

Many factors influence the numbers of Puffins and the fortunes of colonies and populations. At specific sites, man, rats, pollution and many other factors can be linked with declines in numbers. At other places there is no obvious reason for past declines. All the available evidence suggests that these declines were natural and brought about by changes in sea conditions. Such declines in numbers are distressing to humans but there is little we can do about them even if we decide that we should. It seems part of human nature to be pessimistic and to have a morbid interest in disasters. An aura of doom and despondency enshrouds the Puffin as though its days are numbered. Of course we should be concerned about oiling and other pollution, overfishing and the troubles of Lofoten Puffins when year after year they fail to rear young. However, I am optimistic about the Puffin's future and the general state of Puffindom is far better than at any time this century.

APPENDIX A

Scientific names of birds and mammals mentioned in the text

Birds:

Fulmar *Fulmarus glacialis*
Cory's Shearwater *Calonectris diomedea*
Manx Shearwater *Puffinus puffinus*
Audubon's Shearwater *P. therminieri*
Storm Petrel *Hydrobates pelagicus*
Leach's Petrel *Oceanodroma leucorrhoa*
Common Diving-Petrel *Pelecanoides urinatrix*
Peruvian Diving-Petrel *P. garnoti*
Gannet *Sula bassana*
Cormorant *Phalacrocorax carbo*
Shag *Phalacrocorax aristotelis*
Eider *Somateria mollissima*
Shelduck *Tadorna tadorna*
Sea Eagle *Haliaeetus albicilla*
Common Buzzard *Buteo buteo*
Rough-legged Buzzard *B. lagopus*
Gyr Falcon *Falco rusticolus*
Peregrine *F. peregrinus*
Great Skua *Stercorarius skua*
Arctic Skua *S. parasiticus*
Common Gull *Larus canus*
Herring Gull *L. argentatus*
Lesser Black-backed Gull *L. fuscus*
Great Black-backed Gull *L. marinus*
Glaucous Gull *L. hyberboreus*
Black-headed Gull *L. ridibundus*

Kittiwake *Rissa tridactyla*
Common Tern *Sterna hirundo*
Arctic Tern *S. paradisaea*
Roseate Tern *S. dougallii*
Little Tern *S. albifrons*
Snowy Owl *Nyctea scandiaca*
Short-eared Owl *Asio flammeus*
Magpie *Pica pica*
Jackdaw *Corvus monedula*
Carrion/Hooded Crow *C. corone*
Raven *C. corax*

Names of auks are given on p. 23

Mammals:

Hedgehog *Erinaceus europaeus*
Rabbit *Oryctolagus cuniculus*
Black Rat *Rattus rattus*
Brown Rat *R. norvegicus*
Red Fox *Vulpes vulpes*
Arctic Fox *Alopex lagopus*
Otter *Lutra lutra*
Mink *Mustela vision*
Wild Cat *Felix silvestris*
Grey Seal *Halichoerus grypus*
Beluga *Delphinapterus leucas*

APPENDIX B

Sources of counts or estimates used in distribution sections

Scotland
North Rona and Sula Sgeir (Evans 1978), Eilean Mor (S. Murray), Haskeir (D. M. Bryant), Shiant Islands (Brooke 1972b), Mingulay (Sergeant and Whidborne 1951, N. Deely), Berneray (Diamond *et al* 1965), Barra (Bunyard 1922), Rhum (J. Love), Canna (R. L. Swann and A. D. K. Ramsay, Carrick and Waterston 1939), Small Isles (Evans and Flower 1967), Treshnish Islands (C. P. Andrews), Ailsa Craig (Gibson 1951, 1970), Sanda (Borland and Walls 1951), Clo Mor (Pennie 1951), Shetland (Harris 1976b, Venables and Venables 1955), Foula (Furness 1978b), Fair Isle (Williamson 1965), Forth Islands (Baxter and Rintoul 1953, Smith 1961, Scottish Bird Reports), Sule Skerry (Blackburn and Budworth 1976–82, Stark 1967).

England
Farne Islands (Watt 1951, Northumberland Natural History Society, M. Hornung), Coquet Island (J. C. Coulson, RSPB), Bempton (Chislet 1953, RSPB), Dorset (W. T. Hayson, Portland Bird Observatory), Lundy (Perry 1946, Davis 1954, Lundy Field Society Reports), Cornwall (Cornish Bird Report), Grassholm (Lockley 1953), Skomer (Buxton and Lockley 1950, Birkhead and Ashcroft 1975, West Wales Naturalist Trust), Skokholm (Lockley 1953, Dickinson 1958, WWNT), Cardigan Island (Ingram *et al* 1966, P. Davis), Worms Head (Gower Bird Report), Puffin Island (Goldsmith 1774, R. W. Arnold), Ynysgwlan (Bannerman 1963, M. Hornung), South Stack (RSPB), Ormes (Hope Jones and Dare 1976), Cumbria (R. Stokoe).

Isle of Man
Cullen and Slinn 1975, Manx Bird Report.

Ireland
Inishtearaght (Evans and Lovegrove 1974, Kelly and Walton 1977), Great Blasket (Munns 1956), Illanmaster (Irish Bird Report), Bills Rock (Fitter 1940, Cabot 1967), Rathlin (RSPB), Lambay Island and Ireland's Eye (Patterson 1907, Lockley 1953), Puffin Island (H. Brazier).

Sweden
Salomonsen (1944), A. Andersson.

Heligoland
Gatke (1895).

France
E. Pasquet, Guermeur and Monnat (1980), Pénicaud (1979).

Channel Islands
Smith (1879), Potter (1971), M. Hill, R. Long, R. Burrow.

Faeroe Islands
E. Mortensen.

Iceland
A. Petersen (1982), Lockley (1953), M. Sharp.

Norway
Kjør (S. Eldøy), Hengsøy (Holgersen 1950), other Rogaland Islands (S. Eldøy), Utvaer and Nord-Vagsøy (Willgohs 1955), Froan (N. Røv), Heimø (N. Røv), Lovunden (Myrberget 1959), Fugløyi Gildeskål (K-B. Strann), Røst (Brun 1966, 1979), Sør-Fugløy (K. Felsted), Nord-Fugløy (Seligan and Willcox 1940, Brun 1963), Kongsøy (J. Grastveit), Hornøy and Reinøy (R. Barrett), Sklinna (N. Røv), Anda (R. Barrett).

Russia
Norderhaug *et al* (1977), Uspenskii (1958).

West Atlantic
D. N. Nettleship, A. R. Lock, Brown *et al* (1975), Chapdelaine (1980), Nettleship and Lock (1973), Ouellet (1969), Gaboriault (1961), Korschgen (1979), Cameron (1967), Peters and Burleigh (1951).

References

Aikman, E. F. 1958. Auks in the north Atlantic. *Sea Swallow* 11: 31–3.
Albon, S. 1974. Observations on the food and feeding behaviour of the great skua. Univ. East Anglia Expedition 1973/4: 23–6.
Arnason, E. and Grant, P. R. 1978. The significance of kleptoparasitism during the breeding season in a colony of Arctic Skuas *Stercorarius parasiticus* in Iceland. *Ibis* 120: 38–54.
Asbirk, S. 1979. Some behaviour patterns of the Black Guillemot. *Dansk. orn. Foren Tiddsskr.* 73: 287–96.
Ashcroft, R. E. 1976. *Breeding, biology and survival of Puffins.* D. Phil thesis, Oxford.
Ashcroft, R. E. 1979. Survival rates and breeding biology of puffins on Skomer Island, Wales. *Ornis Scand.* 10: 100–10.
Bailey, R. S. 1983. The sandeel fisheries. *Fishery Prospects.* 37–41.
Bannerman, D. A. 1963. *The Birds of the British Isles*, Vol. 12. Oliver and Boyd, Edinburgh.
Bannerman, D. A. 1963. *Birds of the Atlantic Islands*, Vol. 1. Oliver and Boyd, Edinburgh.
Bannerman, D. A. and Bannerman, W. M. 1965–68. *Birds of the Atlantic Islands*, Vols. 2–4. Oliver and Boyd, Edinburgh.
Bannerman, D. A. and Vella-Gaffiero, J. A. 1976. *Birds of the Maltese Archipelago.* Museums Dept., Valletta.
Barrett, R. T. 1979. Small oil spill kills 10–20,000 seabirds in north Norway. *Mar. Pollut. Bull.* 10: 253–5.
Baxter, E. V. and Rintoul, L. J. 1916. Report on Scottish ornithology in 1915. *Scott. Nat.* 1916: 164.
Baxter, E. V. and Rintoul, L. J. 1953. *The Birds of Scotland.* Oliver and Boyd, Edinburgh.
Bédard, J. 1969. Adaptive radiation in Alcidae. *Ibis.* 111: 189–98.
Belopol'skii, L. O. 1961. *Ecology of sea colony birds of the Barents Sea.* Moscow, trs Israel program for Scientific translations.
Bennett, G. R. 1960. Rubber bands in Puffin's stomach. *Br. Birds* 53: 222.
Berland, B. 1971. Pigghå og lundefugl med gummistrikk. *Fauna* 24: 35–7.
Beverton, R. J. H. and Lee, A. J. 1965. Hydrographic fluctuations in the North Atlantic Ocean and some biological consequences. *Symp. Inst. of Biology* 14: 79–107.
Birkhead, T. R. 1977. The effects of habitat and density on breeding success in the Common Guillemot (*Uria aalge*). *J. Anim. Ecol.* 46: 751–64.
Birkhead, T. R. and Ashcroft, R. E. 1975. Auk numbers on Skomer. *Nature in Wales* 14: 222–33.
Birkhead, T. R. and Taylor, A. M. 1977. Moult of the Guillemot (*Uria aalge*). *Ibis* 119: 80–5.
Birnie, G. W. V. 1972. A census of puffins (*Fratercula arctica*) on Hirta and Dun (St Kilda), July, 1969. Unpubl.
Blackburn, A. and Budworth, D. 1976–82. An ornithological survey of Sule Skerry. *Seabird Report* 5: 27–33. Also unpublished updates.
Boddington, D. 1960. Unusual mortality of young puffins on St Kilda, 1959. *Scott. Birds* 1: 218–20.
Borland, J. F. and Walls, F. D. E. 1951. Notes on the birds of Sanda Island. *Scott. Nat.* 63: 178–82.
Bourne, W. R. P. 1976a. The mass mortality of common murres in the Irish Sea in 1969. *J. Wildl. Manage.* 40: 789–92.
Bourne, W. R. P. 1976b. Seabirds and pollution in Johnston, R. (ed), *Marine Pollution.* Academic Press, London.
Boyd, J. M., Tewnion, A. and Wallace, D. I. M. 1957. The birds of St Kilda, mid-summer 1956. *Scott. Nat.* 69: 94–112.
Brëhm, C. L. 1831. *Handbuch der Naturgeschite aller Vögel Deutschlands.* Ilmenau.
Brooke, M. de L. 1972a. Population estimates for Puffins on Soay and Boreray and assessment of the rate of predation by gulls. *Brathay Exploration Group Report*, 1971: 4–13.
Brooke, M. de L. 1972b. The Puffin populations of the Shiant Islands. *Bird Study* 19: 1–6.
Brooke, M. de L. 1978. The dispersal of female Manx Shearwaters *Puffinus puffinus*. *Ibis* 120: 545–51.

Brown, R. G. B. and Nettleship, D. N. 1984. Capelin and seabirds in the northwest Atlantic. In *Marine birds: their feeding ecology and commercial fisheries relationships.* Canadian Wildlife Service Ottawa.

Brown, R. G. B., Gillespie, D. I., Lock, A. R., Pearce, P. A. and Watson, G. H. 1973. Bird mortality from oil slicks off eastern Canada, February–April 1970. *Can. Fld. Nat.* 87: 225–34.

Brown, R. G. B., Nettleship, D. N., Germain, P., Tull, C. E. and Davis, T. 1975. *Atlas of Eastern Canadian Seabirds.* Canadian Wildlife Service, Ottawa.

Brun, E. 1963. Ornithological features of North-Fugløy and Sør-Fugløy. *Astarte* 22: 1–13.

Brun, E. 1966. Hekkebestanden av lunde *Fratercula arctica* i Norge. *Sterna* 7: 1–17.

Brun, E. 1971. Census of Puffins (*Fratercula arctica*) on Nord-Fugløy, Troms. *Astarte* 4: 41–5.

Brun, E. 1979. Present status and trends in population of seabirds in Norway, in Bartonek, J. C. and Nettleship, D. N. (eds), *Conservation of Marine Birds of Northern North America.* Fish and Wildlife Service, Washington.

Bull, K. R., Murton, R. K., Osborn, D., Ward, P. and Cheng, L. 1977. High levels of cadmium in Atlantic seabirds and sea-skaters. *Nature* 269: 507–9.

Bunyard, P. F. 1922. On the eggs of the Puffin *Fratercula arctica. Ibis* 4: 256–8.

Bureau, L. 1877. De la mue du bec et des ornements palpebraux. *Bull. Soc. Zool. France* 2: 377–99.

Bureau, L. 1879. Sur la mue du bec des oiseaux de la famille des mormonides. *Bull. Soc. Zool. France* 4: 1–4.

Buxton, J. and Lockley, R. M. 1950. *Island of Skomer.* Staples, London.

Cabot, D. 1967. The birds of Bills Rocks, Co. Mayo. *Ir. Nat. J.* 15: 359–61.

Cameron, A. W. 1967. Birds of the St Pierre et Miquelon Archipelago. *Nat. Can. (Que.)* 94 389–420.

Carrick, R. and Waterston, G. 1939. The birds of Canna. *Scott. Nat.* 1939: 5–22.

Chapdelaine, G. 1980. Onzième inventaire et analyse des fluctuations des populations d'oiseaux marins dans les refuges de la côte nord du Golfe Saint Laurent, *Canad. Field-Nat.* 94: 34–42.

Chipman, J. K. and Walker, C. H. 1979. The metabolism of dieldrin and two of its analogues *Biochem. Pharm.* 28: 1337–45.

Chislett, R. 1953. *Yorkshire Birds* Brown, London.

Clarke, W. E. 1912. *Studies of Bird Migration.* Gurney and Jackson, London.

Collett, R. 1921. *Norges fugle* Vol. 3. Kristiania.

Conder, P. J. 1950. On the courtship and social displays of three species of auk. *Br. Birds.* 43: 65–9.

Coombs, S. H. 1975. Continuous plankton records show fluctuations in larval fish abundance during 1948–72. *Nature* 258: 134–6.

Corkhill, P. 1972. Measurements of Puffins as criteria of sex and age. *Bird Study* 19: 193–201.

Corkhill, P. 1973. Food and feeding ecology of Puffins. *Bird Study* 20: 207–20.

Cott, H. B. 1951–54. The palatability of the eggs of birds. *Proc. Zool. Soc. Lond.* 121: 1–41, 122 1–54, 124: 335–463.

Coues, E. 1868. A monograph of the Alcidae. *Proc. Acad. Nat. Sci. Philad.* 20: 2–81.

Coulson, J. C. 1957. The effect of age on the breeding ecology of the Kittiwake *Rissa tridactyla. Ibis* 100: 40–51.

Coulson, J. C. 1968. Differences in the quality of birds nesting in the centre and on the edges of colonies. *Nature* 217: 478–9.

Coulson, J. C., Potts, G. R., Deans, I. R. and Fraser, S. M. 1968. Exceptional mortality of Shags and other seabirds caused by paralytic shellfish poison. *Br. Birds* 61: 381–404.

Cramp, S., Bourne, W. R. P. and Saunders, D. 1974. *The Seabirds of Britain and Ireland.* Collins London.

Cramp, S. and Simmons, K. E. L. (eds) in press. *The Birds of the Western Palearctic, Vol. 4.* Oxford University Press.

Cullen, J. P. and Slinn, D. J. 1975. *The Birds of the Isle of Man.* Manx Mus. and National Trust Douglas.

Dacker, H. 1948. Mortality of birds in Scotland in the cold weather of January–March, 1947. *Scott Nat.* 60: 171–6.

Danchin, E. 1983. La posture de post-atterrissage chez le macareux moine (*Fratercula arctica*). *Biol of Behav.* 8: 3–10.

Darling, F. F. 1947. *Highlands and Islands*, Collins, London.

Davis, P. 1954. *A list of the Birds of Lundy.* Lundy Field Society, Exeter.

Dement'ev, G. P., Meklenburtsev, R. N., Sudilovskaya, A. M. and Spangenberg, E. P. 1951–4. *The Birds of the Soviet Union.* Israel Program for Scientific translations, Jerusalem.
Diamond, A. W., Douthwaite, R. J. and Indge, W. J. E. 1965. Notes on the birds of Berneray, Mingulay and Pabbay. *Scott. Birds* 3: 397–404.
Dickinson, H. 1958. Puffins and burrows. *Skokholm Bird Observatory Report* 1958: 27–34.
Dickson, R. R. and Lee, A. 1972. Recent hydro-meteorological trends on the North Atlantic fishing grounds. *Fish Industry* 2: 4–11.
Dickson, R. R., Lamb, H. H., Malmberg, S. A. and Colebrook, J. M. 1975. Climatic reversal in northern North Atlantic. *Nature* 256: 479–81.
Dixon, C. 1896. *British Sea Birds.* Bliss, Sands and Foster, London.
Dobson, R. 1952. *The Birds of the Channel Islands.* Staples, London.
Drane, R. 1894. Natural history notes from Grassholm. *Cardiff Nat. Soc. Trans.* 26: 1–13.
Duncan, N., Taylor, K., Wanless, S. and Wood, V. 1982. The birds of Boreray. *Seabird Report* 1977–81: 18–25.
Duncombe, F. and Reille, A. 1980. Expérience de transplantation de macareux. *Le Courier de la Nature* 1980: 13–7.
Eggeling, W. J. 1960. *The Isle of May.* Oliver and Boyd, London.
Elliott, J. S. 1895. Observations on the fauna of St Kilda. *Zoologist* 19: 218–86.
Evans, A. H. and Buckley, T. E. 1899. *A Vertebrate Fauna of the Shetland Islands.* Douglas, Edinburgh.
Evans, P. G. H. 1975. Gulls and puffins on North Rona. *Bird Study* 22: 239–47.
Evans, P. G. H. 1978. The birds of North Rona and Sula Sgeir *Hebridean Nat.* 1978: 21–36.
Evans, P. G. H. and Lovegrove, R. R. 1974. The birds of the South West Irish Islands. *Ir. Bird. Rep.* 1973: 33–64.
Evans, P. R. and Flower, W. U. 1967. The birds of the Small Isles. *Scott. Birds.* 4: 404–45.
Fisher, J. 1947. St Kilda, 1947. *Bull. Brit. Orn. Club* 68: 66–71.
Fitter, F. S. R. 1940. Notes on the birds of Achill Island and Bill Rock, Co. Mayo. *Br. Birds* 34: 133–4.
Flegg, J. J. M. 1972. The Puffin on St Kilda, 1969–71. *Bird Study* 19: 7–17.
Forrest, H. E. 1907. *The Vertebrate Fauna of North Wales.* Witherby, London.
Furness, R. W. 1977. Studies on the breeding biology and population dynamics of the Great Skua (*Catharacta skua Brünnich*). Ph. D. thesis, Durham.
Furness, R. W. 1978. Kleptoparasitism by Great Skua (*Catharacta skua* Brünn) and Arctic Skua (*Stercorarius parasiticus* L.). *Anim. Behav.* 26: 1167–77.
Furness, R. W. 1981. Seabird populations of Foula *Scott. Birds* 11: 237–53.
Gaboriault, W. 1961. Les oiseaux aux Iles-de-la-Madeleine. *Nat. Can. (Que.)* 88: 166–224.
Galliard, L. O. 1875. Letter to Editor. *Ibis* 5: 267–9.
Gaston, A. J. and Malone, M. 1980. Range extension of Puffin and Razorbill in Hudson Strait. *Canad. Field-Nat.* 94: 328–9.
Gatke, H. 1895. *Heligoland as an Ornithological Observatory.* Douglas, Edinburgh.
Gerasimova, T. D. 1961. (Results of counts of colonial seabirds and Eider on the Murmansk Coast). *Vop Organ i Melody Ilcheta Res. Fauny Razemnykh Posvovochrykh Moscow.* 118–9.
Gibson, J. A. 1951. The breeding distribution, population and history of the birds of Ailsa Craig. *Scott. Nat.* 63: 73–100.
Gibson, J. A. 1970. Population studies of Clyde Seabirds. *Trans. Buteshire Nat. Hist. Soc.* 8: 21–30.
Gibson-Hill, C. A. 1948. Sociable little birds. *The Field* 1948: 490.
Gill, R. and Sanger, G. A. 1979. Tufted Puffins nesting in estuarine habitat. *Auk* 96: 792–4.
Goldsmith, O. 1774. *A History of the Earth and Animated Nature.* Nourse, London.
Grant, P. R. 1971. Interactive behaviour of Puffins and Skuas. *Behav.* 40: 263–281.
Gray, R. 1871. *The Birds of the West of Scotland.* Murray, Glasgow.
Gray, R. and Anderson, T. 1869. *The Birds of Ayrshire and Wigtownshire.* Murray, Glasgow.
Greenwood, J. J. D., Donally, R. J., Feare, C. J., Gordon, N. J. and Waterston, G. 1971. A massive wreck of oiled birds: north-east Britain, winter 1970. *Scott. Birds* 6: 235–50.
Gudmundsson, F. 1953. Islenzkír fuglar V. Lundi (*Fratercula arctica* L.). *Natturufraedingurinn* 23: 43–6.
Guermeur, Y. and Monnat, J-Y. 1980. *Histoire et geographie des oiseaux nicheurs de Bretagne.* ed. Appege. Clermont-Ferrand.

Haftorn, S. 1971. *Norges Fugler.* Universit., Oslo.

Harris, M. P. 1969. Food as a factor controlling the breeding of *Puffinus lherminieri. Ibis* 111: 139–56.

Harris, M. P. 1970. Differences in the diet of British auks. *Ibis* 112: 540–1.

Harris, M. P. 1976a. The present status of the Puffin in Britain and Ireland. *Br. Birds* 69: 239–64.

Harris, M. P. 1976b. The seabirds of Shetland in 1974. *Scott. Birds* 9: 37–68.

Harris, M. P. 1976c. Lack of a 'desertion period' in the nestling life of the Puffin *Fratercula arctica. Ibis* 118: 115–8.

Harris, M. P. 1977. Puffins on the Isle of May. *Scott. Birds* 9: 285–90.

Harris, M. P. 1978. Supplementary feeding of young puffins *Fratercula arctica. J. Anim. Ecol.* 47: 15–23.

Harris, M. P. 1979. Measurements and weights of British Puffins. *Bird Study* 26: 179–86.

Harris, M. P. 1980. Breeding performance of puffins *Fratercula arctica* in relation to nest density, laying date and year. *Ibis* 122: 193–209.

Harris, M. P. 1981. Age determination and first breeding of British Puffins. *Br. Birds* 74: 246–56.

Harris, M. P. 1982a. The breeding seasons of British Puffins. *Scott. Birds* 12: 11–7.

Harris, M. P. 1982b. Seasonal variation in fledging weight of the Puffin *Fratercula arctica. Ibis* 124: 100–3.

Harris, M. P. 1983a. Biology and survival of the immature Puffin, *Fratercula arctica.* Ibis 125: 56–73.

Harris, M. P. 1983b. Parent-young communication in the Puffin. *Fratercula arctica. Ibis* 125: 109–114.

Harris, M. P. and Hislop, J. R. G. 1978. The food of young puffins *Fratercula arctica. J. Zool. Lond.* 185: 213–36.

Harris, M. P. and Murray, S. 1977. Puffins on St Kilda. *Br. Birds* 70: 50–65.

Harris, M. P. and Murray, S. 1978. *Birds of St Kilda.* Institute of Terrestrial Ecology, Cambridge.

Harris, M. P. and Murray, S. 1981. Monitoring Puffin numbers at Scottish colonies. *Bird Study* 28: 15–20.

Harris, M. P. and Osborn, D. 1981. Effect of a polychlorinated biphenyl on the survival and breeding of Puffins. *J. appl. Ecol.* 18: 471–9.

Harris, M. P. and Wanless, S. 1984. The effects of the wreck of seabirds in February 1983 on auk populations on the Isle of May. *Bird Study* 31:

Harris, M. P. and Yule, R. F. 1977. The moult of the Puffin *Fratercula arctica. Ibis* 119: 535–41.

Hartert, E. 1917. A note on the British Puffin. *Br. Birds* 11: 163–6, 235–7.

Harvie-Brown, J. A. 1887. The Isle of May: its faunal position and bird-life. *Proceeds roy. phys. soc. Edinb.* 9: 303–25.

Harvie-Brown, J. A. and Buckley, T. E. 1887. *A Vertebrate Fauna of Sutherland, Caithness and West Cromarty.* Douglas, Edinburgh.

Harvie-Brown, J. A. and Buckley, T. E. 1888. *A Vertebrate Fauna of the Outer Hebrides,* Douglas, Edinburgh.

Harvie-Brown, J. A. and Buckley, T. E. 1892. *A Vertebrate Fauna of Argyll and the Inner Hebrides.* Douglas, Edinburgh.

Harvie-Brown, J. A. and Buckley, T. E. 1895. *A Fauna of the Moray Basin.* Douglas, Edinburgh.

Harvie-Brown, J. A. and Macpherson, H. A. 1904. *A Vertebrate Fauna of the north-west Highlands and Skye.* Douglas, Edinburgh.

Hislop, J. R. G. and Harris, M. P. 1984. Recent changes in the food of young Puffins *Fratercula arctica* on the Isle of May in relation to fish stocks. *Ibis* 126:

Holdgate, M. W. 1971. The seabird wreck in the Irish Sea, autumn 1969. *N.E.R.C. Ser. C.* 4: 1–17.

Holgersen, H. 1950. Seabird studies in Rogaland 1949–50. *Stavanger Mus. Årb* 1950: 61–76.

Holt, G., Frøslie, A. and Norheim, G. 1979. Mercury, DDE and PCB in the avian fauna in Norway 1965–76. *Acta Vet. Scand. Sup.* 70: 1–28.

Hornung, M. 1976. Soil erosion on the Farne Islands. Institute of Terrestrial Ecology Annual Report for 1975: 57–61.

Hornung, M. 1981. Burrow excavation and infill in the Farne Island puffin colony. *Trans. Nat. Hist. Soc. Northumb.* 43: 45–54.

Hornung, M. in press. Burrow dimensions and architecture in the Farne Island puffin colony. *Trans. Nat. Hist. Soc. Northumb.*

Hornung, M. and Harris, M. P. 1976. Soil water levels and delayed egg-laying of puffins. *Br. Birds* 69: 402–8.

Hortling, I. 1929. *Ornithologisk Hanbok*, Hortling, Helsingfors.

Hudson, P. J. 1979a. The parent-chick feeding relationship of the puffin, *Fratercula arctica. J. Anim. Ecol.* 48: 889–98.

Hudson, P. J. 1979b. Survival rates and behaviour of British auks. D. Phil. thesis, Oxford.

Hudson, P. J. 1983. The variation and synchronization of daily weight increments of Puffin chicks *Fratercula arctica. Ibis* 125: 557–61.

Hughes, M. R. 1970. Some observations on ion and water balance in the Puffin, *Fratercula arctica. Can. J. Zool.*, 48: 479–82.

Ingram, G. C., Salmon, H. M. and Condry, W. M. 1966. *Birds of Cardiganshire*, West Wales Naturalists' Trust, Haverfordwest.

Jackson, E. E. 1966. Birds of Foula. *Scott. Birds.* 4: suppl.

Joensen, A. H. and Preuss, N. O. 1972. Report on the ornithological expeditions to northwest Greenland 1965. *Meddel. Grønland* 191: 1–57.

Jones, P. Hope 1980. Beached birds at selected Orkney beaches 1976–8. *Scott. Birds* 11: 1–12.

Jones, P. Hope and Dare, P. J. 1976. *Birds of Caernarvonshire.* Cambrian Ornithological Society, Llandudno Junction.

Jones, P. Hope, Howells, G., Rees, E. I. S. and Wilson, J. 1970. Effect of 'Hamilton Trader' oil on birds in the Irish Sea in May 1969. *Br. Birds* 63: 97–110.

Jones, P. Hope, Monnat, J-Y., Cadbury, C. J. and Stowe, T. J. 1978. Birds oiled during the Amoco Cadiz Incident. *Mar. Pollut. Bull.* 9: 307–10.

Jones, R. and Hislop, J. R. G. 1978. Further observations on the relation between food intake and growth of gadoids in captivity. *J. Cons. int. Explor. Mer.* 38: 244–51.

Jordan, R. and Fuentes, H. 1966. Las poblaciones de aves guaneras y su situacion actual. *Instituto del Mar del Peru:* no. 10.

Kaftanovskii, Y. M. 1941. Comparative characteristics of the breeding biology of some alciformes. *Sen'Ostrovov Glav Uprav. po Zapoved* 1941: 53–72, trs British Library.

Kaftanovskii, Y. M. 1951. Alcidine birds of the East Atlantic. *Mater. Pozn. Fauny Flory SSR. Zool.* 28: 1–170.

Kartaskew, N. N. 1960. *Die Alkenvögel des Nordatlantiks* Ziemsen, Wittenberg Lutherstadt.

Kearton, R. 1906. *With Nature and a Camera.* Cassell, London.

Kelly, T. C. and Walton, G. A. 1977. The auk population crash of 1968–69 on Inishtearaght – a review. *Ir. Birds* 1: 16–36.

Kolsrud, K. 1976. Lundefangst, *Norveg. J. Ethol.* 19: 1–97.

Korneyeva, T. M. 1967. On the reproduction of the puffin on the Ainov Islands. *Forest Industry* (Moscow): 178–84.

Korschgen, C. E. 1979. Coastal water-bird colonies: Maine. *U.S. Fish and Wildlife Service Report* FWS/OBS-79/09.

Korte, J. de, 1972. Netherlands Spitsbergen Expedition *Beaufortia* 20: 23–55.

Kozlova, E. V. 1957. Fauna of USSR, birds. *Acad. Sci. USSR* Moscow, trs. Israel Program for Scientific translation.

Kress, S. W. 1977. Establishing Atlantic Puffins at a former breeding site, in Temple, S.A. (ed), *Endangered birds: management techniques for preserving threatened species.* Univ. of Wisconsin Press.

Kress, S. W. 1978–82. *Egg Rock Up-date.* Nat. Audubon Soc., Ithaca.

Lack, D. 1954. *The Natural Regulation of Animal numbers.* Clarendon Press, Oxford.

Lees, D. R. 1982. Kleptoparasitism by Herring and Lesser Black-backed Gulls on Puffins. *Skomer and Skokholm Bull.* 4: 9.

Lid, G. 1981. Reproduction of the Puffin on Røst in the Lofoten Islands in 1964–1980. *Fauna. Norv. Ser. C. Cinclus* 4: 30–9.

Lid, G., Bentz, P-G. and Michaelson, J. 1979. *Foreløpig rapport om Røstprosjeket* 1979. Zool. Mus. Oslo.

Lloyd, C. S. 1972. Attendance at auk colonies during the breeding season. *Skokholm Bird Observatory Report* 1972: 15–23.

Lloyd, C. S. 1976. Bird kill. *Birds* 6: 23.

Lloyd, C. S. 1982. The seabirds of Great Saltee. *Irish Birds* 2: 1–37.

Lloyd, C., Bogan, J. A., Bourne, W. R. P., Dawson, P. and Parslow, J. L. F. 1974. Seabird mortality in the north Irish Sea and Firth of Clyde early in 1974. Mar. Polln. Bull. 5: 136–40.

Lockley, R. M. 1934. On the breeding-habits of the Puffin: with special reference to the incubation- and fledging-period. *Br. Birds* 27: 214–23.

Lockley, R. M. 1938. *I Know an Island.* Harrap, London.
Lockley, R. M. 1953. *Puffins.* Dent, London.
Lockley, R. M. 1964. Grassholm: Some facts and a legend. *Nature in Wales* 3: 382–8.
Løvenskiold, H. L. 1964. Avifauna Svalbardensis. *Norsk Polarinstitutt* Skrifter: no. 129.
Mackenzie, N. 1905. Notes on the birds of St Kilda. *Ann. Scott. Nat. Hist.* 1905: 75–80.
Macaulay, K. 1764. *The History of St Kilda*, Beckett and de Hondt, London.
Manning, A. 1979. *An Introduction to Animal Behaviour.* London.
Martin, D. M. 1792. *Statistical Account of Scotland, the Parish of Kilmuir.* Creech, Edinburgh.
Mathew, M. A. 1894. *The Birds of Pembrokeshire and its Islands.* Porter, London.
Maurice, M. C. P. 1958. Flying speeds of seabirds. *Sea Swallow* 11: 16–17.
Mead, C. J. 1974. Results of ringing auks in Britain and Ireland. *Bird Study* 21: 45–86.
Mead, C. J. 1978. Amoco Cadiz oil disaster. The ringing recoveries. *B.T.O. News* 93: 1–2.
Meinertzhagen, R. 1955. The speed and altitude of bird flight. *Ibis* 97: 81–117.
Moltoni, E. 1973. Gli uccelli fino ad oggi rinvenuti o notati all'Isola di Pantelleria. *Riv. Ital Di Orn.* 43: 173–437.
Monaghan, P. and Coulson, J. C. 1977. Status of large gulls nesting on buildings. *Bird Study* 24: 89–104.
Monnat, J.-Y. 1982. Intérêt ornithologique de l'archipel de Molène. *Penn ar Bed* 13: 134–43.
Mudge, G. P. 1979. The cliff-breeding seabirds of East Caithness in 1977. *Scott. Birds* 10: 247–61.
Munns, D. J. 1956. Further notes on the birds of the Blasket Islands. *Bird Study* 3: 248–50.
Munsterhjelm, I. 1911. Beobachtungen während einer ornithologischen Studienreise nach dem Nordpolarmeer und Spitzbergen im sommer 1910. *Ofvers. finska Vetensk Soc. Förh.* 1910–11, no. 20.
Murray, J. and Burt, J. R. 1969. The composition of fish. *Torry Advisory Note* No. 38. H.M.S.O.
Mylne, C. K. 1960. Techniques of Herring Gulls and Jackdaws preying on Puffin. *Br. Birds* 53: 86–8.
Myrberget, S. 1959. Lundeura på Lovunden, og lundebestanden der. *Fauna* 12: 143–56.
Myrberget, S. 1959. Vekslinger i Antall Lundefugle inne ved kolonien. *Fauna* 3: 239–70.
Myrberget, S. 1962. Contribution to the breeding biology of the Puffin (*Fratercula arctica* L.). *Meddr St. Viltunders* 11: 1–51.
Myrberget, S. 1962. Lundens seksuelle og sociale adferd. *Fauna* 15: 1–10.
Myrberget, S. 1963. Systematic position of *Fratercula arctica* from a north Norwegian colony. *Nytt. Mag. Zool.* 11: 74–84.
Myrberget, S. 1973. Merking av Toppskarv og Lunde på Røst. *Sterna* 12: 307–15.
Myrberget, S. 1980. Criteria of physical condition of fledging Puffins. Proceed. 2nd Nordic Ornith. Congress.
Nelson, J. B. 1978. *The Sulidae.* Aberdeen University Press, Oxford.
Nettleship, D. N. 1972. Breeding success of the Common Puffin (*Fratercula arctica*) on different habitats at Great Island, Newfoundland. *Ecol. Mongr.* 42: 239–68.
Nettleship, D. N. 1977. Seabird resources of eastern Canada, in Mosquin, T. and Suchal, C. (eds) *Proc. Symp. on Canada's threatened species and habitats:* 96–108.
Nettleship, D. N. 1980. A guide to the major seabird colonies of eastern Canada. Canadian Wildlife Services, Dartmouth.
Nettleship, D. N. and Lock, A. R. 1973. Tenth census of seabirds on the sanctuaries of the north shore of the Gulf of St Lawrence. *Can. Fld. Nat.* 87: 395–402.
Newton, A. 1865. Notes on the birds of Spitsbergen. *Ibis* 7: 199–219.
Nicholson, E. M. and Fisher, J. 1940. A bird census of St Kilda, 1939. *Br. Birds* 34: 29–35.
Norderhaug, M., Brun, E. and Møllen, G. U. 1977. Barentshavets sjøfuglressurser. *Meddn Polar Inst.* 104: 1–119.
Nørrevang, A. 1977. *Fuglefangsten på Faerøerne.* Rhodes, Copenhagen.
Nørrevang, A. 1978. Ecological aspects of fowling in the Faeroes. *Ibis* 120: 109–10.
Ogilvie-Grant, W. R. 1898. The Steganopodes, Pygopodes, Alcae and Impennes in the collection of the British Museum. Catalogue of the Birds in the British Museum, vol. 26.
Ohlendorf, H. M., Risebrough, R. W. and Vermeer, K. 1978. Exposure of marine birds to environmental pollutants. *U.S. Fish and Wildlife Research Report* No. 9.
Ouellet, H. 1969. Les Oiseaux de Ile Anticosti, Province de Quebec, Canada. *Natl. Mus. Sci. Publ. Zool.* No. 1.
Palmer, R. S. 1949. Maine Birds. *Bull. mus. comp. Zool. Harv.* 1–656.

Parslow, J.. L. F. and Jefferies, D. J. 1972 Elastic thread pollution of Puffins. *Mar. Poll. Bull.* 3: 43–5.

Parslow, J. L. F. and Jefferies, D. J. 1973. Relationship between organochlorine residues in livers and whole bodies of guillemots. *Environ. Pollut.* 5: 87–101.

Parslow, J. L. F., Jefferies, D. J. and French, M. C. 1972. Ingested pollutants in Puffins and their eggs. *Bird Study* 19: 18–33.

Patterson, R. 1907. Contribution to the natural history of Lambay, County Dublin. *Ir. Nat. J.* 16: 23–30.

Pearson, H. J. 1904. *Three summers among the Birds of Russian Lapland.* Porter, London.

Penhallurick, R. D. 1969. *Birds of the Cornish Coast, including the Isles of Scilly.* Bradford Barton, Truro.

Penhallurick, R. D. 1978. *The Birds of Cornwall and the Isles of Scilly.* Headland Publications, Penzance.

Pénicaud, P. 1979. Contribution a l'etude du peuplement d'oiseaux de mer de la reserve des Sept-Iles. *Tierre Vie* 33: 591–610.

Pennie, I. D. 1948. Summer bird notes from Foula. *Scott. Nat.* 60: 157–63.

Pennie, I. D. 1951. The Clo Mor bird cliffs. *Scott. Nat.* 63: 26–32.

Perry, R. 1946. *Lundy, Isle of Puffins.* Drummond, London.

Perry, R. 1948. *Shetland Sanctuary.* Faber and Faber, London.

Peters, H. S. and Burleigh, T. D. 1951. *The Birds of Newfoundland.* Dept. of Natl. Res., St Johns.

Petersen, A. 1976a. Age of first breeding in Puffin *Fratercula arctica. Astarte* 9: 43–50.

Petersen, A. 1976b. Size variable in Puffins, *Fratercula arctica* from Iceland and bill features as criteria of age. *Ornis. Scand.* 7: 185–92.

Petersen, A. 1982. Icelandic Seabirds. In Gardarsson, A. (ed.) Icelandic seabirds. *R. Landverndar* 8: 15–60.

Pethon, P. 1967. The systematic position of the Norwegian Common Murre (*Uria aalge*) and Puffin (*Fratercula arctica*). *Nytt. Mag. Zool.* 14: 84–95.

Pettingill, O. S. 1959. Puffins and eiders in Iceland. *Me Fld. Nat.* 15: 58–71.

Pierotti, R. 1983. Gull-Puffin interactions on Great Island, Newfoundland. *Biol. Conserv.* 26: 1–14.

Potter, B. C. 1971. A visit to Burhou, Channel Islands. *Seabird Rep.* 1970: 33–4.

Raeburn, H. 1888. The summer birds of Shetland. *Proc. R. phys. Soc. Edinb.* 9: 542–62.

Rankin, M. N. and Duffey, E. A. G. 1948. A study of the bird life of the North Atlantic. *Br. Birds* 4: suppl.

Richardson, F. 1961. Breeding biology of the Rhinoceros Auklet on Protection Island, Washington. *Condor* 63: 456–73.

Rintoul, L. J. and Baxter, A. V. 1917. Reports on Scottish Ornithology in 1916. *Scott. Nat.* 1917: 200.

Roi, O. le 1911. Die avifauna der Bären-Insel und des Spitzbergen–Archipels in Koenig, A. (ed), *Avifauna Spitzbergensis.* Koenig, Bonn.

Rosenius, P. 1942. *Sveriges Fåglar och Fågelbon.* Gleezups, Lund.

Ruttledge, R. F. 1966. *Irelands Birds.* Witherby, London.

Salomonsen, F. 1935. *The Zoology of the Faeroes: Aves.* Copenhagen.

Salomonsen, F. 1944. The Atlantic Alcidae. *Göteborgs Kungl. Vitterhets Samhälles Handlingar.* 6.

Salomonsen, F. 1950. *Grønlands Fugle.* Rhodos, Copenhagen.

Salomonsen, F. 1979. Marine birds in the Danish Monarchy and their conservation, in Bartonek, J. C. and Nettleship, D. N. (eds.), *Conservation of marine birds in northern North America.* Fish and Wildlife Service, Washington: 267–87.

Salomonsen, F. 1979. Thirteenth preliminary list of recoveries abroad of birds ringed in Greenland. *Dansk orn. Foren. Tidsskr.* 73: 191–206.

Sands, J. 1878. *Out of the World.* Maclachlan and Stewart, Edinburgh.

Saxby, H. H. and Saxby, S. H. 1874. *The Birds of Shetland.* Maclachlan and Stewart, Edinburgh.

Schofield, P. 1975. Puffins on St Kilda in 1972. *Bird Study* 22: 233–7.

Sclater, W. L. and Praed, C. W. M. 1917. A note on the British Puffin. *Br. Birds* 11: 162–3, 214.

Seligman, O. R. and Willcox, J. M. 1940. Some observations on the birds of Jan Mayen. *Ibis* 4: 464–70.

Sergeant, D. E. and Whidborne, R. F. 1951. Birds on Mingulay in the summer of 1949. *Scott. Nat.* 63: 18–25.

Skokova, N. N. 1962. Puffins in the Ainov Islands. *Ornitologiya* 5: 7–12, trs. British Library.

Skokova, N. N. 1967. On the factors which determine the state of the population of puffins during the nesting period. *Forest Industry (Moscow)* 5: 155–77.

Smith, C. 1879. *The Birds of Guernsey and the neighbouring islands.* Porter, London.

Smith, R. W. J. 1961. The spread of some sea-bird colonies in the Forth. *Scott. Birds* 1: 475–9.

Southern, H. N. 1938. A survey of the vertebrate fauna of the Isle of May, Firth of Forth. *J. Anim. Ecol.* 7: 144–54.

Southward, A. J., Butler, E. I. and Pennycuick, L. 1975. Recent cyclic changes in climate and in the abundance of marine life. *Nature* 253: 714–7.

Storer, R. W. 1960. Evolution of the diving birds. *Proc. 12th Intern. Ornith. Congr.*: 55–70.

Stark, D. M. 1967. A visit to Stack Skerry and Sule Skerry. *Scott. Birds* 4: 548–53.

Stresemann, E. and Stresemann, V. 1966. Die Mauser der Vogel. *J. fur Orn.* 107: suppl.

Swennen, C. and Duiven, P. 1977. Size of food objects of three fish-eating seabird species: *Uria aalge, Alca torda,* and *Fratercula arctica* (Aves/Alcidae). *Netherlands. J. Sea. Res.* 11: 92–8.

Tatarinkova, I. P. 1982. On 'desertion period' in the nestling life of the Puffin. *Abstracts 18th Intern. orn. congr.:* 297.

Taylor, G. K. 1982. *Predator-prey interactions between Great Black-backed Gulls and Puffins and the evolutionary significance of Puffin grouping behaviour.* Ph.D. thesis, University of St Andrews.

Thearle, R. F., Hobbs, J. T. and Fisher, J. 1953. The birds of the St Tudwal Islands. *Br. Birds* 46: 182–8.

Thompson, W. 1851. *The Natural History of Ireland,* vol. 3. Reeve and Benham, London.

Timmermann, G. 1949. Die Vögel Islands. *Soc. Scien. Islandica* 28: 239–524.

Toft, G. O. 1983. Changes in the breeding seabird population in Rogaland, S.W. Norway, during 1949–1979. *Fauna norv. Ser. C. Cinclus* 6: 8–13.

Tschanz, B. 1979. Zur Entwicklung von Papageitaucherküken *Fratercula arctica* in Freiland und Labor bei unzulänglichem und ausreichendem Futterangebot. *Fauna norv. Ser. C. Cinclus* 2: 70–94.

Tschanz, B. and Barth, E. K. 1978. Svingninger i lomvibestanden på Vedøy på Røst. *Fauna* 31: 205–19.

Turle, W. H. 1891. A visit to the Blasket Islands and the Skellig Rocks. *Ibis* 3: 1–12.

Udvardy, M. D. F. 1963. Zoogeographical study of the Pacific Alcidae, in Gressit, J. L. (ed.), Pacific Basin Biogeography, a symposium: 85–111.

Uspenskii, S. M. 1958. The bird bazaars of Novaya Zemlya. *Russian Game Dept. Report.* no. 4. trs. Canad. Dept. of Northern Affairs.

Vaurie, C. 1965. *The Birds of the Palearctic Fauna, non-passeriformes.* Witherby, London.

Venables, L. S. V. and Venables, U. M. 1955. *Birds and Mammals of Shetland.* Oliver and Boyd, London.

Vermeer, K., Cullen, L. and Porter, M. 1979. A provisional explanation of the reproductive failure of Tufted Puffins *Lunda cirrhata* on Triangle Island, British Columbia. *Ibis* 121: 348–54.

Vian, J. 1876. Le starique-perroquet en Suede. *Bull. Soc. Zool. France* 1: 1–11.

Walker, C. H. 1980. Species variations in some hepatic microsomal drug metabolising enzymes. *Prog. in Drug. Metab.* 5: 113–64.

Walker, C. H. and Knight, G. C. 1981. The hepatic microsomal enzymes of seabirds and their interaction with liposoluble pollutants. *Aquatic toxicology* 1: 343–54.

Walker, T. C. 1868. Remarks on the birds of Ailsa Craig. *Zoologist* 1868: 1365–73.

Ward, P. and Zahavi, A. 1973. The importance of certain assemblages of birds as 'information-centres' for good-finding. *Ibis* 115: 517–34.

Warman, S., Warman, C. and Todd, D. 1983. Razorbills robbing Puffins. *Brit. Birds* 76: 349–50.

Watson, G. E. 1968. Synchronous wing and tail molt in diving petrels. *Condor* 70: 182–3.

Watt, G. 1951. *The Farne Islands.* Country Life, London.

Wehle, D. H. S. 1980. The biology of the puffins: Tufted Puffin (*Lunda cirrhata*), Horned Puffin (*Fratercula corniculata*), Common Puffin (*F. arctica*) and Rhinoceros Auklet (*Cerorhinca monocerata*). Ph.D. thesis, Alaska.

Whatmough, F. 1949. Abnormal eggs of the southern puffin. *Ool. Rec.* 23: 17–19.

Wiglesworth, J. 1903. *St. Kilda and its Birds.* Tinling, Liverpool.

Willgohs, J. F. 1955. Om forekomstene av en del kyst-og sjøfugl på Vestlandet. *Fauna* 8: 16–27.

Williams, G. 1978. Notes on the birds of Grassholm. *Nature in Wales* 16: 2–15.

Williamson, K. 1945. The economic importance of sea-fowl in the Faeroe Islands. *Ibis* 87: 249–69.

Williamson, K. 1965. *Fair Isle and its Birds.* Oliver and Boyd, Edinburgh.

Williamson, K. 1970. *The Atlantic Islands*. Routledge and Kegan Paul, London.
Wilson, J. 1842. *A Voyage round the coasts of Scotland and the Isles*, Black, Edinburgh.
Wintle, W. J. 1925. Some Caldey birds. *Pax* 1925: 133–9.
Wynne-Edwards, V. C. 1962. *Animal Dispersion in Relation to Social Behaviour*. Oliver and Boyd, Edinburgh.
Zedlitz, O. G. 1911. Ornithologische Notizen von der "Zeppelin-Studienfahrt Spitzbergen Sommer 1910. *J. für Ornith.* 49: 300–27.

Tables 1–20

TABLE 1: *Number of grooves on the bills of Puffins of known age and on breeding Puffins*

		No. of grooves								
	Age (years)	Trace	<1	1	1+	1½	2	2+	2½	3 or more
Isle of May	1	1								
	2	3	13	17	7	2				
	3			2	2	24	11			
	4					2	12	5		
	5						2	1	1	
	6						2	1	1	2
	7									3
	8						1	1	1	
	Breeding			1	1	6	124	233	191	183
St Kilda	2	1	1							
	3			1	2	1	2			
	4						5			
	Breeding					3	136	118	158	88
Westman Is.	2	11								
	3				27					
	4						3	27		6
	5						2	1		5

NOTE: The breeding birds with less than two grooves all had adult-shaped beaks. Data from Petersen (1976a) and personal observations.

TABLE 2: *Measurements (in mm) of male and female Puffins*

	No.	Male Mean	SE	No.	Female Mean	SE
Isle of May						
Wing length	43	161.6	0.59	39	160.4	0.54
Bill length	47	29.9	0.17	46	29.0	0.14
Bill depth	47	37.0	0.20	46	34.6	0.18
St Kilda						
Wing length	20	157.1	1.29	20	156.0	0.68
Bill length	21	28.6	0.22	20	28.1	0.21
Bill depth	21	35.3	0.31	20	32.2	0.37

202

TABLE 2: *continued*

	No.	Male Mean	SE	No.	Female Mean	SE
Skomer						
Wing length	88	159.7	0.21	70	156.9	0.24
Bill length	88	29.8	0.12	70	28.6	0.15
Bill depth	88	36.4	0.12	70	33.6	0.19
Lovunden						
Wing length	96	168.9	0.38	94	166.4	0.37
Bill length	96	48.2	0.14	94	46.0	0.13
Bill depth	96	28.0	0.07	94	27.2	0.08
Great Island						
Wing length	91	173.0	0.46	134	170.3	0.41

NOTES: 1. Birds were sexed by dissection or (Skomer) by cloacal examination.
2. The Lovunden bill length is the upper bill measurement; this and the bill depth includes the cere.
3. Data from Myrberget (1963), Nettleship (1972), Corkhill (1972), Harris (1979 and unpublished).

TABLE 3: *see overleaf*

TABLE 4: *Dates when Puffins first seen on the sea and ashore, and last recorded time on land or carrying fish on Skokholm, Wales. (Skokholm Bird Observatory records)*

	On sea	Ashore	Last ashore		On sea	Ashore	Last ashore
1928	28 March	4 April	22 August	1964	22 March	22 March	13 August
1929	25 March	6 April	16 August	1965			21 August
1930	31 March	8 April	18 August	1966	15 March		20 August
1931	25 March	6 April	15 August	1967	15 March		20 August
1932	22 March	4 April	24 August	1968	19 March		17 August
1933	29 March	3 April	26 August	1969	21 March		20 August
1947	25 March	10 April	25 August	1970	26 March		18 August
1948	28 March	3 April	25 August	1971	23 March		22 August
1949	23 March	10 April	16 August	1972	31 March		28 August
1950	31 March	1 April	22 August	1973	19 March	4 April	20 August
1951	3 April	12 April	21 August	1974	29 March	5 April	26 August
1952	26 March	3 April	24 August	1975	23 March	10 April	15 August
1955	28 March	2 April	18 August	1976	29 March		19 August
1956	27 March	3 April	15 August	1977	4 March		21 August
1957	20 March	2 April	14 August	1978		10 April	18 August
1958	26 March	31 March	19 August	1979	31 March	13 April	
1959	21 March	27 March	11 August	1980	30 March	4 April	17 August
1960	14 March		23 August	1981	19 March	1 April	16 August
1961	22 March		15 August	1982	19 March	2 April	13 August
1962	25 March		24 August	1983	17 March	29 March	23 August
1963	23 March		22 August				

TABLE 3: *Measurements of Puffins (all in mm)*

	Wing length				Straight bill length				Source
	No.	Mean	Range	SE	No.	Mean	Range	SE	
Britain									
Farne Is.	31	162.6	158–168	0.51	31	29.3	27.3–31.1	0.16	
Isle of May	1,615	161.8	149–176	0.14	464	29.5	27.1–32.0	0.07	
Fair Isle	61	160.0	154–167	0.48	63	28.6	27.4–30.8	0.13	R. Broad
Hermaness	197	161.4	151–173	0.28	66	29.6	27.0–32.2	0.15	University of East Anglia
Sule Skerry	31	159.0	153–168	0.67	0				D. Budworth; A. C. Blackburn
Shiant Is.	129	158.6	148–170	0.39	0				Shiant Auk Ringing Group
Flannan Is.	81	159.1	148–166	0.41	38	28.2	25.1–31.2	0.17	S. Murray
St Kilda	495	158.2	144–170	0.19	276	28.2	25.5–30.7	0.07	
Skomer Is.	158	158.3	146–170	0.51	158	29.3	25.0–32.5	0.10	Corkhill (1972)
Skomer Is.	209	159.3	152–171	0.23	360	28.6	25.2–31.4	0.10	Ashcroft (1976)
Channel Is.	12	157.9	152–162	1.62	8	29.5*	27.9–31.9	0.53	
Elsewhere									
Faeroe Is.	29	160.1	156–166	0.63	11	29.1*	27.4–31.3	0.37	Petersen (1976b); K. Taylor
Westman Is. Iceland	21	162.6*	154–172	0.77	21	28.8*	26.6–32.1	0.34	Petersen (1976b)
Baer, North Iceland	13	168.3*	159–173	1.25	13	30.8*	28.5–32.2	0.31	Petersen (1976b)
Grimsey, North Iceland	4	170.8	169–173	0.85	0				K. Taylor
Rott-Begla, Norway	16	162.7*	158–173	1.03	0				Pethon (1967)
Kjor, Norway	38	163.5	?	1.27	5	27.9	26.1–29.5	0.59	O. Johansen
Runde, Norway	41	167.4	160–175	0.63	41	29.3	26.5–31.6	0.17	
Runde, Norway	22	167.4*	160–175	0.87	0				Pethon (1967)
Lofoten Is., Norway	84	168.5*	160–180	0.49	0				Pethon (1967)
Lovunden, Norway	190	167.7	158–178	0.28	0				Myrberget (1963)
Troms, Norway	12	173.4*	165–178	1.15	0				Pethon (1967)
Gjesvaer, Norway	33	175.0	168–184	0.66	33	30.1	27.4–33.2	0.23	R. Barrett

	Wing length				Straight bill length				
	No.	*Mean*	*Range*	*SE*	*No.*	*Mean*	*Range*	*SE*	
Murmansk, USSR	38	173.7*	150–190	?	0				Dement'ev et al (1951)
Novaya Zemlya	14	175.6*	162–188	?	0				Dement'ev et al (1951)
North-west Greenland	?	?	175–194		14	32.0	30.0–34.0	0.34	Salomonsen (1950)
Spitzbergen	14	184.0*	178–187	1.01	14	31.9	29.6–34.8	0.36	Pethon (1967)
Spitzbergen	9	185.4*	180–194	?	4	32.0	30.6–32.7	0.46	Vaurie (1965)
Spitzbergen	48	183.8	175–195	?	0				Vaurie (1965)
Jan Mayen	7	175.2	164–181	?	0				Vaurie (1965)
Bear Island	6	167.5	162–177	?	0				
Newfoundland	225	171.4	161–182	0.31	16	28.3*	26.1–30.8	0.29	Nettleship (1972)

NOTES: 1. Measurements marked * were taken from dried specimens. Wings would have been about 1.6 mm shorter than when fresh.

2. Sexes have been lumped.

3. Measurements were of breeding birds or birds with more than two bill grooves except those from Pethon ('adults'), Myrberget and Ashcroft (birds with two or more grooves), Corkhill (obvious immatures excluded), Vaurie, Salomonsen and Dement'ev et al (unknown ages).

TABLE 5: *First and last dates of Puffins in Grampian, and on the Isle of May and Fair Isle. Dates in brackets are where no observers were present earlier in the year*

	Grampian	Isle of May			Fair Isle	
	First ashore	First ashore	Last ashore	On sea	First ashore	Last ashore
1966		(2 April)	15 August	3 April	3 April	17 August
1967		(2 April)	12 August	3 April	7 April	23 August
1968		(31 March)	17 August	28 March	28 March	27 August
1969		(3 April)		2 April	4 April	28 August
1970		10 March	20 August	2 April	3 April	26 August
1971		1 April	17 August	14 March	1 April	
1972		(23 March)	16 August	20 March	1 April	
1973		(24 March)	20 August	26 March	9 April	28 August
1974	(23 February)	(19 March)	24 August	23 March	26 March	26 August
1975	(23 February)	1 March	26 August	28 March	28 March	25 August
1976	(14 February)	19 February	15 September	31 March	31 March	26 August
1977	(20 February)	6 March	19 August	1 April	1 April	28 August
1978	(24 February)	(14 March)	20 August	24 March	29 March	27 August
1979	24 February	(13 March)	11 September	31 March	1 April	29 August
1980	23 February	(21 March)	29 August	19 March	29 March	23 August
1981	23 February	20 February		30 March	30 March	Mid-August
1982	23 February	(27 March)		26 March	28 March	27 August
1983		5–10 March	20 August	31 March	31 March	22 August

Details from Bird Observatory and personal records.

TABLE 6: *Ages of Puffins the first time they were found breeding*

	Age (years)				
	3	4	5	6	older
Isle of May	1	8	13	25	36
St Kilda	0	3	7	1	2
Farne Islands	0	0	3	5	34
Skomer	0	1	4	?	?
Westman Islands	0	0	5	3	6
Gulf of Maine islands	0	9	14	4	?

Details from Ashcroft (1979), Petersen (1976a), Kress (1981, pers. comm.) and Harris (1983b). A Puffin aged 3 years and 10 months when it laid is considered to be 4 years old, etc.

TABLE 7: *Measurements of eggs of Puffins*

		Length			Breadth		
	No.	Mean	SE	No.	Mean	SE	Source
Isle of May	54	61.5	0.32	54	42.8	0.17	author
St Kilda	171	61.0	0.16	170	42.7	0.08	author
Farne Islands and Bempton	53	61.6	0.31	53	42.6	0.19	author
Skomer	47	61.0	0.30	47	42.7	0.19	R. E. Ashcroft
Ireland, Wales and S.W. England	40	60.3	0.36	39	42.2	0.20	author
France	20	61.1	0.47	20	42.0	0.24	author
West Scotland	24	61.9	0.37	24	42.5	0.28	author
Orkney and Shetland Islands	25	60.9	0.48	25	42.6	0.22	author
Sweden	13	62.9	?	13	42.7	?	Rosenius (1942)
Faeroe Islands	36	61.0	0.44	36	43.0	0.23	author
Iceland	25	64.0	?	25	44.4	?	Timmermann (1949)
Iceland	15	63.7	0.73	15	44.3	0.39	author
Lovunden, Norway	77	64.0	0.27	77	44.1	0.17	Myrberget (1963)
Murmansk Coast, USSR	89	64.0	?	89	44.4	?	Kaftanovskii (1951), Hortling (1929)
Spitzbergen	4	67.3	0.54	4	45.9	0.79	author
Bear Island	11	61.1	0.75	11	43.3	0.40	Roi (1911), author
Novaya Zemlya	6	63.4	?	6	44.2	?	Uspenskii (1956)
Greenland*	33	64.2	0.44	33	44.2	0.33	author
Gulf of St Lawrence	26	63.2	0.45	26	44.5	0.25	author
Labrador	15	62.7	0.51	15	45.2	0.31	author
Newfoundland	150	62.9	0.17	150	44.6	0.09	Nettleship (1972)

NOTE: *includes eggs from the range of both *F. a. arctica* and *F. a. naumanni*.

TABLE 8: *Fledging periods of Puffins*

	No.	Mean (days)	Range (days)	Source
Isle of May	312	41	34–50	personal records
St Kilda	214	44	35–57	personal records
Skokholm	3	49	47–51	Lockley (1934)
Skomer	241	38	34–44	Ashcroft (1979)
Russia	?	?	36–46	Kaftanovskii (1951)
Eastern Murmansk	?	?	38–45	Kartaschew (1960)
Norway	32	48	43–52	Myrberget (1962)
Canada	180	53	39–83	Nettleship (1972)

NOTE: Most measurements were made to ± 1 or 2 days.

TABLE 9:   *Breeding success of Puffins at various colonies*

	Year	No. nests before laying	No. eggs laid (%)	No. eggs laid	No. eggs hatch (%)	No. young fledge (%)	No. young fledge/ pair laying
Newfoundland							
Great Island	1968			90	58(64)	25(43)	0.28
	1969			200	151(75)	101(67)	0.51
Funk Island	1969			106	?	?	0.87
Small Island	1969			147	?	?	0.93
Wales							
Skomer Island	1973	54	51(95)	51	38(75)	35(93)	0.66
	1974	129	108(84)	108	84(78)	61(74)	0.61
	1975	87	80(92)	80	61(76)	73(96)	0.66
Scotland							
St Kilda	1974	192	148(79)	148	113(76)	102(90)	0.69
	1975	191	160(84)	202	162(81)	158(96)	0.78
	1976	185	140(81)	133	118(89)	99(84)	0.74
	1977	185	153(83)	153	?	?	0.84
	1978	165	130(79)	130	?	?	0.69–0.90
Isle of May	1973			58	?	?	0.74
	1977			51	?	?	0.73
	1978			100	?	?	0.87
	1979			139	?	?	0.90
	1980			119	?	?	0.76
	1981			35	?	?	0.89
	1982			124	?	?	0.92
	1983			168	?	?	0.79

NOTE: Although Great Island and St Kilda data refer to the best part of the colony, the bulk of the populations nest in these areas so the results are fairly representative of the population as a whole. Details are from Nettleship (1972), Ashcroft (1979) and Harris (1980, unpublished).

TABLE 10:   *Dates when known-aged immature Puffins first seen ashore*

Isle of May	1st year	2nd year	3rd year	4th year	5th year
1974	0	—	—	—	—
1975	0	17 June	—	—	—
1976	29 July	4 July	17 May	—	—
1977	0	15 June	30 April	11 April	—
1978	16 July	1 June	13 April	30 March	29 March
1979	0	16 May	8 May	10 April	9 April
1980	14 July	27 June	16 April	7 April	31 March
1981	4 July	8 June	25 April	9 April	9 April

TABLE 11: *Last dates when known aged Puffins were ashore on the Isle of May*

	1978	1979
One year old	3 August	None ringed
Two years old	2 August	15 August
Three years old	9 August	15 August
Four years old	9 August	9 August
Five years old	9 August	15 August
Six years old	None ringed	15 August
Last observation	10 August	15 August

TABLE 12: *Percentages of various fish brought to young Puffins in Britain expressed as number and biomass*

	No. of fish	Sandeel		Sprat		Saithe or Whiting		Rockling	
		No.	Wt.	No.	Wt.	No.	Wt.	No.	Wt.
Isle of May									
1973	350	92.6	90.2	2.9	6.9	0.6	0.4	3.1	1.4
1974	588	69.7	47.6	27.6	50.6	1.2	1.1	0.9	0.2
1975	476	21.0	13.5	73.5	85.6	1.3	0.3	4.0	0.4
1976	735	55.1	38.1	29.4	52.6	14.2	9.1	0.3	+
1977	581	50.9	30.0	41.6	65.8	2.9	1.1	2.9	0.3
1978	508	53.9	43.1	40.3	50.7	2.7	1.4	0	
1979	434	68.2	73.3	21.5	22.9	3.2	1.9	0	
1980	330	78.8	75.4	2.4	6.9	0		2.7	0.2
1981	457	65.2	70.0	3.3	8.2	0.9	3.7	2.0	0.2
1982	422	51.9	59.8	1.7	5.8	3.8	4.4	6.2	0.6
St Kilda									
1973	359	32.0	13.9	0.8	14.0	32.3	62.4	27.0	8.5
1974	820	58.8	27.4	16.6	14.5	18.3	52.0	5.6	2.8
1975	992	9.2	10.3	75.8	83.8	2.0	1.4	12.4	4.2
1976	2,143	37.5	26.8	40.6	57.9	0.7	1.0	20.8	13.8
1977	557	15.6	3.9	29.8	69.1	40.2	24.8	14.4	2.1
1978	272	7.0	0.5	30.5	71.2	36.9	22.5	19.1	2.9
1980	723	20.6	19.6	3.0	0.1	24.6	57.0	47.4	17.8

NOTE: Saithe were found only on the Isle of May, whiting only on St Kilda

TABLE 13:　*Mean lengths (mm) of fish brought to young Puffins on the Isle of May and St Kilda*

	Sandeel				Sprat				Rockling		Whiting/ Saithe	
	Large		Small		Large		Small					
	No.	Length	No.	Length	No.	Length	No.	Length	No.	Length	No.	Length
Isle of May												
1972	0		47	66	4	75	0		52	36	1	44
1973	2	177	322	79	10	81	0		11	47	2	53
1974	47	115	360	62	29	107	133	62	5	34	7	58
1975	9	124	91	72	11	113	339	69	19	33	6	44
1976	9	110	396	72	12	104	204	71	2	33	104	51
1977	54	103	242	69	75	96	167	67	17	37	17	45
1978	104	102	170	75	25	97	180	69	0		14	53
1979	103	127	191	83	17	110	76	64	0		14	61
1980	46	109	214	82	8	95	0		9	34	0	
1981	88	116	210	84	4	113	11	86	9	38	4	51
1982	83	132	136	66	7	99	0		26	38	16	65
St Kilda												
1971	0		125	40	0		0		218	33	17	43
1973	0		115	48	3	118	0		97	31	116	54
1974	0		482	50	0		136	43	46	37	150	63
1975	4	169	87	40	19	118	733	41	123	33	20	39
1976	0		803	47	1	101	869	41	446	32	14	42
1977	1	187	86	38	0		166	79	80	40	224	48
1978	0		19	37	33	125	50	45	52	28	113	47
1980	34	118	149	40	1	46	20	29	343	31	172	50

NOTES: 1. Large and small sandeels and sprats are kept separate because they belong to different age classes.
2. Only whiting were recorded on St Kilda, only saithe on the Isle of May.

TABLE 14:　*Annual mean weights of loads of fish, number of fish per load and frequency of feeds brought to young Puffins on Isle of May and St Kilda*

	Weight (g)		Fish/load		No. of feeds/day	
	No.	Mean	No.	Mean	No. of days	Mean
Isle of May						
1972	0		15	6.0	0	
1973	23	8.5	59	5.3	0	
1974	102	9.7	105	5.4	0	
1975	137	8.2	136	3.7	1	7.0
1976	169	8.2	171	5.0	2	4.5
1977	121	9.5	121	4.6	3	6.8
1978	107	10.4	107	4.4	3	4.0
1979	107	10.1	96	3.4	3	4.6
1980	56	10.3	59	4.6	4	2.6
1981	95	8.8	96	4.0	1	4.9

TABLE 14: *continued*

Isle of May	Weight (g) No.	Mean	Fish/load No.	Mean	No. of feeds/day No. of days	Mean
1982	104	10.4	109	3.8	1	5.2
1983	140	9.5	142	4.3	1	4.9
St Kilda						
1971	16	4.3	16	22.4	0	
1974	73	5.9	81	10.5	1	6.8
1975	132	5.8	132	10.3	3	10.4
1976	219	4.4	219	13.2	4	8.2
1977	82	5.8	83	8.2	0	
1978	63	10.0	65	4.4	0	
1980	82	5.3	82	11.7	0	

TABLE 15: *Peak and fledging weights, ages the peak weights were attained and fledging periods of young Puffins*

	Peak weight (g) No.	Mean	SE	Fledging weight (g) No.	Mean	SE	Age at peak (days) No.	Mean	SE	Fledging period (days) No.	Mean	SE
of May												
1974	48	323.7	3.4	42	289.3	4.4	48	31.9	0.7	42	42.1	0.5
1975	65	330.5	3.2	65	293.4	3.6	65	32.8	0.5	65	39.6	0.4
1976	0			13	303.7	11.8	0			0		
1977	27	325.8	4.6	23	280.6	5.6	26	36.1	0.7	22	42.5	0.7
1978	56	329.0	4.1	38	289.8	5.1	54	32.0	0.7	40	40.8	0.6
1979	71	325.5	2.8	60	278.0	2.6	69	33.0	0.6	62	40.0	0.4
1980	34	323.5	4.2	24	284.8	6.4	24	33.0	0.8	24	39.6	0.4
1981	34	314.9	3.5	28	271.6	3.9	27	34.2	1.1	23	40.8	1.0
1982	31	322.0	5.0	27	278.9	5.0	31	32.9	0.8	29	39.9	0.6
Kilda												
1974	21	282.6	7.2	31	269.1	8.1	30	39.6	0.8	25	45.3	0.8
1975	37	300.7	3.6	37	278.8	3.2	37	36.6	0.6	37	41.2	0.5
1976	30	278.5	4.4	30	272.2	4.7	41	40.9	0.9	53	44.7	0.7
1977	27	306.0	5.3	19	278.8	5.2	20	35.5	1.0	17	41.5	0.8
omer												
1970	13	309.1	7.2	13	284.0	6.0	?			?		
1973	63	317.1	3.0	63	290.1	3.5	?			?		
1974	110	314.6	2.2	110	287.5	2.1	?			?		
1975	68	319.8	3.0	68	296.6	3.0	?			?		
1978	20	328.7	4.8	20	295.3	5.5	20	34.2	0.7	20	40.0	0.3
vunden, Norway												
1955	20	327.7	8.5	20	277.2	5.7	20	37.5	0.6	20	39.2	0.6
eat Island, Newfoundland												
1968	0			25	261.4	6.5	0			25	59.7	2.1
1969	0			101	261.8	3.5	0			101	52.3	0.7

NOTES: 1. The St Kilda and Great Island weights are from the densest parts and steepest slopes of the colony respectively; chicks elsewhere grew less well.
2. Results from Corkhill (1973), Ashcroft (1976), Myrberget (1962) and Hudson (1979).
3. Lovunden figures refer to last time the young were weighed.

TABLE 16:   *Weights of normal and manipulated young Puffins*

	No.	Peak weight (g)	Fledging weight (g)	Age at peak (days)	Fledging age (days)
St Kilda 1975					
Unlimited food	5	365	305	31	?
Supplementary feed	11	316	296	31	40
Normal	37	301	279	37	41
Single adult	3	240	237	39	46
Isle of May 1975					
Unlimited food	6	367	342	?	?
Supplementary feed	10	344	315	33	41
Normal	65	331	293	33	40
Single adult	4	303	267	41	44
Isle of May 1974					
Normal	42	324	289	32	42
Twin	2	307	302	43	47
Skomer 1970					
Normal	13	309	284	?	37
Twin	4	279	267	?	45
Skomer 1973					
Normal	63	317	290	?	38
Single adult	2	298	263	?	42
Skomer 1977					
Unlimited food	5	354	312	33	41
Normal quantity	5	310	300	36	41
80 g per day	5	290	273	35	42

From Corkhill (1973), Ashcroft (1979), Hudson (1979a) and Harris (1978).

TABLE 17:   *Percentages of loads of fish being brought to young Puffins which were stolen by gulls*

Place	Year	No. of arrivals	% loads lost to gulls
Great Island, Newfoundland	1968–69		
(i) Slope		601	4.4
(ii) Flat		775	13.5
Skomer	1969	1,293	0.3*
	1974–75	3,518	1.2
	1977	?	1.4
Skokholm	1982	479	2.9

TABLE 17: *continued*

Place	Year	No. of arrivals	% loads lost to gulls
Isle of May	1974	151	15.2
	1975	155	18.7
	1977	509	12.6
	1978	1,064	8.3
	1979	1,065	7.8
	1980	518	16.4
	1981	200	2.1
	1982	150	4.6
St Kilda	1974–77	1,847	0
	1978	?	very few
Hermaness	1974	809	1.1
Vik, Iceland	1969	?	<10
	1973	?	ca. 4

*NOTE: a few additional loads were lost to Jackdaws.
Data from Corkhill (1973), Ashcroft (1976), Grant (1971), Arnason and Grant (1978), Nettleship (1972), Hudson (1979), Lees (1982) and personal records.

TABLE 18: *Major British oiling incidents between September 1976 and June 1979 where Puffins were found dead*

		No. Puffins	Other auks
16 February 1977	Bempton	3	920
26 January 1978	Northumberland	15	4,228
3 February 1978	Firth of Forth	1	178
18 March 1978	Holy Island and Firth of Forth	4	201
1 May 1978	Northumberland	12	170
6 May 1978	East Norfolk	1	112
12 October 1978	South Wales and Devon	8	2,182
8 December 1978	Caithness and Orkney	7	438
30 December 1978	Sullom Voe, Shetland	39	1,064
2 January 1979	East Norfolk	2	67
10 February 1979	North Orkney	7	465
24 February 1979	Orkney	5	309
4 April 1979	St Abbs Head	2	273
10 April 1979	Caithness and Orkney	31	661
20 June 1979	Cape Wrath, Sutherland	36	145

Data from RSPB – Seabird Group Beached Bird Survey.

TABLE 19:   *Concentrations of chemicals in livers of Puffins*

	Year	No. examined	Mercury	PCB	DDE	Dieldrin
Found Dead						
North Sea coasts	1969–74	22	1.8 ± 0.4	18.0 ± 7.0(21)	1.9 ± 0.3	0.4 ± 0.14(9)
West coast of Britain	1972–74	11	2.0 ± 0.2	10.0 ± 5.0(9)	1.8 ± 0.4(10)	0.3 ± 0.1(6)
North Scotland	1971–73	5	1.5 ± 0.6	3.0 ± 2.0(3)	0.6 ± 0.4	0
Norway	1977	1	2.7	25	3.3	?
Killed						
Isle of May	1973–74	5	0.6 ± 0.8	1.1 ± 0.6(2)	0.3 ± 0.02	0.1 ±0.01(3)
Isle of May	1977–79	37	0.6 ± 0.1(34)	5.0 ± 2.2(5)	0	0
St Kilda	1977	10	1.5 ± 0.2	0.9 ± 0.4(9)	0	0
West coast of Britain	1973–74	8	1.1 ± 0.2	1.1 ± 0.1(5)	0.4 ± 0.1	0
Faeroe Is.	1971	5	?	0.4 ± 0.1	0.07 ± 0.02	?
Norway	1972	4	1.2 ± 0.3	0.4 ± 0.1	0.1 ± 0.04	?
Spitzbergen	1972	2	?	0.3 ± 0.1	0.03 ± 0.03	?

NOTES: 1. Concentrations are expressed as mean ppm wet weight ± s.e.
2. In the calculation of means, concentrations where the pollutant was detected at such a low level that it could not be measured were taken as half the levels of possible measurement.
3. Means were calculated using only birds where the substance involved was detected. If the sample size was lower than the number of birds examined, this is given in brackets.. The true means are, therefore, smaller than those shown.
4. Analyses were undertaken by Monks Wood Experimental Station laboratories except for the birds from Faeroe Island and Spitzbergen (Bourne 1976b, pers. comm.) and Norway (Holt *et al* 1979, pers. comm.).

TABLE 20:   *Concentrations of PCB, DDE, dieldrin and mercury in Puffin eggs*

		No. of eggs	Mercury	PCB	DDE	Dieldrin
Isle of May	1973	15	0.6 ± 0.03(14)	6.6 ± 0.8(13)	0.7 ± 0.03	0.2 ± 0.03(13)
Isle of May	1974	8	0.6(1)	12.9 ± 2.2	1.3(1)	0.4(1)
Isle of May	1978	18	?	8.4 ± 2.6	0	0
Isle of May	1979	6	0.4 ± 0.02	1.4 ± 0.3	0	0
Skomer	1974	7	0.7 ± 0.1	6.1 ± 0.9	0.8 ± 0.1	0.1 ± 0.05
Fair Isle	1973	6	0.6 ± 0.1	2.7 ± 1.0	0.9 ± 0.3	0
North Rona	1972	2	0.6 ± 0.1	0	0.9 ± 0.4	0.03(1)
St Kilda	1969	5	0.6 ± 0.04	0	0.2 ± 0.04	0
St Kilda	1973–74	8	0.5 ± 0.05	6.5 ± 1.1(4)	1.1 ± 0.3(7)	0.1 ± 0.002(2)
Shiant Is.	1973	6	0.6 ± 0.1	0	0.3 ± 0.1	0

NOTES: See Table 19.

Index

Consult Appendix A and p. 23 (auks) for scientific names.

217